™

MW01121350

References for the Rest of Us! ®

BESTSELLING BOOK SERIES FROM IDG

Are you intimidated and confused by computers? Do you find that traditional manuals are overloaded with technical details you'll never use? Do your friends and family always call you to fix simple problems on their PCs? Then the *...For Dummies*® computer book series from IDG Books Worldwide is for you.

...For Dummies books are written for those frustrated computer users who know they aren't really dumb but find that PC hardware, software, and indeed the unique vocabulary of computing make them feel helpless. *...For Dummies* books use a lighthearted approach, a down-to-earth style, and even cartoons and humorous icons to diffuse computer novices' fears and build their confidence. Lighthearted but not lightweight, these books are a perfect survival guide for anyone forced to use a computer.

> *"I like my copy so much I told friends; now they bought copies."*
>
> — Irene C., Orwell, Ohio

> *"Quick, concise, nontechnical, and humorous."*
>
> — Jay A., Elburn, Illinois

> *"Thanks, I needed this book. Now I can sleep at night."*
>
> — Robin F., British Columbia, Canada

Already, millions of satisfied readers agree. They have made *...For Dummies* books the #1 introductory level computer book series and have written asking for more. So, if you're looking for the most fun and easy way to learn about computers, look to *...For Dummies* books to give you a helping hand.

™

IDG BOOKS
WORLDWIDE

Server Objects

Request and Response objects

See the section "Using the Request and Response Objects" in Chapter 9 for more information.

```
Response.Write "<h1>This is a header</h1>"
```

Writes HTML to a Web page at the current cursor position.

```
Response.Cookie("Music")("Style") = "Alternative"
```

Sets the `Music` cookie's key `Style` to a value of `Alternative`.

```
<% If Request.Cookie("Music")("Style") = _
   "Alternative" Then %>
```

Retrieves the `Style` key from the `Music` cookie to test its value.

```
<a href="greet.asp?Name=Fred>
```

Passes an argument on the URL as you open the page greet.asp.

```
<h1>Good To See You, <%=Request.QueryString("Name")%></h1>
```

Within the page greet.asp, this line retrieves the argument passed and uses it in its header.

Application and Session objects

See the section "Using the Application and Session Objects" in Chapter 9 for more information.

```
Session("UserName") = "Amber"
```

Creates a session variable `UserName` (if it didn't exist before) and assigns the value `Amber` to it. This variable will last as long as the current user is using the application.

```
Application("NumHits") = 0
```

Creates an application variable `NumHits` (if it didn't exist before) and assigns the value 0 to it. This variable will last as long as the application runs. This one variable servers *all* users.

Server Components

See "Putting Server Components to Work" in Chapter 9 for more information.

```
Set browser = Server.CreateObject("MSWC.BrowserType")
```

Creates a Browser Capabilities component and stores it in a local variable for use on this page.

```
<OBJECT RUNAT=Server SCOPE=Session ID=browser
PROGID="MSWC.BrowserType">
```

This tag, located in the global.asa file, creates a Browser Capabilities component that can be used on all pages for as long as the current user is logged in.

Visual InterDev™ 6 For Dummies®

Cheat Sheet

BESTSELLING BOOK SERIES FROM IDG

Keyboard Shortcuts

Page Editor

Project/File commands

New Project	Ctrl+N
Open Project	Ctrl+O
New File	Ctrl+Shift+N
Open File	Ctrl+Shift+O
Save current file	Ctrl+S
Save all open files	Ctrl+Shift+S
Print	Ctrl+P

Switching Windows

Project Explorer	Ctrl+Alt+J
Properties	F4
Toolbox	Ctrl+Alt+X
Task List	Ctrl+Alt+K
Script Outline	Ctrl+Alt+S

Other

Run your application	F5
Break your application	Ctrl+Break
Find	Ctrl+F
Find the next occurrence	F3
Select the entire page	Ctrl+A
Cut	Ctrl+X
Copy	Ctrl+C
Paste	Ctrl+V
Undo	Ctrl+Z
Redo	Ctrl+Y

Site Diagram Editor

New HTML Page	Ctrl+Shift+H
New ASP Page	Ctrl+Shift+A
Add an existing page	Ctrl+Shift+E
Add current page to Global Navigation Bar	Ctrl+Shift+G
Detach current page from its parent	Ctrl+Shift+D

IDG BOOKS WORLDWIDE

...For Dummies: #1 Computer Book Series for Beginners

VISUAL INTERDEV™ 6 FOR DUMMIES®

by Bill Hatfield

IDG BOOKS WORLDWIDE

IDG Books Worldwide, Inc.
An International Data Group Company

Foster City, CA ♦ Chicago, IL ♦ Indianapolis, IN ♦ New York, NY

Visual InterDev™ 6 For Dummies®

Published by
IDG Books Worldwide, Inc.
An International Data Group Company
919 E. Hillsdale Blvd.
Suite 400
Foster City, CA 94404
www.idgbooks.com (IDG Books Worldwide Web site)
www.dummies.com (Dummies Press Web site)

Library of Congress Catalog Card No.: 96-77074

ISBN: 0-7645-0010-4

Printed in the United States of America

10 9 8 7 6 5 4 3 2 1

1O/RY/QZ/ZY/IN

Distributed in the United States by IDG Books Worldwide, Inc.

Distributed by Macmillan Canada for Canada; by Transworld Publishers Limited in the United Kingdom; by IDG Norge Books for Norway; by IDG Sweden Books for Sweden; by Woodslane Pty. Ltd. for Australia; by Woodslane (NZ) Ltd. for New Zealand; by Addison Wesley Longman Singapore Pte Ltd. for Singapore, Malaysia, Thailand, Indonesia and Korea; by Norma Comunicaciones S.A. for Colombia; by Intersoft for South Africa; by International Thomson Publishing for Germany, Austria and Switzerland; by Toppan Company Ltd. for Japan; by Distribuidora Cuspide for Argentina; by Livraria Cultura for Brazil; by Ediciencia S.A. for Ecuador; by Ediciones ZETA S.C.R. Ltda. for Peru; by WS Computer Publishing Corporation, Inc., for the Philippines; by Unalis Corporation for Taiwan; by Contemporanea de Ediciones for Venezuela; by Computer Book & Magazine Store for Puerto Rico; by Express Computer Distributors for the Caribbean and West Indies. Authorized Sales Agent: Anthony Rudkin Associates for the Middle East and North Africa.

For general information on IDG Books Worldwide's books in the U.S., please call our Consumer Customer Service department at 800-762-2974. For reseller information, including discounts and premium sales, please call our Reseller Customer Service department at 800-434-3422.

For information on where to purchase IDG Books Worldwide's books outside the U.S., please contact our International Sales department at 650-655-3200 or fax 650-655-3297.

For information on foreign language translations, please contact our Foreign & Subsidiary Rights department at 650-655-3021 or fax 650-655-3281.

For sales inquiries and special prices for bulk quantities, please contact our Sales department at 650-655-3200 or write to the address above.

For information on using IDG Books Worldwide's books in the classroom or for ordering examination copies, please contact our Educational Sales department at 800-434-2086 or fax 317-596-5499.

For press review copies, author interviews, or other publicity information, please contact our Public Relations department at 650-655-3000 or fax 650-655-3299.

For authorization to photocopy items for corporate, personal, or educational use, please contact Copyright Clearance Center, 222 Rosewood Drive, Danvers, MA 01923, or fax 978-750-4470.

About the Author

Bill Hatfield is the author of *Active Server Pages For Dummies* (published by IDG Books Worldwide, Inc.) and the bestselling *Developing PowerBuilder Applications*. He is also the author of *Creating Cool VBScript Web Pages* and co-author of the bestselling *Visual Basic 4 Unleashed*.

In addition to writing, Bill is a Certified Visual Basic Instructor and a Certified PowerBuilder Instructor, and he frequently does training and consulting for a wide variety of Internet, intranet, and client/server development projects.

Bill is also the editor of Pinnacle Publishing's *Delphi Developer,* a technical journal for professional Borland Delphi programmers.

He and his wife Melanie live in Indianapolis, where they are both surrounded by a large number of animals and computers. ("Get the chinchilla off that power supply!")

ABOUT IDG BOOKS WORLDWIDE

Welcome to the world of IDG Books Worldwide.

IDG Books Worldwide, Inc., is a subsidiary of International Data Group, the world's largest publisher of computer-related information and the leading global provider of information services on information technology. IDG was founded more than 25 years ago and now employs more than 8,500 people worldwide. IDG publishes more than 275 computer publications in over 75 countries (see listing below). More than 90 million people read one or more IDG publications each month.

Launched in 1990, IDG Books Worldwide is today the #1 publisher of best-selling computer books in the United States. We are proud to have received eight awards from the Computer Press Association in recognition of editorial excellence and three from *Computer Currents'* First Annual Readers' Choice Awards. Our best-selling *...For Dummies®* series has more than 50 million copies in print with translations in 38 languages. IDG Books Worldwide, through a joint venture with IDG's Hi-Tech Beijing, became the first U.S. publisher to publish a computer book in the People's Republic of China. In record time, IDG Books Worldwide has become the first choice for millions of readers around the world who want to learn how to better manage their businesses.

Our mission is simple: Every one of our books is designed to bring extra value and skill-building instructions to the reader. Our books are written by experts who understand and care about our readers. The knowledge base of our editorial staff comes from years of experience in publishing, education, and journalism — experience we use to produce books for the '90s. In short, we care about books, so we attract the best people. We devote special attention to details such as audience, interior design, use of icons, and illustrations. And because we use an efficient process of authoring, editing, and desktop publishing our books electronically, we can spend more time ensuring superior content and spend less time on the technicalities of making books.

You can count on our commitment to deliver high-quality books at competitive prices on topics you want to read about. At IDG Books Worldwide, we continue in the IDG tradition of delivering quality for more than 25 years. You'll find no better book on a subject than one from IDG Books Worldwide.

John Kilcullen
CEO
IDG Books Worldwide, Inc.

Steven Berkowitz
President and Publisher
IDG Books Worldwide, Inc.

*Eighth Annual
Computer Press
Awards ≥1992*

*Ninth Annual
Computer Press
Awards ≥1993*

*Tenth Annual
Computer Press
Awards ≥1994*

*Eleventh Annual
Computer Press
Awards ≥1995*

IDG Books Worldwide, Inc., is a subsidiary of International Data Group, the world's largest publisher of computer-related information and the leading global provider of information services on information technology. International Data Group publishes over 275 computer publications in over 75 countries. More than 90 million people read one or more International Data Group publications each month. International Data Group's publications include: **ARGENTINA:** Buyer's Guide, Computerworld Argentina, PC World Argentina; **AUSTRALIA:** Australian Macworld, Australian PC World, Australian Reseller News, Computerworld, IT Casebook, Network World, Publish, Webmaster; **AUSTRIA:** Computerwelt Osterreich, Networks Austria, PC Tip Austria; **BANGLADESH:** PC World Bangladesh; **BELARUS:** PC World Belarus; **BELGIUM:** Data News; **BRAZIL:** Annuario de Informática, Computerworld, Connections, Macworld, PC Player, PC World, Publish, Reseller News, Supergamepower; **BULGARIA:** Computerworld Bulgaria, Network World Bulgaria, PC & MacWorld Bulgaria; **CANADA:** CIO Canada, Client/Server World, ComputerWorld Canada, InfoWorld Canada, NetworkWorld Canada, WebWorld; **CHILE:** Computerworld Chile, PC World Chile; **COLOMBIA:** Computerworld Colombia, PC World Colombia; **COSTA RICA:** PC World Centro America; **THE CZECH AND SLOVAK REPUBLICS:** Computerworld Czechoslovakia, Macworld Czech Republic, PC World Czechoslovakia; **DENMARK:** Communications World Danmark, Computerworld Danmark, Macworld Danmark, PC World Danmark, Techworld Danmark; **DOMINICAN REPUBLIC:** PC World Republica Dominicana; **ECUADOR:** PC World Ecuador; **EGYPT:** Computerworld Middle East, PC World Middle East; **EL SALVADOR:** PC World Centro America; **FINLAND:** MikroPC, Tietoverkko, Tietoviikko; **FRANCE:** Distributique, Hebdo, Info PC, Le Monde Informatique, Macworld, Reseaux & Telecoms, WebMaster France; **GERMANY:** Computer Partner, Computerwoche, Computerwoche Extra, Computerwoche FOCUS, Global Online, Macwelt, PC Welt; **GREECE:** Amiga Computing, GamePro Greece, Multimedia World; **GUATEMALA:** PC World Centro America; **HONDURAS:** PC World Centro America; **HONG KONG:** Computerworld Hong Kong, PC World Hong Kong, Publish in Asia; **HUNGARY:** ABCD CD-ROM, Computerworld Szamitastechnika, Internetto online Magazine, PC World Hungary, PC-X Magazin Hungary; **ICELAND:** Tolvuheimur PC World Island; **INDIA:** Information Communications World, Information Systems Computerworld, PC World India, Publish in Asia; **INDONESIA:** InfoKomputer PC World, Komputek Computerworld, Publish in Asia; **IRELAND:** ComputerScope, PC Live!; **ISRAEL:** Macworld Israel, People & Computers/Computerworld; **ITALY:** Computerworld Italia, Macworld Italia, Networking Italia, PC World Italia; **JAPAN:** DTP World, Macworld Japan, Nikkei Personal Computing, OS/2 World Japan, SunWorld Japan, Windows NT World, Windows World Japan; **KENYA:** PC World East African; **KOREA:** Hi-Tech Information, Macworld Korea, PC World Korea; **MACEDONIA:** PC World Macedonia; **MALAYSIA:** Computerworld Malaysia, PC World Malaysia, Publish in Asia; **MALTA:** PC World Malta; **MEXICO:** Computerworld Mexico, PC World Mexico; **MYANMAR:** PC World Myanmar; **NETHERLANDS:** Computer! Totaal, LAN Internetworking Magazine, LAN World Buyers Guide, Macworld Netherlands, Net, WebWereld; **NEW ZEALAND:** Absolute Beginners Guide and Plain & Simple Series, Computer Buyer, Computer Industry Directory, Computerworld New Zealand, MTB, Network World, PC World New Zealand; **NICARAGUA:** PC World Centro America; **NORWAY:** Computerworld Norge, CW Rapport, Datamagasinet, Financial Rapport, Kursguide Norge, Macworld Norge, Multimediaworld Norge, PC World Ekspress Norge, PC World Nettverk, PC World Norge, PC World ProduktGuide Norge; **PAKISTAN:** Computerworld Pakistan; **PANAMA:** PC World Panama; **PEOPLE'S REPUBLIC OF CHINA:** China Computer Users, China Computerworld, China InfoWorld, China Telecom World Weekly, Computer & Communication, Electronic Design China, Electronics Today, Electronics Weekly, Game Software, PC World China, Popular Computer Week, Software Weekly, Software World, Telecom World; **PERU:** Computerworld Peru, PC World Profesional Peru, PC World SoHo Peru; **PHILIPPINES:** Click!, Computerworld Philippines, PC World Philippines, Publish, Seti; **POLAND:** Computerworld Poland, Computerworld Special Report Poland, Cyber, Macworld Poland, Networld Poland, PC World Komputer; **PORTUGAL:** Cerebro/PC World, Computerworld/Correio Informático, Dealer World Portugal, Mac*In/PC*In Portugal, Multimedia World; **PUERTO RICO:** PC World Puerto Rico; **ROMANIA:** Computerworld Romania, PC World Romania, Telecom Romania; **RUSSIA:** Computerworld Russia, Mir PK, Publish, Seti; **SINGAPORE:** Computerworld Singapore, PC World Singapore, Publish in Asia; **SLOVENIA:** Monitor; **SOUTH AFRICA:** Computing SA, Network World SA, Software World SA; **SPAIN:** Communicaciones World España, Computerworld España, Dealer World España, Macworld España, PC World España; **SRI LANKA:** Infolink PC World; **SWEDEN:** CAP&Design, Computer Sweden, Corporate Computing Sweden, Internetworld Sweden, it.branschen, Macworld Sweden, MaxiData Sweden, MikroDatorn, Nätverk & Kommunikation, PC World Sweden, PCaktiv, Windows World Sweden; **SWITZERLAND:** Computerworld Schweiz, Macworld Schweiz, PCtip; **TAIWAN:** Computerworld Taiwan, Macworld Taiwan, NEW ViSiON/Publish, PC World Taiwan, Windows World Taiwan; **THAILAND:** Publish in Asia, Thai Computerworld; **TURKEY:** Computerworld Turkiye, Macworld Turkiye, Network World Turkiye, PC World Turkiye; **UKRAINE:** Computerworld Kiev, Multimedia World Ukraine, PC World Ukraine; **UNITED KINGDOM:** Acorn User UK, Amiga Action UK, Amiga Computing UK, Apple Talk UK, Computing, Macworld, Parents and Computers UK, PC Advisor, PC Home, PSX Pro, The WEB; **UNITED STATES:** Cable in the Classroom, CIO Magazine, Computerworld, DOS World, Federal Computer Week, GamePro Magazine, InfoWorld, I-Way, Macworld, Network World, PC Games, PC World, Publish, Video Event, THE WEB Magazine, and WebMaster; online webzines: JavaWorld, NetscapeWorld, and SunWorld Online; **URUGUAY:** InfoWorld Uruguay; **VENEZUELA:** Computerworld Venezuela, PC World Venezuela; and **VIETNAM:** PC World Vietnam.   5/7/98

Dedication

To my wife of ten, more or less, fantastic years. I really do love you. And to you, I renew my vows — for better or for worse . . . I do!

Author's Acknowledgments

First, a big thanks to Doug Miller — a new friend and boss. Thanks for allowing me the time off to give this project my full attention. And thanks for the opportunity to work with you and the other great folks at Cybo. There have been precious few times in my life when I've actually been *excited* about going to work in the morning!

And thanks to my Monday boys-night-out gang: Brad, Mike, and Curtis. You guys are all right — for a bunch of geeks! (Pot, kettle, black — I know.)

Thanks to my wife for her patience with me through yet another painful book birthing process. We'll get around to that other kind of birthing process soon — I promise!

And to my parents for your continuing love and friendship throughout my writing of this book — and throughout my life!

And most importantly, thanks to all the great folks at IDG — especially Kel Oliver and Joyce Pepple and all the rest of the IDG staff that helped make this book possible. Thanks also to my technical editor, Greg Guntle, for his thoughtful contribution. It has been great working with you all. Let's all get together and do it again sometime.

Publisher's Acknowledgments

We're proud of this book; please register your comments through our IDG Books Worldwide Online Registration Form located at http://my2cents.dummies.com.

Some of the people who helped bring this book to market include the following:

Acquisitions, Editorial, and Media Development

Project Editor: Kelly Oliver

Acquisitions Editor: Joyce Pepple

Technical Editor: Greg Guntle

Media Development Editor: Marita Ellixson

Associate Permissions Editor: Carmen Krikorian

Editorial Manager: Mary Corder

Media Development Manager: Heather Heath Dismore

Editorial Assistant: Paul Kuzmic

Production

Associate Project Coordinator: Tom Missler

Layout and Graphics: Lou Boudreau, Linda M. Boyer, J. Tyler Connor, Angela F. Hunckler, Anna Rohrer, Brent Savage, Janet Seib

Proofreaders: Christine Berman, Kelli Botta, Nancy Price, Nancy L. Reinhardt, Rebecca Senninger, Janet M. Withers

Indexer: Ann Norcross

Special Help

Valery Bourke, Donna Love, Suzanne Thomas

General and Administrative

IDG Books Worldwide, Inc.: John Kilcullen, CEO; Steven Berkowitz, President and Publisher

IDG Books Technology Publishing: Brenda McLaughlin, Senior Vice President and Group Publisher

Dummies Technology Press and Dummies Editorial: Diane Graves Steele, Vice President and Associate Publisher; Mary Bednarek, Director of Acquisitions and Product Development; Kristin A. Cocks, Editorial Director

Dummies Trade Press: Kathleen A. Welton, Vice President and Publisher; Kevin Thornton, Acquisitions Manager

IDG Books Production for Dummies Press: Michael R. Britton, Vice President of Production and Creative Services; Beth Jenkins Roberts, Production Director; Cindy L. Phipps, Manager of Project Coordination, Production Proofreading, and Indexing; Kathie S. Schutte, Supervisor of Page Layout; Shelley Lea, Supervisor of Graphics and Design; Debbie J. Gates, Production Systems Specialist; Robert Springer, Supervisor of Proofreading; Debbie Stailey, Special Projects Coordinator; Tony Augsburger, Supervisor of Reprints and Bluelines

Dummies Packaging and Book Design: Robin Seaman, Creative Director; Jocelyn Kelaita, Product Packaging Coordinator; Kavish + Kavish, Cover Design

◆

The publisher would like to give special thanks to Patrick J. McGovern, without whom this book would not have been possible.

◆

Contents at a Glance

Cartoons at a Glance

By Rich Tennant

page 301

page 7

page 315

page 325

page 201

page 107

Fax: 978-546-7747 • **E-mail:** the5wave@tiac.net

Table of Contents

Part II: Making Your Web Pages Smarter with Scripts.... 107

Chapter 6: Using Scripts 109

Chapter 7: Discovering Objects 123

Introduction

● ●

*W*elcome to *Visual InterDev 6 For Dummies!* This book is your fast track to creating exciting, dynamic Web applications with the most exciting Web development tool out there: Microsoft Visual InterDev 6.

Making use of a smorgasbord of technologies including Active Server Pages (ASP), database access with Active Data Objects (ADO) and Microsoft's Open Database Connectivity (ODBC), client- and server-side ActiveX components, and many more, Visual InterDev 6 empowers you as no other development environment can. But the real trick is that Visual InterDev makes using all these technologies pretty darn easy!

Who Are You?

Looking into my crystal ball, I bet I can make a few guesses about whom you may be . . .

- ✔ You may be the Webmaster or developer for an Internet site who wants to create dynamic Web pages to increase traffic, sell information or products, or simply get your ideas across more clearly.

- ✔ You may be the Webmaster or developer for an intranet site who is developing internal corporate applications to make other employees' jobs easier or more efficient.

- ✔ Or you may just be one of those incurable techie types who always has to have your fingers in all the newest and coolest technologies. They ought to lock you guys up!

In any case, I'm going to assume that you have some experience developing Web pages. You probably already know HTML, and you may have done some programming using a Web scripting language such as JavaScript or Perl. Or maybe you've done some traditional programming with a language such as Visual Basic, PowerBuilder, Delphi, Java, or C/C++.

Because of these (perhaps foolish) assumptions, I don't show you how to write HTML in this book. If you want to brush up on that topic, you should check out *HTML For Dummies,* 3rd Edition, by Ed Tittel (published by IDG Books Worldwide, Inc.). I also don't cover the JavaScript language for use in client-side scripting. But again, *JavaScript For Dummies,* 2nd Edition, by Emily A. Vander Veer (also published by IDG Books Worldwide, Inc.) can give you everything you need to know. I do include an appendix that covers VBScript, if you don't already know it, because you'll use that a lot in your server-side scripting. Finally, if you want to dig deeper into the mysteries of Active Server Pages in general, I happen to know of a really good book on that topic, too: *Active Server Pages For Dummies* (by yours truly and published by IDG Books Worldwide, Inc.).

Why Use Visual InterDev 6?

Visual InterDev 6 is only one of the many tools designed to make your Web pages easier to create. So why settle on it? Actually, I can think of many good reasons.

Other tools are focused on making your Web pages prettier. Visual InterDev 6 is more focused on helping you easily create more powerful and productive Web applications — pages that actually *do* something.

Setting up flexible applications that allow you to view and update the information in a database, for example, is one of the specialties of Visual InterDev 6.

If you are familiar with Visual Basic, Visual C++, or Visual J++, you'll find that the Visual InterDev 6 development environment looks very familiar. This common look and feel makes Visual InterDev 6 easy to learn, and that makes you more productive!

Why Read This Book?

Okay, so you've decided on Visual InterDev 6. So why read this book? Good question. In this book, I show you how to quickly dive right in and make Visual InterDev 6 work for you. No long, drawn-out conceptual chapters, and no dwelling on insignificant details. Instead, I focus on the concepts and techniques you need to know to get your work done and look like a genius.

How This Book Is Organized

This book is divided into six parts, and each part consists of several chapters. In general, the book starts off with the basics and then moves on to more complex topics. But that doesn't mean you have to read it from front to back. If you already know the topic a particular chapter covers, skip ahead. Or skip right to the topics that interest you most, if you want. I won't tell anyone. But just remember, if you run across something that is confusing or doesn't make sense, you may want to look back at an earlier chapter. I try to point you to related material or stuff-you-need-to-know-to-understand-this-stuff wherever appropriate.

The next sections describe the parts and tell you what each part covers.

Part I: Creating a Web Site

This part is the foundation to all the rest. It introduces you to the user interface and tells you what all the little doohickies on the screen do. It also describes how Visual InterDev is organized and how you can use it to design your Web site and start creating really cool Web pages.

Part II: Making Your Web Pages Smarter with Scripts

If all you want to do is create the Web equivalent to a sales brochure or annual report, you can do that easily enough. But if you want to create real Web applications that actually do cool stuff, then you need to go beyond HTML into the world of client- and server-side scripting. In this part, I introduce the concept of scripting and how it works. Then I show you how to do it in Visual InterDev 6. You find out about all the cool stuff you can do when you have a real programming language and lots of cool objects to play with.

Part III: Accessing the Database

Databases enable you to keep track of lots and lots of information in an orderly way. And because Web pages are probably the best way to see and distribute information, databases and the Web are a match made in heaven! In this part, you find out how to make that match happen. Don't worry; it's much easier than it looks.

The highlight of your database journey is the tour of Billy-Bob's Internet Auction Application. That's right — now you can host auctions on your own Web site to sell all your precious stuff to the highest bidder. This application demonstrates a lot of cool database techniques and gives you a foundation for creating your own database Web applications.

Part IV: Wrapping It Up!

Unless you are a lot closer to perfect than I am, your scripting is going to be quickly followed up by debugging. And in this part, you discover the Visual InterDev integrated debugging capabilities.

You also get tips and instructions on the best way to finally deploy your application so that the world can see your masterpiece!

Part V: The Part of Tens

And now, the part you've all been waiting for: The Part of Tens! In The Part of Tens, you discover the ten best of everything Visual InterDev-related. Nope, I'm not giving away any secrets. And no fair jumping to The Part of Tens first!

Part VI: The Appendixes

Finally, the appendixes cap off the book with a few handy places to look for need-to-know information.

First, you explore all the secrets of VBScript. In Appendix A, I boil down this language to its essentials so that you can quickly pick it up, read through it, and be scripting your own Web pages in no time.

In Appendix B, I offer a few tips and thoughts on installing Visual InterDev. If you haven't already completed this step, you may want to check here before you do. I don't have all the answers, and the process is a little complicated, but I definitely point you in the right direction and give you a good shove.

Last but not least is the "What's on the CD" appendix. I packed the CD with useful components and other stuff to make your Web application life easier. Check it out!

How To Read This Book

Actually, I'm quite sure you know how to read this book. It works much like any other book — you start with the first word, proceed to the second, and go on like that until there are no more words.

But a few things may trip you up here and there. When I want to show you a portion of a Web page or some script from a page, it looks like this.

```
<% Response.Cookie("Music")("Style") = "Alternative" %>
```

I refer to something you should type by using a bold font, like this:

Type this in the text box: **Pookie**.

I refer to something you see on screen, like the title of a window, by using a monofont typeface, like this:

Look for the window titled `Active Window`.

Also, scattered throughout the coming chapters, you find step-by-step descriptions of how to do almost anything you want to do in Visual InterDev. The steps always start with a line that describes what the steps will do, followed by a colon. Then the things you are supposed to do are in bold. The things that happen in response and all descriptions are in regular type.

I refer to items on the menu bar that I want you to select by using a command arrow that looks like this: File⇨Open.

Finally, sometimes I refer you to the Visual InterDev online Help system for more information. The online Help is organized into a big tree-like structure. So to tell you where a specific Help topic is, I start with the root and then tell you each branch to take until you get to the specific document. It looks something like this.

MSDN Library Visual Studio 6.0⇨Visual InterDev Documentation⇨ Reference⇨Scripting Object Model⇨Script Objects⇨ Recordset Script Object

Visual Contact!

I'm a feedback junky! Send me all your comments — good or bad. I want to hear them — I need to hear them! You can reach me via e-mail at

`billhatfield@worldnet.att.net`

You can also visit one of the best software developer Web sites at:

`www.edgequest.com`

In fact, on that very site, you find a link to a Web site that is completely dedicated to this book:

`www.edgequest.com/VIDFD`

There, you find cool Visual InterDev 6 examples; book corrections, if there are any (like I would ever make a mistake!); and links to other great Web development sites.

What's on the CD

The CD included in the back of this book includes the complete Internet Auction application (discussed in Chapter 14) and a lot of shareware, demo, and freeware components and examples.

Icons Used in This Book

Like bacon without eggs. Like the Captain without Tenille. What would a ...*For Dummies* book be without those cute little icons in the margin of almost every page? But they're not there just to make the page look more interesting. They actually mean something! What do they mean? I'm glad you asked. . . .

This icon indicates technical trivia that is interesting (to me, at least!) but not at all necessary to understanding Visual InterDev 6. If I go off on a techie rant, I promise to at least warn you with one of these icons so that you can skip it if you want.

Look next to these icons for a hint or quick idea that can help make your life just a little simpler.

Danger, Will Robinson! This icon labels important information that can help you avoid impending doom. Ignore these tidbits at your own peril.

Indicates important tidbits to tuck away for quick reference in your brain.

If I designed the world, everything would be nice, sane, and normal. And it would all make sense. Unfortunately, no one has offered me that gig yet, so the world is still a very messy and confusing place. However, I can at least point out the places where things work in a — shall we say — *non-intuitive* way by using this icon. (By the way, I think this icon is by far the coolest-looking one of the bunch.)

Find this icon to locate cool components and examples in their already-typed form on the CD.

Part I
Creating a Web Site

The 5th Wave By Rich Tennant

"NIFTY CHART, FRANK, BUT NOT ENTIRELY NECESSARY."

In this part . . .

*F*rom designing your site organization, to creating pages, to standardizing your look and feel, Visual InterDev has all the tools you need. In this part, you discover the Visual InterDev flexible page editor, site diagramming tools, the Cascading Style Sheets editor, as well as all the secrets for using themes and layouts to give your site a professional touch in no time.

Chapter 1

What Is Visual InterDev?
(And Why Does It Have
Such a Funny Name?)

● ●

In This Chapter

▶ The history of Visual InterDev

▶ The origin of the (how should we say?) *unique* name

▶ What Visual InterDev does

▶ Microsoft's goals in developing the product

▶ How Visual InterDev fits in with other tools

● ●

*T*he World Wide Web started as a simple idea — text pages, tags, graphics, and the ever-present hyperlink, which enables users to skip and hop from one page to the next.

But the development of this idea resulted in the nagging impression that so much more was possible. And so this simple technology has grown into a complex web of new ideas, implemented as new technologies, to make the Web faster, more graphical, more engaging, more informational, and, above all, more interactive.

But all these technologies have their own tools and their own way of integrating into the Web world. Bringing everything together to fulfill the promise of the Web has been a challenge — until now.

Visual InterDev 6 is the first tool to truly integrate all the essential features needed to make interactive Web pages not only possible, but actually pretty easy to create! By integrating simple scripting languages with object-oriented concepts, Visual InterDev 6 takes a giant step forward in the goal of making Web applications as interactive and full-featured as any other computer application.

What Is Visual InterDev 6?

Visual InterDev 6 is a development environment that is designed to make creating and maintaining Web applications for the Internet and corporate intranets easy.

Here's the scoop on the background, the name, and the version

When Microsoft first began working on the Visual InterDev project, it was referred to by the ominous name *Blackbird*. It was originally imagined as a tool for developing content using Microsoft's proprietary technologies in Microsoft Network. But Microsoft quickly realized that an Internet based on its proprietary technologies would not be taken seriously in an Internet industry that already had very good standards in place.

So, Microsoft switched gears and decided that its new approach would be to "embrace and extend" the already-existing Internet standards and technologies. This, as it turns out, was exactly the right move. And with this new, kinder, gentler approach, Microsoft decided to change what was once called Blackbird. Now code-named *Internet Studio,* this new development application was being designed to bring together all the best tools for creating Web content and put them under one roof. The product would also make database access from Web pages not only possible, but actually *easy.*

After much development, many sneak previews, and more than a little ballyhoo, Microsoft released a new product in early 1997: Visual InterDev 1.0. Until the announcement of the product, many rumors about the product's name were circulating. Some favored continuing with the bland Internet Studio, while others touted the cryptic Visual I++ —

to maintain continuity with Visual C++ and Visual J++ (other Microsoft programming products). The final name was quite a surprise — it's a combination of the words *Internet* and *Development.* Although some may find the name clumsy and even a little ugly, it is unique enough to be copyrighted and, after all, this is business.

Visual InterDev 1.0 was an unusual product. It seemed to glom a variety of tools all together. And, like the name, the result wasn't very pretty. But it *was* surprisingly productive. No single environment put the capabilities of all these tools so readily at hand. Visual InterDev quickly became the favorite Web development tool for many.

Then in September of 1998, Microsoft released Visual InterDev 6.

Now wait a minute! What happened to Visual InterDev 2 through 5? A very good question. The answer is that they simply never existed. Visual InterDev is a part of a larger package called Visual Studio that includes products such as Visual Basic, Visual C++, and Visual J++. Microsoft decided to release the new version of all these products at once and to make the version number of all the products the same. So Visual InterDev aged five generations in just over a year. For more information on Visual Studio, see "Okay, So What's Visual Studio?" later in this chapter.

Visual InterDev 6 is different from other Web page creation tools because it's designed like an application development environment — like Visual Basic or Visual C++. It not only looks similar to these tools, but it also works in much the same way. It is designed to create Web *applications,* not just Web pages (see Figure 1-1 for an example of a Web application).

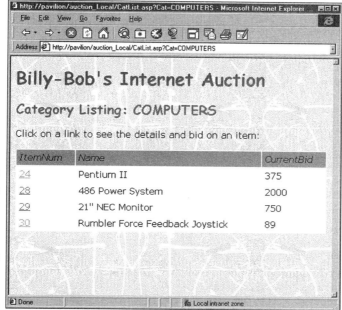

Figure 1-1: This Web site example shows a list of items up for sale.

The difference between a set of pages and an application is that an application *does something.* It doesn't just display information. For example, a real estate Web site that shows houses for sale is just a Web page, but a Web site that can actually calculate your mortgage payment based on your down payment and the length of the loan is a Web *application.* Applications can be simple or complex, obvious or subtle. But they transform Web technologies from passive information storage and retrieval to an active, intelligent platform.

Microsoft's Goals for Visual InterDev (And Why You Should Care!)

If you make your living at computer programming, the decisions you make about what tools to work with are very important. If you work with a development environment for three years, and it ends up being abandoned or its company ends up going out of business, then you have three years of experience in a development environment that no one cares about. That can be a problem!

So when you are looking at a new development tool like Visual InterDev, it is essential that you know what it is and how its company is positioning the product for the future before you dive in and start using the product. To help you decide if Visual InterDev is for you, I'm giving you a list here of what Microsoft's stated goals are for the product and what those goals mean to you as a developer.

Because Visual InterDev is a development environment, its goals are very different from other Web page development tools. What you want out of Visual InterDev is similar to what you want out of Visual Basic, PowerBuilder, or other client/server development environments. Specifically, you want:

- ✔ **A rapid prototyping and development environment.** The speed of business just keeps getting faster and faster. So it's absolutely essential that prototypes and completed applications are delivered as quickly as possible. Visual InterDev makes many common activities automatic. Tedious tasks are often turned into a simple drag-and-drop.

- ✔ **Complete integration of the database into the development environment.** Client/server databases are a very important part of the development process — you need easy access to data. Visual InterDev offers an easy-to-use visual interface for creating tables, adding and modifying data, and creating queries. In addition, Visual InterDev enables the application to easily keep track of changes the user makes to the data on the page, and then automatically make the corresponding updates in the database.

- ✔ **An easy-to-understand, coherent programming model.** Because the Web often uses a variety of technologies and a variety of platforms, Web development can quickly become a very complicated process. Microsoft has forged a new way to tame this complexity while still providing the broadest flexibility possible. A new technology introduced with Visual InterDev 6 is called the *Scripting Object Model (SOM)*, and it creates a simplified, yet powerful way to speed development of complex applications.

- ✔ **Team development features.** A Web application is different from other software development projects — not everyone working on the project is a programmer. You are just as likely to have page layout designers, graphic artists, and content writers all working together on the same project. Because of that, it is important to have an easy way for many people with many different backgrounds to work together on the same project, without getting in each other's way. Visual InterDev allows each user to check out certain parts of the project on their own workstation and tinker with it there. Then when the user is ready to share her work with the world, she can check it back in to the server.

✔ **Ability to create *industrial-strength*, *enterprise-wide*, or *mission-critical* applications.** These terms are often used to separate simple, single-user applications from important corporate applications. Industrial-strength, enterprise-wide, or mission-critical applications involve the following issues:

- **Scalability:** The capability of an application to work with a small or large number of users

- **Reliability:** The assurance that the application will always be available and that it will always work as you expect it to

- **Client/server database accessibility:** The secure, multi-user data storage that assures data integrity

- **Distributed capabilities:** The possibility that it may be used by users across the company or across the world

- **Support for diverse technologies:** The capability to access to older mainframe computer systems or databases that hold or maintain information that needs to be integrated

- **Team development support:** The capability to share information, source code, and ideas

All these goals add up to a very tall order for the second version of a product — even if it does have "6" after its name! But Visual InterDev 6 is a very big step toward meeting all these goals. The fact that such a strong product was developed in such a short time is astonishing!

And I think it's safe to say that Microsoft intends to continue to keep this product at the front and center of its development tools. Microsoft's goal is that Visual InterDev will do for Web development exactly what Visual Basic did for Windows development — make it fast, easy, and very productive.

Okay, So What's Visual Studio?

Microsoft Visual Studio 6 is the latest version of Microsoft's complete suite of software development tools. Visual Studio collects together all the tools you need to develop software in the same way that Microsoft Office collects together all the most commonly used business applications. Among the development tools in Visual Studio are:

✔ Visual InterDev

✔ Visual J++

✔ Visual Basic

✔ Visual C++

Visual InterDev is one of the newest additions to be added to Visual Studio. Microsoft designed it to provide a general platform for creating complex Web pages and Web applications to meet the needs of Internet and intranet developers.

Visual J++ is also a relatively new addition to this suite. It's a Java development environment that enables you to create both client-side and server-side Java programs for use in Web applications, as well as completely stand-alone Java applications. Web components created in Visual J++ can be easily integrated into a Visual InterDev project.

Visual Basic is another Visual Studio component designed to work closely with Visual InterDev. You can use Visual Basic to create ActiveX components that, like Java components, can run on either the client or the server. The Visual Basic language is extremely popular and very easy to learn. Because of this, the Visual InterDev/Visual Basic combination offers probably the quickest and easiest way to create complete Web-based applications to meet almost any need.

Finally, Visual C++ is the granddaddy in Visual Studio. It has been around in one form or another for many years and is the most popular platform for low-level development on the market.

How Are Visual InterDev 6 and FrontPage Different?

You may have heard of Microsoft FrontPage. It's also a tool for helping you create Web pages. So you may be wondering, "Why does Microsoft have two products to do essentially the same thing?" The main reason is because FrontPage and Visual InterDev are designed for two different kinds of people.

Microsoft FrontPage (see Figure 1-2) is a *very* easy-to-use package. In fact, it works very much like a word processor. You simply type in the text, add styles, insert graphics, and save your creation as a new Web page. Using FrontPage, *anyone* can begin creating pages after only a few minutes of instruction.

But FrontPage can't do everything. Although it is very flexible and makes a lot of complex tasks easy, it isn't designed for creating pages that access and process data from databases or for easily creating other kinds of complex Web applications.

Figure 1-2:
Microsoft
FrontPage
in action.

That's where Visual InterDev comes in. Visual InterDev is also pretty easy to use, but it's definitely not designed for the average Microsoft Word user. It's a product designed for software developers who are familiar with products such as Visual Basic, PowerBuilder, or Delphi.

In exchange for this added complexity, though, Visual InterDev provides a vast array of capabilities for creating powerful Web applications that would be very difficult to do without it. It cuts the time for creating database and client/server Web applications into a fraction of the time it would take using other Web development tools.

But here's the best news: Visual InterDev and FrontPage work together seamlessly! They access the same Web projects in the same way and can easily be used together. So the content providers and graphic artists can work in FrontPage while the programmers use Visual InterDev. Each can use the environment that most directly meets his or her needs.

Chapter 2

Creating Webs, Projects, and Solutions

In This Chapter

▶ Discovering what webs, projects, and solutions are

▶ Creating a new project

▶ Opening an existing project

*T*he applications you create in Visual InterDev are unlike applications you've created using any other development environment. Instead of being made up of forms and code, they are made up of many pages, script, graphics, ActiveX components, and lots of other little files. Keeping track of all these pieces and how they fit together is no small task.

But Visual InterDev has created a complete and easy to understand system for organizing this complexity. In this chapter, you discover what *webs, projects,* and *solutions* are and how they work together to organize your development.

Taking a Step Back Before You Begin

I'm assuming that you already have Visual InterDev installed and working. That's a mighty big assumption because installing Visual InterDev isn't nearly as easy as just running Setup and putting in the right CD-ROM. Server components need to be installed on the server, and client and server components need to be installed on your workstation. Ain't computers great?

If you don't have Visual InterDev installed yet, be sure to check out Appendix B. There, you find some guidelines that help you figure out what needs to go where.

Defining the Terms

Before I dive into Visual InterDev itself, I want to tell you about a few terms that I use all the time when working on Web applications in Visual InterDev. They aren't complicated, but be sure you understand them before you go on — don't make me give you a pop quiz!

A *web* is a collection of files *on a Web server* that work together to form a Web site or Web application. You can create a new web on a server using Visual InterDev or Microsoft FrontPage.

A *project* is a collection of files *on your workstation* that correspond to a web on the server. Often, you don't want to work directly with the files on the server as you are changing them. So you make a copy of these files on your workstation; you can work with that copy until you are done. All those copies and other files on your workstation that work together are called a *project*. The project is always directly associated with a web on the server, and the project often has the same name as the web. You can think of the project as a mirror on your workstation of a web on the server.

A *solution* is a collection of one or more projects. You can have only one solution open in Visual InterDev at a time. But a solution can have as many projects in it as you like.

When you create a new project in Visual InterDev, you usually create a new solution, too. But when you are working on a project in a solution, you can always add another project to the current solution. Then you can have both projects open at once. You can also create a whole new project to be a part of the solution you have open.

Finally, a specific project can be a part of more than one solution, if you want.

See Figure 2-1 for a diagram of how all these pieces fit together.

Before you do any work in Visual InterDev, you must have a solution open with at least one project in it. I discuss how to create a new project and solution in the next few sections of this chapter.

Looking at the New Project Dialog Box

The New Project dialog box (see Figure 2-2) usually appears when you first start Visual InterDev.

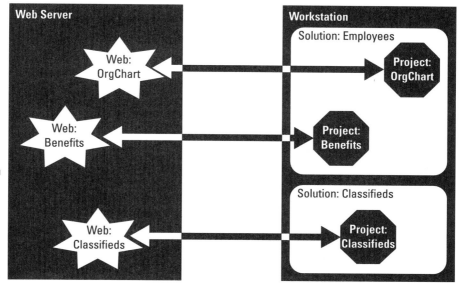

Figure 2-1:
How webs,
projects,
and
solutions all
fit together.

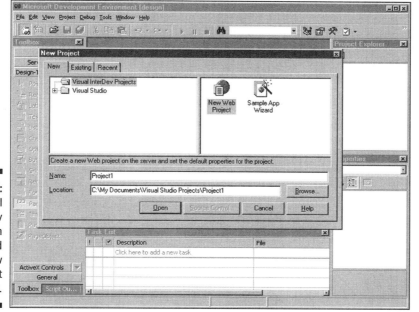

Figure 2-2:
The Visual
InterDev
main
window and
the New
Project
dialog box.

The three tabs along the top of the New Project dialog box are:

- ✔ **New:** Allows you to create a new project from scratch.
- ✔ **Existing:** Allows you to open any project that you've created in the past.
- ✔ **Recent:** Provides an easy way to open a project that you just recently worked with.

You can stop the New Project dialog box from appearing every time you start up by clicking the check box at the very bottom of the dialog box that says `Don't show this dialog in the future`. If you do that, a blank primary window will appear in the future.

Creating a New Project and Solution

When you create a new project in Visual InterDev, you *automatically* create a new solution to hold the project. When you open an existing project, again, a new solution is created to hold it.

You can also open an existing solution, and whatever projects were a part of that solution when it was saved appear there. See "Opening an Existing Project or Solution" for more information on this.

To create a new project:

1. **Click the New tab on the New Project dialog box.**

   For information on using this dialog box to open existing projects, see "Opening an Existing Project or Solution" later in this chapter.

2. **Click the folder on the left that's labeled Visual InterDev Projects.**

3. **Click the icon on the right that's labeled New Web Project.**

4. **Click in the text box labeled Name Below and type the name you want to give to the new project.**

5. **Click Open.**

   The Web Project Wizard appears (see Figure 2-3).

The Web Project Wizard, Step 1

The Web Project Wizard (see Figure 2-3) is designed to quickly gather all the information needed to create a brand new Visual InterDev project.

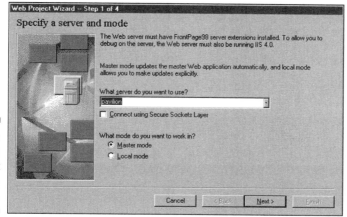

Figure 2-3:
The Web
Project
Wizard,
Step 1.

To fill in the Web Project Wizard, Step 1:

1. **Enter the name of the Web server where your final Web site will be stored.**

   The information you enter here could be the name of a Web server on your intranet (like Dana or Pluto) or the actual Web address of a server you have access to on the Web (like www.myserver.com).

2. **If your server supports secure sockets and you need a secure connection, click the Connect Using Secure Sockets Layer check box.**

3. **Choose whether you want to work in Master mode or Local mode.**

   In *Master mode,* you work directly with the files on the Web server. Every time you save the files, they are updated on the server. And when you run your application, it runs off the server.

   Local mode enables you to make changes and test pages on your own computer before sending them up to the server.

   Local mode is almost always preferable.

   You *can* change modes after you create the project.

4. **Click Next.**

   A small window appears to inform you that Visual InterDev is trying to connect to the server.

   The Web Project Wizard, Step 2 window appears.

The Web Project Wizard, Step 2

Step 2 (see Figure 2-4) enables you to create a brand new web on the server or simply connect to an already-existing web.

If you are creating a brand new project from scratch, you'll want to create a new web on the server. If you simply want to work on a project that is already started and is on the server, then you'll want to connect to an already-existing web.

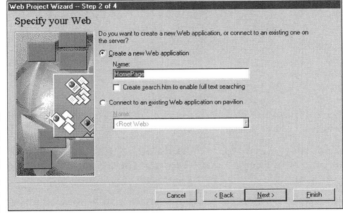

Figure 2-4:
The Web
Project
Wizard,
Step 2.

Connecting to an existing web

To fill in the Web Project Wizard, Step 2, to connect to an existing web:

1. **Choose the Connect to an Existing Web Application radio button.**

2. **Choose which existing web on the server you want to connect this project to.**

3. **Click Finish.**

The Visual InterDev primary window appears containing a new solution and a new project connected to the web you specified. You are finished creating your new project and ready to begin work on it. Because you've connected to an existing web, you don't need to go on to Steps 3 and 4 of the Web Project Wizard.

Creating to a new web

To fill in the Web Project Wizard, Step 2, to create a new web:

1. **Click the Create a New Web Application radio button.**

2. **Give your web a name.**

   This is the name that your web is known by on the *server.* You already told Visual InterDev in Step 1 what you wanted to name this *project,* and so it just uses that name as the default for the Name edit box.

   It's a good idea to always name the web the same thing as the project that works with that web.

3. **If you want, click the Create Search.htm to Enable Full Text Searching check box.**

   This option automatically creates a page called search.htm and sets up your application so the user can easily search through the Web pages for information he is interested in.

4. **Click Next.**

   The Web Project Wizard, Step 3 window appears.

The Web Project Wizard, Step 3

Step 3 (see Figure 2-5) enables you to apply a layout to this Web application. A *layout* is a configuration of buttons used throughout the application to make it easy to navigate. These buttons are created automatically and added to each page with minimal input from you. The layout makes adding simple sight navigation a no-brainer!

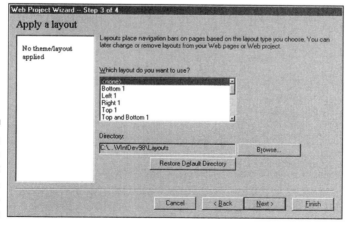

Figure 2-5:
The Web
Project
Wizard,
Step 3.

To fill in the Web Project Wizard, Step 3:

1. **Click the various options in the list box.**

   As you do, the associated layout appears in the preview box on the left. The preview box shows you exactly where the navigation buttons will appear in your application and what they will do.

2. **Click the name of the layout that you want to use.**

3. **Click Next.**

   The Web Project Wizard, Step 4, window appears.

The Web Project Wizard, Step 4

Step 4 (see Figure 2-6) enables you to apply a theme to your Web application. A *theme* is a description of what the pages will look like, including:

✔ The background graphic

✔ The text size, font, and color used for headings

✔ The graphics used for bullets

A theme helps give your pages a distinctive look and feel that is common throughout the entire Web application.

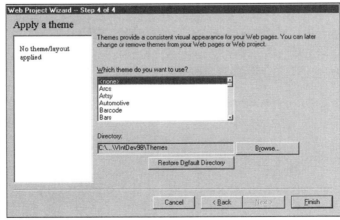

Figure 2-6: The Web Project Wizard, Step 4.

To fill in the Web Project Wizard, Step 4:

1. **Click the various options in the list box.**

   As you do, the associated theme appears in the preview box on the left. The preview box shows you exactly how your pages will look.

2. **Click the one you like best, or, if you don't like any of them, click <none>.**

3. **Click Finish.**

   A window appears to tell you that the Wizard is creating the different parts of your project.

4. **If your Web server requires you to log in to access and update the pages, you need to enter that information in the login dialog box that appears (see Figure 2-7).**

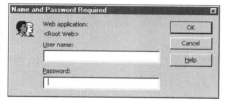

Figure 2-7:
The Login
dialog box.

A window appears to keep you updated about all the things Visual InterDev is doing to set up the Web on your server and the project on your workstation.

This setup may take a couple of minutes.

Finally, the Visual InterDev primary window appears, in all its glory.

For information on the various parts of the development environment, what they do and how they work, see Chapter 3.

Opening an Existing Project or Solution

To open an existing project:

1. **Click the Open Project button on the toolbar or choose File⇨Open Project from the menu bar.**

2. **The Open Project dialog box appears (see Figure 2-8).**

   This dialog box is almost identical to the New Project dialog box you saw when you first opened Visual InterDev. The only difference is that the title bar says Open Project and the tab that appears first is the Existing tab.

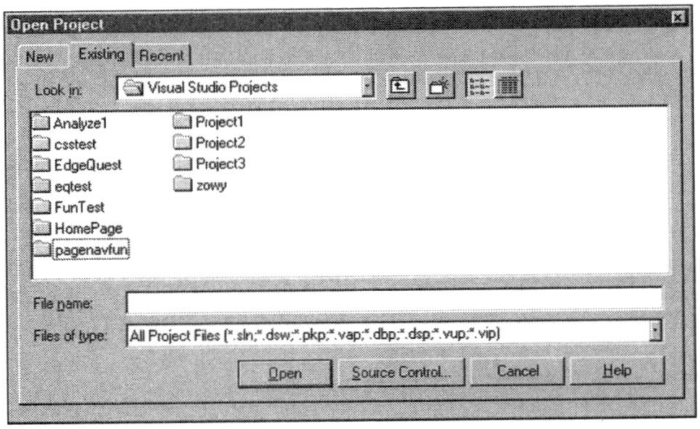

Figure 2-8:
The Existing
tab on the
Open
Project
dialog box.

3. **Find the folder with the name of the project or solution you want to open. Double-click it.**

   Inside the folder, you may find both a solution file and a project file. The solution has the extension .sln, and the project has the extension .vip.

4. **Double-click a project or solution file to close the current solution and open the new one.**

   Or you can click the Add to Current Solution radio button and then double-click a project file.

   That project is then added to your current solution.

   If you don't have another solution already open, the radio buttons do not appear.

To open an existing project that you've worked on recently:

1. **Click the Open Project button on the toolbar or choose File⇨Open Project from the menu bar.**

2. **The Open Project dialog box appears (refer to Figure 2-8).**

3. **Click the Recent tab (see Figure 2-9).**

4. **Double-click a project or solution to close the current solution and open the new one.**

   Or you can click the Add to Current Solution radio button and then double-click a project file.

   That project is then added to your current solution.

   If you don't have another solution already open, the radio buttons do not appear.

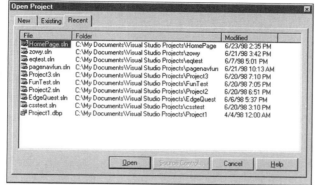

Figure 2-9:
The Recent
tab on the
Open
Project
dialog box.

Closing a Project

To close a project, choose File⇨Close All. The current solution and all the
projects in that solution close.

You must open another project before you can do any more work in Visual
InterDev.

Chapter 3

Navigating Visual InterDev and Creating Web Pages

*V*isual InterDev is a very complete, well-designed development environment. It is also very rich — which is to say, there's a lot to it! If you are familiar with other Visual Studio development tools such as Visual Basic, Visual C++, or Visual J++, then much of the information in this chapter is already familiar to you, and you can probably just skim over this chapter.

However, if you haven't used development tools like this before, give this chapter a more careful read. Nothing about the interface is tricky, but it has a lot of pieces, and you'll be more productive if you know how they all fit together!

In this chapter, you explore all the important windows like the Project Explorer and Toolbox. You also find all the key toolbar buttons and menu items in Visual InterDev. In the process, you discover all the techniques you need to create Web pages that use tables, ActiveX components, graphics, and more using the capabilities that Visual InterDev places at your fingertips.

Windows, Windows Everywhere!

Figure 3-1 shows Visual InterDev and each of the major windows. I refer to the windows throughout this book by the names that you see in their title bar.

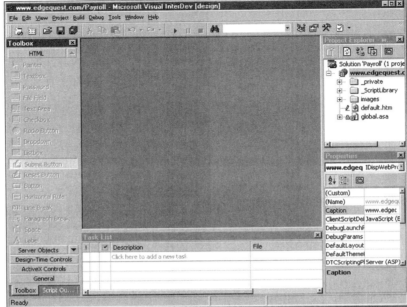

Figure 3-1:
Visual
InterDev
and all its
windows.

The first thing to notice is that the Visual InterDev user interface isn't a typical Multi-Document Interface (MDI) user interface like Word or Excel. It's made up of windows that are *docked,* or attached, to the primary window. If you move your mouse cursor between two of the windows that are docked next to each other, the mouse cursor turns into a double-headed arrow, and you can then change the relative size of both windows.

You can also move the cursor to any edge of a window and drag it to make it larger or smaller. Finally, you can grab the title bar of a window and drag the entire window to a different location. You can dock it in another location, or you can make it a free-floating window by dropping it in the middle of the primary window.

You can even drag it outside of the primary window and make it completely separate.

The docking ability is really the thing that distinguishes this user interface from other MDI-type interfaces. This addition allows you to place windows in a certain location and assure that they will stay there and not get in the way of other windows.

Using the Menu Bar

Like most other Windows applications, Visual InterDev has a menu bar and a toolbar. (I cover the toolbar in the next section.) The primary menu bar has nine top-level menus to choose from:

- ✔ **File:** This menu provides options for opening, closing, and creating new projects and files within the projects.

- ✔ **Edit:** Along with the typical Cut, Copy, Paste, and Delete options, the Edit menu includes the potential lifesavers Undo and Redo. You can also use Find and Replace to quickly search and make global changes to your Web page. Finally, Apply Theme and Layout enables you to add or change your theme or layout on the current page.

- ✔ **View:** This menu provides Open and Browse options that enable you to easily edit or preview the selected file in the Project Explorer window (see the section "Using the Project Explorer" later in this chapter for more about this feature). Additional options allow you to easily identify links (broken and otherwise) and to display or hide all the available windows.

- ✔ **Project:** The options on this menu enable you to add a variety of new files and objects to the current project. The Project menu provides access to a Source Control submenu, deployment options, and a variety of other project- and file-specific commands.

- ✔ **Build:** Provides the options to build your application in preparation to run it in either debugging mode or a release mode.

- ✔ **Debug:** In this menu, you can access all the commands necessary for the full-scale client- and server-side debugging features in Visual InterDev. For more information on debugging, see Chapter 16.

- ✔ **Tools:** The commands in the Tools menu enable you to customize Visual InterDev and provide access to the Add-In Manager and the Visual InterDev Options dialog box.

- ✔ **Window:** The options in this menu enable you to dock, hide, cascade, tile, and otherwise manipulate the windows in Visual InterDev.

- ✔ **Help:** The Help files, About box, and a variety of interesting and useful Web pages on the Microsoft Web site can be found here.

When you edit an HTML page, an Active Server Pages (ASP) page, a style sheet, or a site diagram, additional menus are added to the menu bar to provide options for these tasks.

Using the Standard Toolbar

The most important commands from the menus appear on the toolbar (see Figure 3-2). You should become familiar with all of these toolbar buttons — you'll use them all the time!

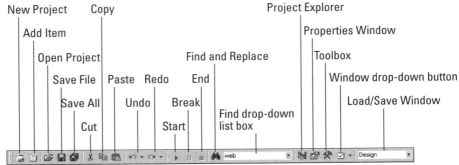

Figure 3-2:
The toolbar
buttons.

Here's a list of the buttons and what each does:

✔ **New Project:** Clicking this button opens the New Project dialog box, which enables you to create a new project or open an existing one. For more information on the New Project dialog box, see Chapter 2.

✔ **Add Item:** Click this button to add a new item to your project. *Items* include HTML pages, ASP pages, style sheets, and site diagrams. For more information on adding pages to your site, see "Adding an HTML Page or ASP Page" later this chapter.

✔ **Open:** Use this button to open the Open Project dialog box, which is almost identical to the New Project dialog box discussed previously. The only difference is that when you click Open, the Existing tab of the dialog box appears first, rather than the New tab. See Chapter 2 for more information.

✔ **Save and Save All:** Clicking the Save button saves the currently open item. Clicking the Save All button saves all open items.

✔ **Cut, Copy, and Paste:** You use these buttons to move or copy text, controls, or graphics to the Clipboard and then paste them somewhere else.

✔ **Undo and Redo:** These essential tools can save your neck in a whole bunch of situations when using Visual InterDev. Whenever you make a mistake, reach for these buttons first. But be aware that they won't bring back files you've deleted — so be careful!

✔ **Start, Break, and End:** These VCR-like buttons enable you to run your application, pause it temporarily, or stop it altogether.

✔ **Find and Replace:** Clicking this button makes a convenient Find/Replace dialog box pop up. But, even more conveniently, you don't have to use the Find/Replace dialog box for simple find operations. Type the text you want to find right into the textbox that appears on the toolbar and hit Enter. Or choose from the drop-down list of items you've searched for in the past.

✔ **Windows buttons:** These buttons enable you to easily show the most commonly used windows in Visual InterDev, including the Project Explorer, Properties window, and Toolbox. In addition, the drop-down button allows you to access and easily show the windows you don't use as often.

✔ **Load/Save Window UI:** This drop-down button allows you to choose from all the user interface configurations that you've saved (or that came with Visual InterDev initially). You can use this button to quickly change configurations as your needs change.

Adding an HTML Page or ASP Page

To create a new HTML or ASP page to your project:

1. **Click the Add Item button on the Standard toolbar.**

2. **The Add Item dialog box appears.**

   Web Project Files is selected on the left. On the right, you see four icons: HTML Page, ASP Page, Style Sheet, and Site Diagram.

3. **Click either the HTML Page or the ASP Page icon to select it.**

4. **Type the name you want to give the page in the Name edit box.**

5. **Click Open.**

   A new page appears in the middle of the primary window (see Figure 3-3). If your page doesn't look like the figure, click the Design tab at the bottom of the editor window. I discuss these tabs in the next section.

   Note that your screen may look different from Figure 3-5, depending on what you chose for a layout, theme, and so on. I chose to create an ASP page with the default name that has no theme or layout.

If you have chosen a theme, the background image for that theme appears on the page automatically.

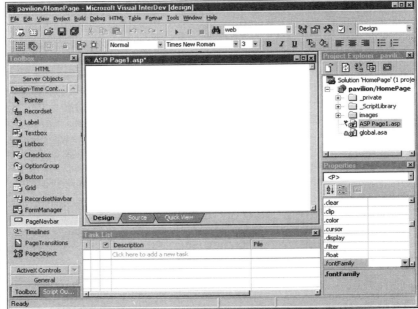

Figure 3-3:
A new
page.

If you have chosen a layout, you see strange bars across your page that look something like those in Figure 3-4. These bars indicate where navigation buttons will appear and where it is safe for you to add your own content. For more information on layouts, see Chapter 5.

Using the Editor

The Editor is the window where your Web page appears. This window looks and works pretty much the same for both HTML pages and ASP pages. You create and modify the Web pages for your Web applications in the Editor. Notice the following three tabs at the bottom of the window: Design, Source, and Quick View. These tabs enable you to switch to three different *views* of your page:

  ✔ **Design view:** You'll probably do most of your Web page designing in Design view (see Figure 3-5). It looks very much like the page will look in the browser when you are done creating it. You can type text here that will appear on the Web page, and you can add other HTML elements from the toolbox and see how they look (more on this later in this chapter).

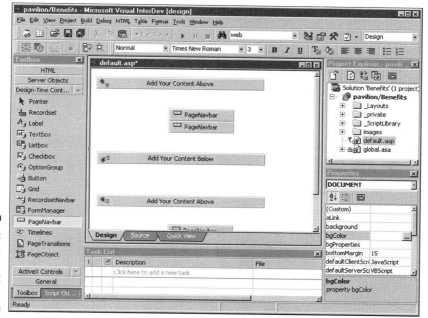

Figure 3-4:
A new page
with a
layout
applied.

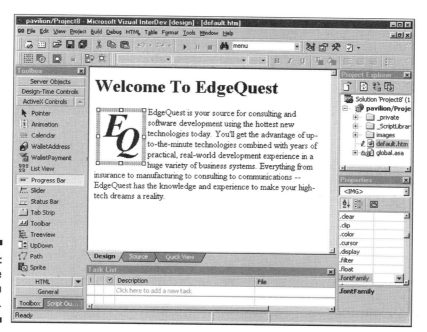

Figure 3-5:
A page
in Design
view.

✔ **Source view:** This is the raw text form of your HTML or ASP page. It shows you all the HTML tags and any server- or client-side script you've written for this page (see Figure 3-6). You'll spend your time here when you are writing ASP code.

✔ **Quick View:** Finally, Quick View (see Figure 3-7) provides an easy way to see more precisely how your Web page will look in the browser. You use this tab to see a preview of the page in its final glory.

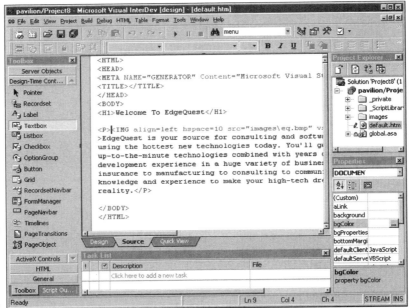

Figure 3-6: A page in Source view.

Using the Design Toolbar and the HTML Toolbar

Another toolbar lives below the Standard toolbar when the Editor is displayed (see the section "Using the Editor" earlier in this chapter for information about the Editor). This toolbar is actually two toolbars side by side: the Design toolbar and the HTML toolbar (see Figure 3-8). If you look closely, you see that each begins with a double vertical bar. The first one is the Design toolbar, and it is shorter — only six buttons. Then the longer HTML toolbar begins.

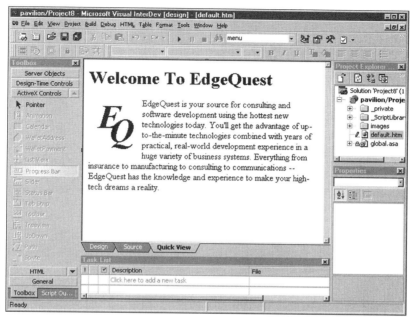

Figure 3-7:
A page in
Quick View.

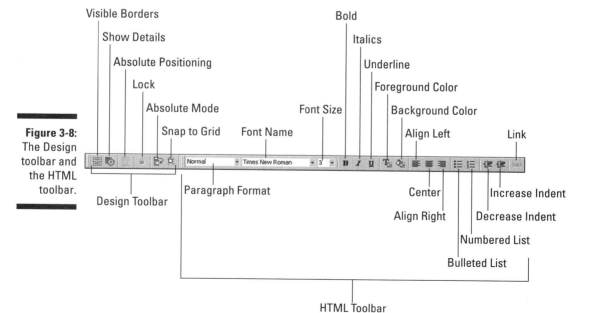

Figure 3-8:
The Design
toolbar and
the HTML
toolbar.

You don't need to use the Design toolbar right away, but the HTML toolbar has a number of features you can use to help you format your page. In fact, you probably recognize most of those buttons. They are nearly identical to the buttons in Microsoft Word.

Using the Project Explorer

The Project Explorer window is in the upper right of the primary window, by default. The Project Explorer window appears as a tree list, so each entry can be expanded and collapsed by clicking the + (plus) and - (minus) that appear beside the entries. Project Explorer shows you what solution you have open. The open solution is always the first entry at the very top of the list. Within it, you can see all its projects. The projects can, in turn, be opened up to show all the files and folders in each project. When you create a new HTML or ASP page, it appears here, inside the project.

The Project Explorer in Figure 3-9 shows you a solution with the single project open within it, the global.asa file that is a part of every project and a single page, named default.htm in the project, along with a few folders.

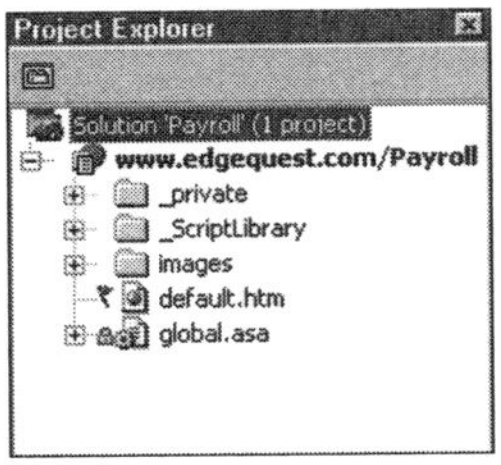

Figure 3-9:
The Project
Explorer.

The Web server in Figure 3-9 is www.edgequest.com. Yours will be whatever you specified in Step 1 of the Web Project Wizard (see Chapter 2).

The Project Explorer is a great place to work from. It gives you an overview of your project, and you can easily double-click a page to open it for editing.

The Project Explorer also shows you the status of your Web page documents. Look closely at the default.htm entry in the project in Figure 3-9. You notice that a little flag appears by the page. This flag indicates that this page has recently been created and added to the project, but it has not yet been added to the Web on the server.

Master mode versus Local mode

When you create a project, you always have the option of choosing Local or Master mode (see Chapter 2). Local is preferable because it enables you to work and test your pages locally on your own workstation and then send them up to the server only when you're done.

If you work in Master mode, your pages are created and edited *on the server.* No distinction exists between the files you have locally and the ones on the server. They are identical.

Throughout this chapter and the rest of the book, I assume you are working in Local mode. In this chapter, I point out how you can tell which files are in sync with the server and which are not, through the Project Manager.

Remember that if you chose Local mode (the preferred option) when you created this application (instead of Master mode), you are dealing with two different sets of files — the project on your machine and the Web on the server. Mostly, these two sets of files are in sync, but not always. And you need to understand which files are in sync and which ones aren't.

Adding an existing file to the Web server

To add a project file to the web on the server:

1. **Right-click the file in the Project Explorer.**

   A pop-up menu appears.

2. **Choose Add to Master Web.**

   Visual InterDev copies the file to the server and adds it to the web. It also turns the icon beside the file into a lock (see Figure 3-10).

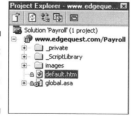

Figure 3-10: The icon turns into a lock.

When a lock appears beside a file, the lock means that the file is on the server, and you don't have write access to it. If you want to edit it, you must first get a working copy.

To get a working copy of a locked file

To get a working copy of a locked file:

1. **Right-click the file in Project Explorer.**
2. **Choose Get Working Copy from the pop-up menu.**

   The page from the server is copied back down to your workstation, and you're free to update it.

   The icon beside the file turns into a pencil (see Figure 3-11).

Figure 3-11:
The icon
turns into
a pencil.

A pencil beside the file means that you have a working copy of the file on the server and are free to edit it.

Releasing a file to the server

When you are done making changes to a file, you should release the file so that others can access it and make their own changes.

To release a file to the server after you're finished making changes:

1. **Right-click the file in Project Explorer.**
2. **Choose Release Working Copy from the pop-up menu.**

   The page is copied from your workstation up to the server. Also, the icon beside the file turns back into a lock.

Deciding to discard changes since the last checkout

If you decide after making changes to the page that you want to simply discard those changes, you also have that option.

To discard all the changes you've made since you got a working copy of a file:

1. **Right-click the file in Project Explorer.**

2. **Choose Discard Changes from the pop-up menu.**

   A dialog box appears, warning you that your changes will be lost.

3. **Click Yes.**

   The page on your workstation is discarded, and the page from the Web server is copied to your workstation.

   Also, the icon beside the file turns back into a lock.

If you are using Visual Source Safe to track your source code, Visual Source Safe stops others from making changes to pages you have a working copy of.

Adding a personal file to the project

Suppose you have a really cool graphic you just designed and saved to your hard disk. How do you take that graphic and make it a part of an already-existing Web project?

To add a personal file to an existing project:

1. **Open a window to the folder where the file is stored.**

2. **Drag the file from that window and drop the file onto the project in the Project Explorer.**

   If you'd rather drop the file in a folder (like Images), drop it there.

   The file is copied to the project. An icon appears beside it, and a flag appears beside the icon.

3. **Copy the file up to the Web server by following the steps in the section titled "Adding an existing file to the Web server" earlier in this chapter.**

Using the handy-dandy file comparison utility

If you don't have Visual Source Safe, then someone else may have made changes to your page on his workstation at the same time you were making changes to it on your workstation. When this happens, Visual InterDev gives you the option of comparing the two files using its built-in, handy-dandy file comparison utility.

You can also access the file comparison utility any time you like by doing the following:

1. **Right-click the file you want to compare to the corresponding file on the Web server.**

2. **Choose Compare to Master Web from the pop-up menu.**

   If the files are different, the file comparison utility appears (see Figure 3-12). If they are identical, Visual InterDev simply tells you so.

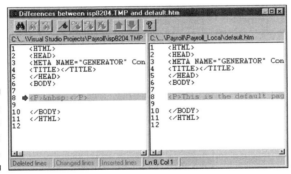

Figure 3-12:
The file
comparison
utility.

You can scroll up and down in the utility to view all the differences between the two files. When you are finished, close the window.

Adding and Manipulating Text on a Page

If you've ever used a Word processor before, you won't have any trouble at all creating Web pages using Design view in the Editor. (For a description of Design view and the other views, see "Using the Editor" earlier this chapter.) Here's the way it works.

Adding text

Adding text to a page in Visual InterDev is as easy as falling off a Web server — just type it in.

To enter text on the page:

1. **Open or create the page you want to edit. (See "Adding an HTML Page or ASP Page" earlier in this chapter for information on how to do this.) Then click the Design tab in the Editor.**

2. **Type a heading.**

   Maybe something like: `Hello and Welcome To Bill Hatfield's Home Page!.`

   Except that you'll want to replace `Bill Hatfield` with your own name, unless *your* name is Bill Hatfield, too.

3. **Press Enter.**

4. **Type an introduction.**

   Maybe something like: `I'm glad you found time to stop by and be a guest in my home page. This page tells you more than you ever wanted to know about anyone. No need to thank me. The opportunity to talk endlessly about myself is all the reward I need.`

5. **Press Enter.**

Making a header

To change text you've already typed into a header:

1. **Select your heading text.**

2. **Click the Paragraph Format drop-down list box (the first button in the HTML toolbar).**

   You see a long list of formatting options that HTML supports. Normally, you have to write tags around the text you want these options to affect. With Visual InterDev, all you have to do is select the text and choose the style from this drop-down list.

3. **Click Heading 1 (or whichever heading style you want).**

   The text is set to the font and size for the heading you chose, in this case, Heading 1 (see Figure 3-13).

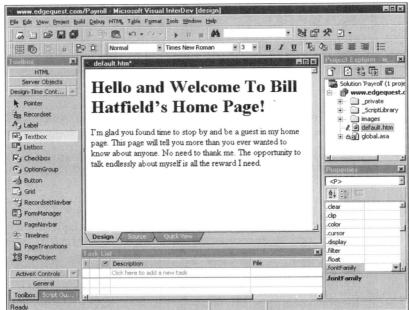

Figure 3-13:
The heading
and some
text.

Changing the text style, color, and alignment

To change the text style:

1. **Select a word or phrase.**

2. **Click any combination of the Bold, Italic, and Underline buttons on the HTML toolbar.**

   The text changes.

To change the text foreground and background color:

1. **Select a word or phrase.**

2. **Click the Foreground Color or Background Color button on the HTML toolbar.**

   The Color Picker window appears (see Figure 3-14).

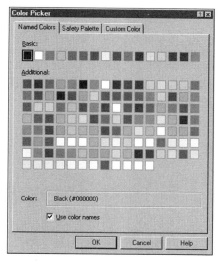

Figure 3-14:
The Color
Picker.

3. **Click different tabs to see named colors, the safety pallet, and a custom color picker.**

   If your application might be viewed by many different browsers, as in a Web application, you should use the safety pallet. These are the colors that browser makers have all agreed to support. If you are building an intranet application that only Internet Explorer browsers will be accessing, then you can choose from the named colors.

4. **Choose the color you want.**

5. **Click OK.**

To change the text alignment:

1. **Select an entire paragraph of text.**

2. **Click one of the alignment buttons on the HTML toolbar: Align Left, Center, or Align Right.**

Adding bullet lists, numbered lists, and indents

You can easily turn a bunch of lines of text into a bulleted or numbered list.

To create a bulleted or numbered list:

1. **Enter several lines of text. Press Enter after each separate line.**
2. **Select the lines of text.**
3. **Click the Bulleted List or Numbered List button on the HTML toolbar.**

   The buttons or numbers appear beside the lines.

To indent or unindent a group of lines:

1. **Select the lines.**
2. **Click the Increase Indent or Decrease Indent button on the HTML toolbar.**

Running Your Application

Any time you like, you can test your application in one of several different ways:

- The Quick View pane
- The Browse With option
- The Start button

I cover these options in the next few sections.

Previewing with Quick View

If you just want to take a quick look at the page as it will look in the browser, click the Quick View tab at the bottom of the editor. The Quick View appears. This is a very close approximation to what this page will look like in Internet Explorer.

This method has a couple of downsides:

- It shows you only how the page will look in Internet Explorer. It may look very different in Netscape Navigator or another browser.
- It only runs the client-side script and shows client ActiveX controls. It ignores the script in an ASP page and any interaction with server components.

Using the Browse With option

To actually view your page in a browser, follow these steps:

1. **Right-click the page in the Project Explorer.**

2. **Choose Browse With from the pop-up menu.**

   The Browse With dialog box appears.

3. **Choose the browser you want to use to view this page from the list at the bottom of the dialog box.**

   If you don't see the browser you want to use, you can click the Add button to find and add a new browser.

4. **Click the Browse button to view the page in the selected browser.**

   The browser launches, and the page appears inside.

This method enables you to try out your page in a variety of different browsers to make sure that it looks good in all of them. But this method also has a disadvantage — like Quick View, this method does not processes ASP server script or any interaction with server components.

The Start button

To launch your application and run it from the local Web server:

1. **Right-click the page you want to execute and choose Set As Start Page from the pop-up menu.**

2. **Click the Start button on the Standard toolbar (it looks like the Play button on a VCR).**

   The Internet Explorer browser launches, and your page appears inside.

This method does execute server scripts and interaction with server components. That's because it sets up your site to work with the local Web server, and the browser interacts with the server, not directly with your page. This setup works a lot more like a normal Web site with the server sending out the pages when browsers request them. This is the preferred way of testing your Web applications.

Using the Toolbox

The Toolbox is the window that stretches down the left side of Visual InterDev. It works much like the Outlook Bar that appears along the left side of Microsoft Outlook. The Toolbox provides access to a large number of items that you may want to drag and drop onto your Web page.

By default, the Toolbox is divided into five tabs:

✔ **HTML:** Objects that translate directly into HTML tags. These are built into HTML and do not require downloading code to see them (as ActiveX controls do). Most of these are controls that appear in HTML forms.

✔ **Server Objects:** Non-visual objects that are used exclusively with ASP server scripting. These object provide access to databases, files on the Web server, e-mail, and other facilities.

✔ **Design-Time Controls:** These are server components that produce HTML tags that show the controls listed. These controls are used to bind HTML form controls to database columns.

✔ **ActiveX Controls:** Controls that are written to the Microsoft's COM standard that are downloaded, automatically installed, and displayed in the client's browser when the page is downloaded.

✔ **General:** This one is pretty much blank and open for you to use for your own purposes. For more information on adding your own elements to the Toolbox, see Chapter 11.

Adding Toolbox Items to a Web Page

The Toolbox provides a host of controls, content, and capabilities for you to add to your Web page. Among the simplest of the controls are the built-in HTML controls.

To add a horizontal rule to your page:

1. **Place the cursor on a line by itself where you want the horizontal rule to appear.**

2. **Click the HTML tab in the Toolbox.**

3. **Press and hold the mouse button while the mouse hovers over the Horizontal Rule option and drag the mouse pointer until it is over the blank line following your introduction on your Web page.**

4. Release the mouse button.

A selected line appears where you dropped it.

All the other HTML components (and most of the other items in the Toolbox, for that matter) are added to your page in the same way — just drag and drop!

Adding ActiveX Controls

ActiveX controls are handy objects that can be added to your page to add snazzy animation, sophisticated graphic controls, or other capabilities. When a user requests the page, the ActiveX control automatically downloads to the user's machine and is installed so that it can be viewed on the page.

Adding ActiveX controls is just as easy as adding HTML elements:

1. Click the ActiveX Controls tab in the Toolbox.

2. Drag the control you want from the Toolbox to the place where you want it to appear on the page, and drop it.

A control appears where you dropped it.

You can check out the ActiveX control in the Quick View tab of the Editor to see how it will work on the final page.

Adding Graphics

To add a graphic to your page:

1. Find the image you want to use using Windows Explorer.

2. Drag the image from its current location (probably somewhere on your hard drive) to the Project Explorer window's Images folder.

Putting the graphic in the Images folder makes the graphic a part of your project.

3. On the Editor's Design tab, place the cursor in the location where you want to put the graphic.

4. Choose HTML⇨Image from the menu bar.

The Insert Image dialog box appears (see Figure 3-15).

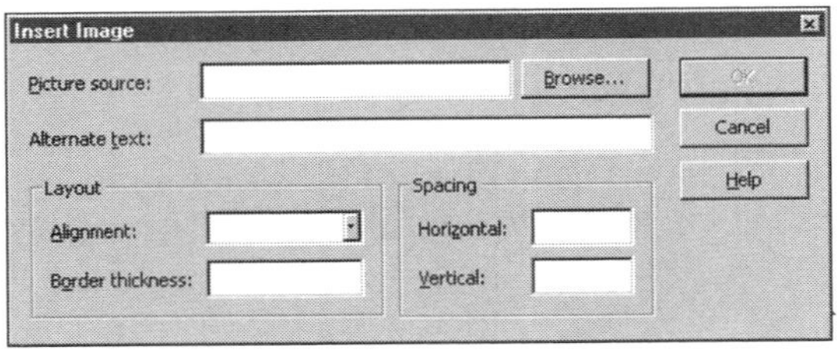

Figure 3-15:
The Insert
Image
dialog box.

5. **Click the Browse button.**

The Create URL dialog box appears (see Figure 3-16).

6. **In Projects list box on the left, click the Images folder.**

Your graphic should appear in the list box on the right.

7. **Click the image to select it, and then click OK.**

The Picture Source edit box in the Insert Image dialog box should contain images/*graphic.jpg,* where *graphic.jpg* is the name of your graphic file.

8. **Fill in the rest of the properties in this dialog box to describe how you want the graphic aligned and what border and spacing options you need.**

9. **Click OK.**

Your graphic appears in the Web page.

10. **If you don't like where the graphic is located just drag and drop it to a new location.**

For information on changing the properties of the graphic, after it is created, see "Using the Properties Window" section later this chapter.

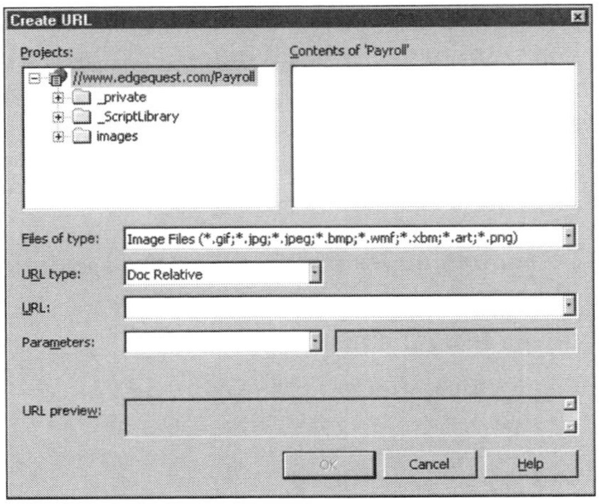

Figure 3-16:
The
Create URL
dialog box.

Adding a Marquee

To add a marquee (scrolling text) to your page:

1. **On the Design tab of the Editor, place the cursor where you want to insert your marquee.**

2. **Choose HTML⇨Marquee from the menu bar.**

   The marquee object is inserted, but it may be invisible.

3. **Click the marquee object.**

   A selection box appears around it, and a cursor flashes inside.

4. **Type the text you want to scroll across the marquee.**

5. **When you are done, you can click the Quick View tab of the Editor to see the marquee in action.**

For information on changing the properties of the marquee after it is created, see "Using the Properties Window" — the next section.

Using the Properties Window

The Properties window is one of the most important windows in Visual InterDev. It enables you to see and change all the key information for every object and HTML tag on your page.

The Properties window is located in the lower right, by default. It always shows the properties for the *currently selected* object or HTML tag.

You can verify which object's properties you are seeing by looking at the drop-down list box at the top of the window. You can also click the drop-down list box to see a list of other objects to choose from.

The Properties window works just like the Visual Basic properties window — the property names are listed in the first column, and their values are listed in the second. You can change the value of any property by clicking in the second column and typing or selecting a new value.

If you ever have a question about a particular property — what it does, what its options are, or how to use it — just click the property and press the F1 key. The online Help appears with information about that specific property.

The next two sections provide examples of how to use the Properties window to make changes to objects on your page.

Changing the properties of a marquee

The marquee object has properties that affect how it displays scrolling text. To change the properties of the marquee:

1. **Click the marquee object.**

   A gray selection bar appears around it.

2. **Scroll down the Properties window and find the property you want to change (a list of commonly used properties and what they do is listed in Table 3-1).**

3. **Click in the second column. If a drop-down button appears (see Figure 3-17), click it and choose an option from the list. Otherwise, just type the value you want into the edit box.**

Figure 3-17: A drop-down button appears in the Properties window.

Some of the more interesting properties for the marquee appear in Table 3-1.

Table 3-1	Marquee Properties
Property	*What It Affects*
scrollDelay	scroll speed
direction	direction of the scrolling
bgColor	the background color of the marquee

You can organize the properties in the Property window by category to more easily find the property you want. Just click the Categorized button — it's the second button from the left in the Properties window.

Changing the properties of a graphic

The graphic object has properties that you can set when you add the graphic to the page. You can also change these properties later by using the Properties window.

To change the properties of a graphic:

1. **Click to select the graphic on your page.**
2. **Scroll down the Properties window and find the property you want to change.**
3. **Click in the second column and change the property value.**

This is how you changed the properties for the marquee. But with graphics, and certain other objects and HTML tags in the Visual InterDev environment, there's an easier way: using the custom properties page.

To change the properties of a graphic using the custom properties page:

1. **Click to select the graphic on your page.**
2. **Scroll all the way to the top of the properties list in the Properties window.**
3. **Click the second column beside Custom.**
4. **Click the button with three dots on it that appears there.**

    A custom tabbed dialog box appears with the properties grouped so they are more easily found and changed (see Figure 3-18).

5. **Change the properties you want, and click OK when you are done.**

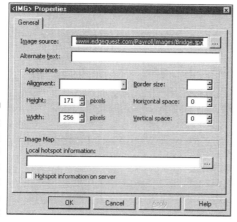

Figure 3-18: The custom properties dialog box for a graphic.

Or you can use a shortcut:

1. **Click to select the graphic on your page.**
2. **Click the Property Pages button — the third button from the left inside the Properties window.**
3. **Change the properties you want, and click OK when you are done.**

You have another option, too! You can also:

1. **Right-click the graphic.**
2. **Choose Properties from the pop-up menu.**
3. **Change the properties you want, and click OK when you're done.**

Not all objects and HTML tags have a custom property window. The marquee, for example, does not. If you select the marquee, the Property Pages button in the Properties window is disabled. And if you right-click the marquee and choose Properties, the focus goes to the normal Properties window.

But for those object and tags that do have the custom properties dialog box, you'll find that it is a much easier way to access and maintain the properties of the object.

Using the Task List

Running along the bottom of Visual InterDev is a window called the Task List. The Task List is like a To Do list that is associated with this solution. It is a convenient place to keep track of enhancements you want to make and bugs you need to fix.

In addition, Visual InterDev itself sometimes places tasks in your Task List when it finds errors in your pages that need to be fixed.

Using the HTML Outline Window

The HTML Outline window doesn't appear in Visual InterDev by default. You have to specifically ask to see it. You can do that by choosing View⇨ Other Windows⇨Document Outline from the menu bar. Also, a drop-down list button on the right of the primary toolbar lists all the available windows. You can choose Document Outline from that list to display the HTML Outline window, too.

Either way, when it appears, the HTML Outline window shows up along the left side of the primary window, covering the Toolbox. If you look at the bottom of the HTML Outline window, you see two tabs that let you switch back and forth between HTML Outline and the Toolbox.

HTML Outline shows a complete breakdown of all the important objects and tags in your HTML page in a tree view. As you click objects in the HTML Outline window, notice that the focus in the Editor hops around, too. If you are looking at the Design tab of the Editor, you see that objects are selected in the Editor as you select them in the HTML Outline window. If you are in the Source tab of the Editor, the tags associated with the HTML Outline elements are selected as you select them in the HTML Outline window.

The HTML Outline is just another way for you to view and navigate though your work on complex HTML and ASP pages. Use it to simplify navigation and selection of objects on complex pages.

Creating Tables

Tables are like grids that you can drop into your Web page to help structure information. They are great for displaying information like a Height/Weight chart or spreadsheet numbers showing your company's performance over the last several months.

But tables can also be used for helping to place and organize information on your page. Because the grid lines of a table don't have to be visible, you can use them to precisely space or position your icons, text, or buttons.

Creating a new table

As you may know, creating complex tables in raw HTML can be quite a challenge. But, as you might have guessed, Visual InterDev makes the whole process a snap.

To create a new table:

1. **Place your cursor on the page where you want your table to go.**

2. **Select Table⇨Insert Table from the menu bar.**

   The Insert Table dialog box appears (see Figure 3-19).

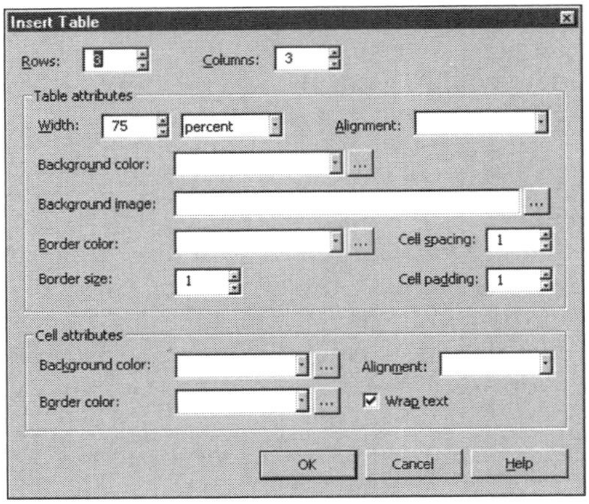

Figure 3-19:
The Insert
Table
dialog box.

3. **Enter the number of rows and columns you want in your table (you can add and delete rows and columns later, if you need to).**

4. **Enter the width of the table, either in pixels or percent.**

5. **Specify whether you want the table aligned left, right, or centered.**

6. **Specify your preferences for the other background, border, or spacing options.**

7. **Click OK.**

   Your table appears on the page.

After you have created your table, you can click in the different cells to enter information there. You can place pictures, ActiveX controls, or even other tables inside the cells.

Manipulating table rows and columns

Often, after you create a table and begin filling it in with information, you realize that you need another row or that you have too many columns. These problems are easy to fix.

To add a new row:

1. **The newly inserted row always appears before the row you're on. So before you insert the row, click the row that you want to appear *after* the new one.**

   For example, if you have five rows and you want to insert a new row after the second, place your cursor on the third row. The new row will be inserted before the third row (where your cursor is) and right after the second row. Clear as mud?

2. Choose Table⇨Insert Row from the menu bar.

The new row appears in the row before the one where your cursor is.

Adding a new column works the same way. Just remember, the new column is inserted before the column where your cursor is. When you're ready, choose Table⇨Insert Column.

To delete a row:

1. Click any of the cells in the row you want to delete.

2. Choose Table⇨Delete Row from the menu bar.

The row you are on is deleted, and the rows after it move up a notch.

Deleting a column works the same way. Click a cell in the column you want to delete and choose Table⇨Delete Column.

Merging and splitting cells

There are times when you need to split an individual cell into two different cells. You could do this by creating another tiny one-row, two-column table inside of that cell, but that solution could throw off your spacing and end up looking odd. The best way to do it is to simply split the cell.

To split a cell:

1. Place the cursor in the cell you want to split.

2. Choose Table⇨Split Cell from the menu bar.

A line appears in the cell, dividing it into two (see Figure 3-20).

The line will not necessarily be in the center, but each part of the cell will grow and shrink as you add information in it.

You can also take two existing cells and merge them into one big cell.

To merge two cells:

1. Select all the information in both cells.

If one of the cells is empty, it may be a good idea to type a bit of text into the cell and make sure it is selected.

2. Choose Table⇨Merge Cells from the menu bar.

The line between the two cells disappears, leaving one large cell (see Figure 3-21).

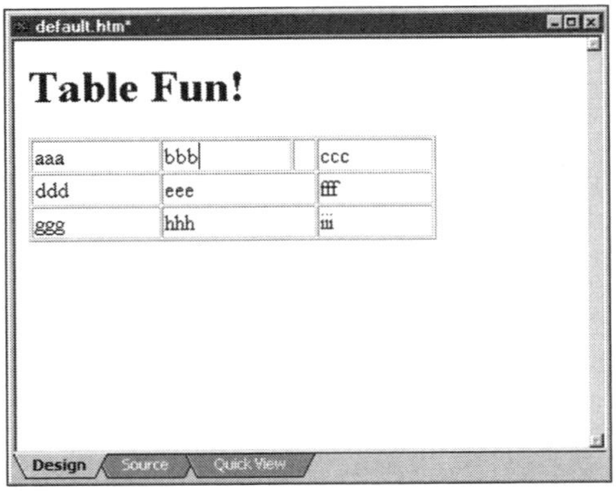

Figure 3-20:
A split cell.

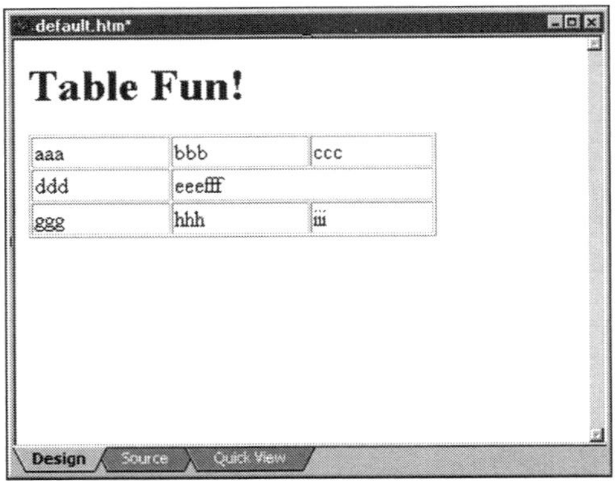

Figure 3-21:
A merged
cell.

Changing table properties

After you've created a table, you may decide you need to change some of those properties you gave it when you created it. Fortunately, it isn't difficult.

To change a table's properties:

1. **Right-click the outer edge of the table.**

   A selection box should appear around the entire table.

2. **Choose Properties from the pop-up menu.**

   The <TABLE> Properties dialog box appears (see Figure 3-22).

3. **Set the properties as you like, and click OK.**

Changing properties of rows and cells is also possible.

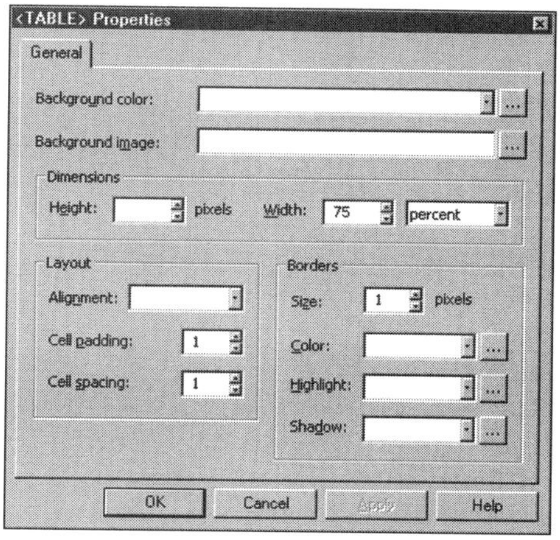

Figure 3-22:
The
<TABLE>
Properties
dialog box.

To change an individual cell's properties:

1. **Right-click the cell.**

2. **Choose Properties from the pop-up menu.**

   The <TD> Properties dialog box appears (see Figure 3-23).

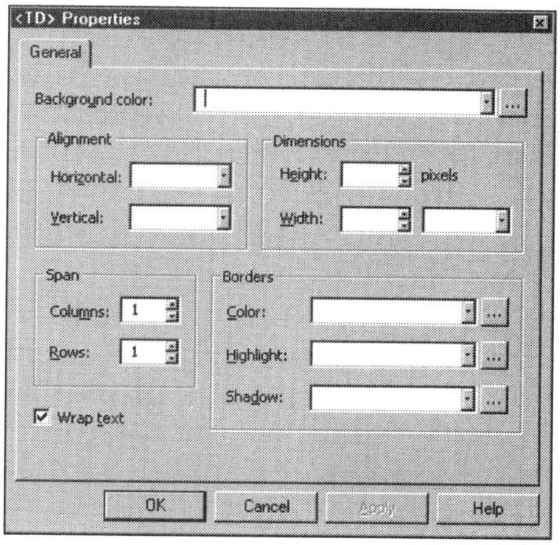

Figure 3-23:
The <TD>
Properties
dialog box.

Changing the row's properties is a little more complicated. The row (<TR>) doesn't have its own custom properties dialog box. Another problem is that there's no obvious place to click on to get row properties.

To change a row's properties:

1. **Click any cell in the row.**
2. **Click the drop-down list box at the top of the Properties window.**
3. **Choose <TR> from the list.**
4. **Scroll to the property you want to change and change it.**

Viewing a 0-Border Table

People commonly want to create tables that have their Border property set to 0 (zero). That makes the table itself invisible but still allows you to put items in the table to control better where they are placed on a page.

The only problem with this is that you can't see the table in Design view. The smart folks at Microsoft included a way around this problem. Just click the first button in the Design toolbar: Show Borders. Now all your tables appear in Design view with borders, even though the borders *won't* appear on the page.

Chapter 4

Designing the Look and Feel of Your Web Application

In This Chapter

▶ Creating and using Cascading Style Sheets

▶ Linking a style sheet to your Web pages

▶ Using themes to quickly dress up your pages

*W*ith all the sexual-harassment lawsuits flying around these days, it's important to define exactly what you mean when you say "look and feel." So I think I should explain that in this chapter, I show you how you enhance the user interface of your Web applications. (Nothing more!)

Visual InterDev is flexible, and although it makes adding snazzy features to your Web site easy, it never forces you into *its* way of doing things. You can always start with its suggestions and then modify them to your own tastes.

In this chapter, you find out how to create a Cascading Style Sheet and apply it to your Web pages. You also discover how themes can create a complete look and feel for your whole site in virtually no time at all.

Watch for Falling Rocks and Cascading Style Sheets

Cascading Style Sheets (CSS) are an easy way for you to create a distinctive look and feel for your pages that is shared among all the pages in your application — without adding a lot of extra work!

Normally, when you enter text or headers that will be displayed in your Web page, the browser determines what font, size, and style to use. When you use a <FONT> tag, Internet Explorer renders normal text in Times New Roman, 10 points, unless you specify otherwise. A Header 1 appears as Times New Roman, 20 points, Bold. Netscape Navigator and other browsers may choose to render these tags differently. Because of this, you never know exactly how your page is going to look on different browsers.

CSS puts you in control of this process. It enables you to tell the browser, "Whenever you see a Header 1, always use Arial 18-point, Bold, and Underline" — or whatever you want. That way, you don't have to use a <FONT> tag or any other indicator every time you want to use *your* header. You just use the normal Header 1, and the page knows how you want it to look.

You can think of CSS as a way of overriding the standard definitions of the tags with your own specific definitions.

Visual InterDev themes have their *own* style sheets built-in. I discuss themes later in this chapter. But in the meantime, if you want to experiment with your own style sheets, start out with a project that doesn't use a theme.

Adding a Style Sheet to Your Project

To use Cascading Style Sheets in Visual InterDev, you first create a *style sheet*. A style sheet is just another type of document that you can add to your Visual InterDev project — just like an HTML page or an ASP page. However, unlike HTML and ASP pages, they are never viewed directly in a browser. Instead, they contain all the information about how you want to format your Web pages. They are then *associated* with your HTML and ASP pages to specify how they should look.

To add a style sheet to your project:

1. **Click the Add Item button on the Standard toolbar.**

   The Add Item dialog box appears.

   Web Project Files is selected on the left. On the right, you see four icons: HTML Page, ASP Page, Style Sheet, and Site Diagram.

2. **Click the Style Sheet icon to select it.**

3. **Type the name you want to give the Style Sheet in the Name edit box.**

4. **Click Open.**

   The CSS editor appears (see Figure 4-1).

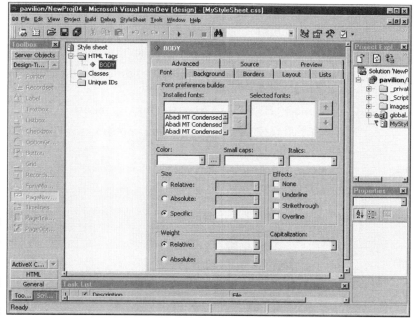

Figure 4-1:
The
Cascading
Style Sheet
editor.

Visual InterDev enables you to very easily create and edit style sheets through its CSS editor. Unlike the HTML and ASP page editor, this window works like a tabbed dialog box. All you have to do is fill in the blanks with the information you want to store, and you're finished!

Assigning Fonts and Styles to Tags

The CSS editor has a simple, familiar user interface: a tree-view list box alongside a tabbed dialog box. But don't let this simplicity fool you. This editor provides a lot of flexibility to define almost any Cascading Style Sheet you want — without having to code it yourself.

In this section, I demonstrate some of the capabilities of this powerful editor. The most obvious, and probably most used, feature of CSS is the ability to assign specific fonts, sizes, and styles to HTML tags. The process is easy.

To assign a font, size, and style to a specific HTML tag:

1. **Add a style sheet to your project.**

   See the previous section for details on how to do this.

2. **Click the Font tab to display it, if it isn't already selected.**

3. **In the tree-view list box on the left, right-click the folder labeled HTML Tags.**

4. **Choose Insert HTML Tag from the pop-up menu.**

   The Insert New HTML Tag dialog box appears (see Figure 4-2).

Figure 4-2:
The Insert
New
HTML Tag
dialog box.

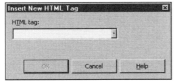

5. **Choose the tag you want to assign a font, size, and style to from the drop-down list box.**

6. **Click OK.**

   The tag is added below the HTML Tags folder and automatically selected.

7. **Now simply change the font information in the Font tab so that it represents how you want that tag displayed.**

The Font Preference Builder at the top of the Font tab enables you to choose from a list of the fonts on your system and add them to a list of selected fonts in any order you want. You can also type additional font names and add those.

The order of the fonts in the Selected Fonts list box determines the order of preference when displaying this tag in the user's browser. If the first font isn't available on the user's system, the browser checks the second, then the third. It uses the first one it comes to that is installed. If none of them are installed, the browser uses the default font for that tag.

Other options on the Font tab enable you to specify the color and whether to use small caps, italic, underline, strikethrough, and other styles. You can change the size of the text, its weight (how bold it appears), and even its capitalization.

After you are finished defining a tag, you can start the process again and specify the information for another tag. Keep doing this until you've specified the font, size, and style information for all the tags that you want to customize.

Also notice that the <BODY> tag appears automatically under HTML Tags. Any changes you make to <BODY> affect the entire document.

After you're done, save all your changes to the style sheet by clicking the Save button on the Standard toolbar.

Behold, Your Masterpiece!

Any time you want, you can preview the changes you are making.

To see a preview of your styles:

1. **Click the Preview tab.**
2. **Scroll down to see what your changes will look like on a Web page.**

    The default preview page shows most of the important tags.

3. **When you're done, click the Font tab again to continue making changes.**

Viewing the CSS Source Code

Cascading Style Sheets are implemented with a simple language extension to HTML. As you make changes in the CSS editor, there's a little CSS scribe that's busy adding and making the changes to the CSS source code that will make your changes a reality.

You don't ever have to view or modify this code if you don't want to. That's the scribe's job. But if you know the CSS language and you are curious about what the scribe's up to, you can view it any time you want.

To view the source code produced by the CSS editor, just click the Source tab in the CSS editor. The source code for all the changes you've made appears there.

You can copy this code to the Clipboard by selecting a portion or all of the code and pressing Ctrl+C.

Linking a Style Sheet to a Page

After you've saved a Cascading Style Sheet in your project that has all your preferences in it, you can easily link it to one or more pages to put your newly created styles to work.

To link a Cascading Style Sheet to a page:

1. **Open the HTML or ASP page.**

2. **Scroll up to the top where the** `<HEAD>` **section is.**

3. **Drag the Cascading Style Sheet file from the Project Manager window and drop it within the** `<HEAD>` **tags.**

   A `<LINK>` tag is created. It looks something like this:

   ```
   <LINK rel="stylesheet" type="text/css"
   href="Style Sheet1.css">
   ```

4. **Preview the page to make sure your changes have taken effect.**

   You should be able to see all your changes in the Quick View tab of the editor.

Classy, Stylish Sheets (And Pillowcases)

In addition to HTML tags, you can also associate attributes to classes. You can apply a class to any tag to change how it is displayed. Whenever it is applied, all the styles associated with that class are assigned to the text for that tag.

For example, you may have a Header 1 defined as Arial 18 point, Bold. You might also have the class `RedText` assigned to be the color red. Whenever you use a Header 1, it appears in the font you specify. But if you also use the class `RedText`, like so:

```
<h1 class=RedText>This is a Red Header 1</h1>
```

the text appears in the font specified and in the color red.

In addition, you could also apply the `RedText` class to a Header 2, even if you haven't specified any special style sheet characteristics to it.

```
<h2 class=RedText>This is a Red Header 2</h2>
```

This text would appear in the default Header 2 style, except that it would be red.

Adding a class to a style sheet

Adding a class works very much like adding an HTML tag.

To add a class to your style sheet:

1. **In the tree-view list box on the left, right-click the folder labeled Classes.**

2. **Choose Insert Class from the pop-up menu.**

   The Insert New Class dialog box appears (see Figure 4-3).

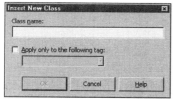

Figure 4-3:
The Insert
New Class
dialog box.

3. **Type the name of the class you want to add.**

   You are free to name your classes anything you like.

4. **Click OK.**

   (I discuss the check box and drop-down list later in this chapter, in the section "Adding a tag-specific class.")

   The class is added below the Classes folder and is automatically selected.

5. **Now simply change the information in the tabbed dialog box to define how text labeled with this class should be displayed.**

Applying the class

After you've created a style, you can apply it to any tag by going to the Source view of the editor and simply adding the following text inside the opening tag:

```
class=ClassName
```

Put the name you gave your class in place of *ClassName*.

You can also apply a class to text that doesn't have any other tags around it. For example, if you wanted a single word in an otherwise normal text paragraph to be red, you could use the `<span>` tag.

```
<p>This text is completely normal.
Well, <span class=RedText>almost</span> completely
normal.</p>
```

The `<span>` tag does nothing to the text by itself. But it allows you to easily apply a class to the code anyplace you like.

The `<div>` tag works the same way, except that the `<div>` tag sets the surrounded text off as a separate paragraph. Basically, `<div>` is like a `<span>` with a `<p>` tag built in.

Applying the class — another way

If you'd rather not muck about in the Source view of the editor if you don't have to (and who can blame you!), you can apply a class to a tag in the Design view of the editor.

To add a class to a tag in the Design view:

1. **In the Design view of the editor, click the element you want to change the class for.**

2. **Click the drop-down list box at the top of the Properties window (in the lower right) and choose the exact tag you want to add a class to.**

3. **Scroll down toward the bottom of the properties and look for the property named** `class`.

4. **Enter the name of the class you want to associate with this tag as the value for class in the Properties window.**

After you go through this process, you can click over to the Source view and see the tag with the new class attribute assigned within it.

Adding a tag-specific class

When you create a class, you have the option of assigning the class to a specific tag. If you do, that class is restricted to being used only with the tag specified.

Using tag-specific classes enables you to create different varieties of a specific tag. For example, you could create different kinds of Header 1s for different locations in your document. This option gives you more flexibility in defining how you want your pages to look.

To create a tag-specific class:

1. **From within the CSS editor, right-click the folder labeled Classes in the tree-view list box on the left.**

2. **Choose Insert Class from the pop-up menu.**

   The Insert New Class dialog box appears (refer to Figure 4-3).

3. **Type the name of the class you want to add.**

   You are free to name your classes anything you want.

4. **Click the Apply Only to the Following Tag check box if you want to make your class tag-specific. If you do, choose the tag you want from the drop-down list box or type the name of the tag in the edit box.**

5. **Click OK.**

   The class is added below the Classes folder and is automatically selected. Notice that the tag you chose appears in front of the class name to identify it as a tag-specific class.

6. **Now simply change the information in the tabbed dialog box to define how text labeled with this class should be displayed.**

Tag-specific classes are used in the same way as other classes. They are simply restricted to being used with the tag specified.

Using Unique IDs

A Unique ID is, as you might guess, a unique name given to a specific control on a page. Styles associated with a Unique ID only affect the *one* control on the page — the one with that Unique ID. Because Unique IDs are so specific, they are nearly as useful as classes.

The process for creating and applying Unique ID styles is almost identical to creating and applying class styles, except that Unique IDs are stored in their own folder in the CSS editor tree list. See the previous section "Classy, Stylish Sheets (And Pillowcases)" for more information.

Conflicts Are a Fact of Life

When you have all these styles that you can specify in different ways, you could have some conflicts. For example, what if you specify that your Heading 2 is Times New Roman, 20 point, Blue, and then you use a `RedText` class with it, which sets the color to red?

CSS has defined a very detailed set of rules for resolving conflicts like this. In this case, the class would take precedence because it is specifically applied to modify the tag. The Header 2 text would appear red (but still in Times New Roman, 20 point).

Instead of spelling out all the gory details describing the rules for resolving conflicts (which you'll never remember anyway), let me instead offer a word of advice: Experiment! If you are curious about how two different ways of combining elements will work, try it out and see what happens.

And, just as important, click over to the Preview tab in the CSS editor or to the Quick View pane in the HTML editor *often* as you are creating and applying style sheets to your pages. Switching back and forth helps you keep it all straight and alerts you to any unexpected combinations or conflicts.

Assigning Other Features to Tags and Styles

In the previous section titled "Applying Fonts and Styles to Tags," I discuss the Font tab of the CSS editor. In this section, I give you a brief overview of the other tabs and tell you what capabilities they offer. For detailed information on individual control settings, see the Visual InterDev online Help system.

Background

The Background tab of the CSS editor (see Figure 4-4) allows you to specify a background color or image for the tag or class.

If you specify an image, you can also specify its exact position and whether it is tiled with the controls at the bottom of the tab.

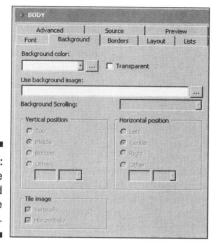

Figure 4-4:
The Background tab in the CSS editor.

Remember that this background only appears on the part of the document spanned by the associated tag or class. If you want to specify a background color or image for the entire document, click BODY under HTML Tags in the CSS editor's tree list and specify the background there.

Borders

The Borders tab of the CSS editor (see Figure 4-5) enables you to specify a border that appears around the element.

Figure 4-5:
The Borders tab in the CSS editor.

Start in the middle of this tab (in the Borders group box) and specify the style, color, and width of the border you want. A preview appears on the right.

By default, you are specifying these attributes for the entire border. If you want the top border to be different from the bottom border, for example, you can click the various buttons representing the specific border sides and set the attributes for them individually.

After you have the border specified as you like it, you can look back up to the top of the tab and set the margins and padding. The margin specifies how much space should be between the HTML element and the border. The padding specifies how much space should be outside the border — between the border and any other elements on the page. To make this clear, let me show you a couple of examples: Figure 4-6 shows a Header 1 with a large margin and a small padding. Figure 4-7 shows the same Header 1 with a small margin and a large padding.

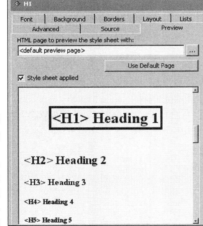

Figure 4-6:
Header 1
with a large
margin
and a small
padding.

Like most of the measurements, you can set the margin and padding using a huge variety of measures including pixels, millimeters, and inches.

Creative use of fonts, background color, and borders options can produce eye-catching, low-bandwidth headlines for your page.

Layout

The Layout tab of the CSS editor (see Figure 4-8) collects a variety of options that allow you to have more precise control of how text is spaced, aligned, and indented on your page.

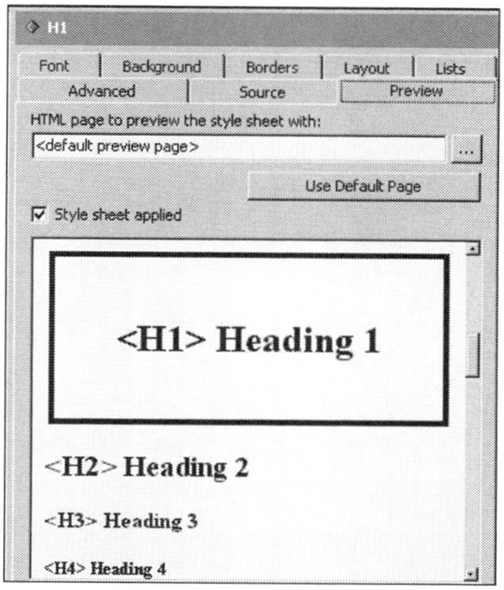

Figure 4-7:
Header 1 with a small margin and a large padding.

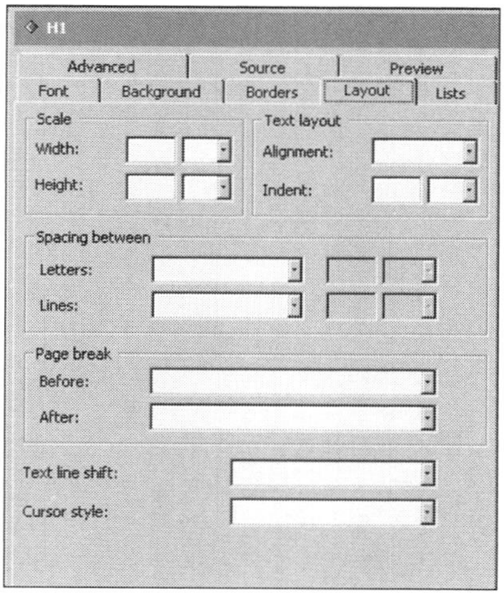

Figure 4-8:
The Layout tab in the CSS editor.

The Scale options enable you to specify a height and a width for your element, and the Text Layout options allow you to left-justify, right-justify, or center the text as well as specify an indent and its size.

The Spacing Between options enable you to control how close characters are together and how far one line is from the next.

You can also specify when page breaks should occur, either before or after the element.

Use the Text Line Shift option to change the vertical position of the text on a line upward (superscript) or downward (subscript).

Finally, the Cursor Style option allows you to specify what the mouse pointer will look like when it moves over the element you are defining.

Lists

The Lists tab of the CSS editor (see Figure 4-9) enables you to specify how ordered (numbered) and unordered (bulleted) lists should be displayed.

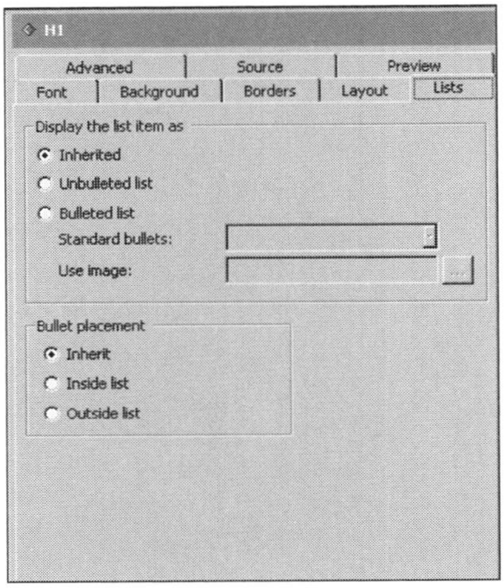

Figure 4-9:
The Lists
tab in the
CSS editor.

You have the option of using no bullets at all, specifying one of the standard types of bullets or numbering schemes, or using any image you like as a bullet. Specifying an image as a bullet can help add character to your pages. That's why all the built-in themes specify a different bullet to be used when you apply them. For more information on themes, see the section "Visiting the Visual InterDev Theme Park" later in this chapter.

You also have the option of having the bullet appear within the text or having the text indented away from the bullets so that they stand out more.

You can easily (and mistakenly) assign a bullet to appear for *ordered* lists (the `<ol>` tag) and a series of numbers to appear for *unordered* lists (the `<ul>` tag). In other words, you could make it very confusing. Don't.

Advanced

The Advanced tab of the CSS editor (see Figure 4-10) offers a number of capabilities for indenting, creating floating text, and creating sidebars (the text that often appears in a box alongside an article in a magazine or a page on the Web).

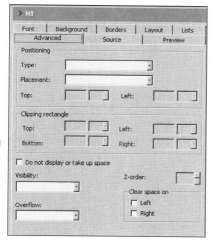

Figure 4-10:
The
Advanced
tab in the
CSS editor.

First, you must decide how you want to position the element you are defining. By default, elements flow onto a page one after another. But CSS enables you to change that.

If you choose the Absolute option, you can give specific coordinates where you want this element placed, and it will appear there, regardless of any other elements on the page. You specify its location using the Top and Left options.

If there are other elements at the location you specify for this element, then the elements are ally displayed on top of each other. The Z-order (at the bottom left part of this tab) determines which element in a pile appears on top.

Relative positioning works like the absolute option, but your coordinates start where ever the last tag ended, rather than at the top left of the document.

Placement determines how text flows around this element. Float on Left puts the element on the left and allows the text to flow around it. Float on Right puts the element on the right. Do not Float does not allow text to flow around the object.

The Clipping rectangle specifies where the element can be seen. If parts of the element would appear outside the clipping rectangle, they aren't seen.

You have two ways to make an object disappear. Obviously, Visibility is one of them. When you set Visibility to Hidden, the object vanishes, but it still takes up space. In other words, the place where it was is simply blank now.

However, if you click the Do not Display or Take Up Space check box, the object not only becomes invisible, but the elements after it flow up to make use of the space, as if the invisible element were never there.

Overflow allows you to deal with situations where the element (such as an image) is larger than the specified height and width for the tag. One option is to only display what's visible and forget about the rest. To do that, choose Hidden. Or if you'd rather allow the user to have scroll bars available to view the rest, choose Scroll. Finally, if you want to completely ignore the height and width properties and display it at its original height and width, choose Visible.

The Clear Space On option determines whether this element is free to flow around floating elements. If it's okay for this element to flow around an element that appears on its left, click Left. If it's okay for this element to flow around an element that appears on its right, click Right.

Visiting the Visual InterDev Theme Park

Themes in Visual InterDev and FrontPage are pre-designed look-and-feel interfaces that you can apply to your pages. A theme usually includes a background image for your pages, a variety of alternative bullets, and a set of Cascading Style Sheets that define the fonts, styles, and sizes for all the common tags. Quite a number of themes come with Visual InterDev, and they are professionally designed to make your pages look good with minimal effort. All you have to do is add a theme to your project or to a particular page, and all the appropriate files are copied and applied automatically.

If you accepted all the defaults when you installed Visual InterDev, you are missing out on a bunch of themes. Only about a third of the themes on the installation CDs are actually installed by default. To get the rest of them installed, run Setup again and choose the Custom Setup option for Visual InterDev. Then you can select the additional themes and get them on your hard drive.

Adding a theme when you create a new project

When you create a new project, you walk through the Web Project Wizard to give Visual InterDev all the information it needs to create the project (see Chapter 2 for more information on this process).

To add a theme when you create a new project:

1. **Click the New Project button on the Standard toolbar.**

2. **Walk through the Web Project Wizard and provide all the information it requests.**

   (For more information on starting and using the Web Project Wizard, see Chapter 2.)

   The last step in the wizard asks you to choose a theme to be used in your new project (see Figure 4-11). As you click different ones, you see how they look in the preview on the left side of the window.

3. **When you find one you like, click it.**

4. **Click Finish.**

Now, each new HTML or ASP page you create in your project will make use of this theme.

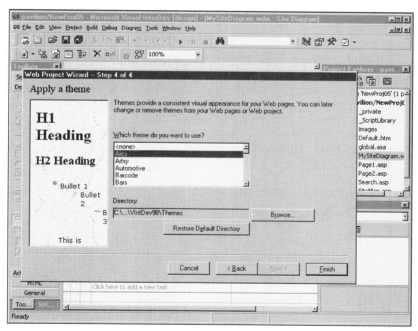

Figure 4-11:
The Web
Project
Wizard,
Step 4.

Adding a theme to an existing project

It's not too late, after you creat a project, to add a theme to it. In fact, it's simple.

To add a theme to an existing project:

1. **Right-click the project itself in the Project Explorer window.**

2. **Choose Apply Theme and Layout from the pop-up menu (see Figure 4-12).**

   The Apply Theme and Layout window appears (see Figure 4-13).

3. **Click the Apply Theme radio button above the list.**

4. **Click the various themes to see them previewed along the right.**

5. **When you decide on one, click it and then click OK.**

   The files for the theme are copied to your project.

The process of copying the files to your project can take time because the files are copied not only to your project but also to the server. Notice that a lock appears beside the files after they are all copied to your project.

From this point on, every time you create a new HTML or ASP page, your newly chosen theme will be applied to it.

Adding a theme to the current page

Adding a theme to a project doesn't force you to use that same theme for each page. Even if you haven't chosen a theme for a project, you can still add a theme to a specific page within that project.

To add a theme to the current page (regardless of whether one exists for the whole project or not):

1. **Open the page in the editor.**

2. **Choose Edit⇨Apply Theme and Layout.**

   The Apply Theme and Layout window appears (see Figure 4-13).

3. **Click the Apply Theme radio button above the list.**

4. **Click the various themes to see them previewed along the right.**

5. **When you decide on one, click it and then click OK.**

   The files for the theme are copied to your project.

   Then you see a dialog box that indicates that the page has been modified outside the editor (see Figure 4-14). The dialog box asks if you want to reload the modified page.

6. **Click Yes.**

   The current page is reloaded with the new theme.

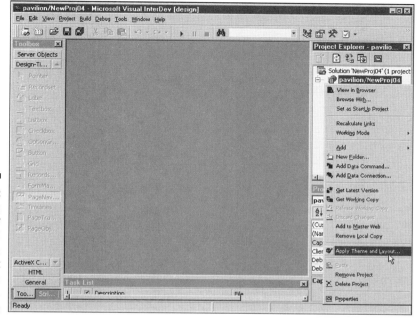

Figure 4-12:
Choosing
Apply
Theme and
Layout from
the project
pop-up
menu.

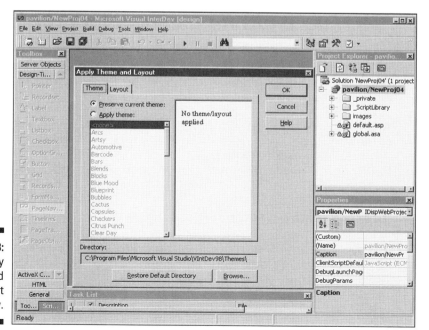

Figure 4-13:
The Apply
Theme and
Layout
window.

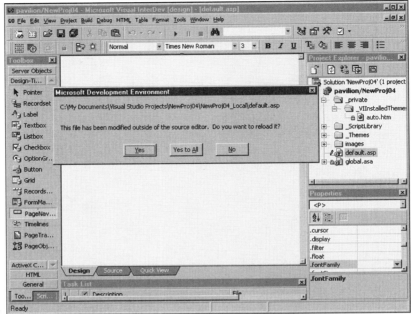

Figure 4-14:
The page
has been
modified
outside
the editor.

Juggling multiple themes in a project

When you experiment with themes, you discover that you can actually have many themes in one project by applying different themes to different pages. New pages are always automatically given the last theme that you applied to the entire project.

Applying a new theme to your project changes all the pages in that project to the theme applied. If you want specific pages to have different themes, you have to go back to those pages and change their theme individually (see the section "Adding a theme to the current page" earlier in this chapter).

Using themes with layouts

You may often use themes and layouts together to create a distinctive identity for your Web applications. Themes provide a look for the page and its text; layouts provide a standard way of organizing the information and navigational links on the page. Layouts take their navigational cues from site diagrams, so I discuss both site diagrams and layouts together in Chapter 5.

Chapter 5

Diagramming Your Site and Applying Layouts

In This Chapter

▶ Creating site diagrams

▶ Using layouts to add uniform navigation to your site

▶ Adding the PageNavbar to your own pages

*I*f your Web site is only a few pages, you shouldn't have trouble keeping track of all your files. But when your site grows to 20, 30, or 100 pages, keeping track of everything becomes a little more complicated. And that's where the Visual InterDev site diagrams and layouts come in handy.

The site diagram is a document that organizes all the pages on your site into a structure so that you can keep track of what pages you have and how they relate to each other.

Layouts can be applied to pages in the same way that themes are applied. Instead of providing font, color, and background information, though, they provide a way of organizing information on the page and a way of navigating to other pages on your site. Layouts provide flexible, easy-to-manage page organization and automatic link creation.

Creating a Site Diagram

A site diagram is a chart that provides an overview of the pages on your site and their relationship to each other. The diagram is added to your project in the form of a file. Like Cascading Style Sheets (which I discuss in Chapter 4), site diagrams aren't directly viewed by those people who visit your site. Instead, they help you design how your site is organized and help you figure out how your users should navigate it.

TIP

Site diagrams — one or many?

You can use one site diagram file to organize all the pages on your site. Or you can have two, three, or more site diagrams, each with some subset of the pages. You could have one site diagram for each major division of your site, for example.

Unless you have a very large site, you probably need only one site diagram file. That way, no one gets confused about where a page goes and what its relationship to other pages is.

If you do choose to use more than one site diagram file, you can include the same page or set of pages in several different site diagram files, if you want. But be aware that what you do in one site diagram can affect other site diagrams. Here's how it works: All the site diagram files in a project work together because Visual InterDev keeps a single picture of what the site looks like internally. The changes you make to your site diagrams affect that single, internal picture. The result is that if you make changes to a page's relationships on one site diagram, it can affect and change other site diagrams that also include that page.

The best way to deal with this situation is to avoid having lots of overlap between your diagrams. If you divide your site into four major divisions and then create a diagram for each, you'll probably have only a few pages that show up in more than one diagram.

The site diagram looks like a company's organizational chart. (In case you haven't seen one, an organizational chart usually starts with the president of the company in a box at the top, and lines connect his box to those who report to him or her. Those boxes, in turn are connected to additional boxes below them, and so forth.) The site diagram includes boxes that stand for Web pages and lines connecting the boxes to indicate how the pages are related.

It's a good idea to create a site diagram first — even before you create your first page. That way, you can organize and plan for all the pages you'll need before you begin.

Why bother?

No one is going to force you to create a site diagram. In fact, you can create many large sites with Visual InterDev without ever creating a site diagram. So why bother? Well, after you've created a site diagram for your site, it serves two purposes:

✔ It organizes your pages into logical hierarchies that show you how the site is arranged and aides you in finding the exact page you want to work with.

✔ The site diagram gives Visual InterDev the information it needs to automatically generate toolbars of buttons or links on each page that provide for all your common site navigation. You can set up the site navigation with layouts, which are discussed later in this chapter. But remember: Before you use a Layout, you must have a site diagram so that Visual InterDev has the information it needs to create the layout.

Adding a site diagram to a project

Adding a site diagram to your Web project works just like adding any other type of file to your project.

To add a site diagram to your project:

1. **Click the Add Item button on the Standard toolbar, or choose Project⇨Add Item from the menu bar.**

   The Add Item dialog box appears (see Figure 5-1).

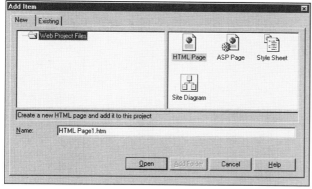

Figure 5-1:
The
Add Item
dialog box.

2. **Click the Site Diagram icon on the right side of the dialog box.**

3. **Enter the name you want to give the site diagram in the Name text box.**

4. **Click Open.**

   If you are working in Local mode, you may see a warning dialog box like the one pictured in Figure 5-2.

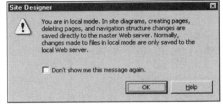

Figure 5-2:
The site diagram warning dialog box.

This dialog box lets you know that when you work with the site diagram editor, you are changing pages on the Web server, not just the pages in your local project. You need to remember this when you work with a site diagram. By default, you see this dialog box each time you enter the site diagram editor. If you don't want to see it in the future, click the Don't Show Me This Message Again check box.

5. **Click OK.**

   The new site diagram appears in the site diagram editor (see Figure 5-3).

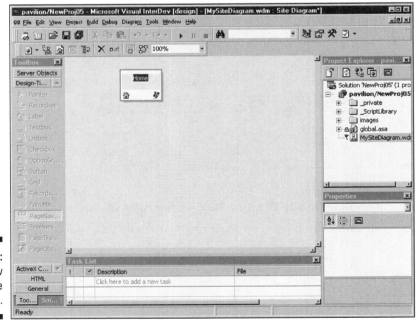

Figure 5-3:
The new site diagram.

You may see a Home page appear automatically on your new diagram. Visual InterDev automatically generates this page. For more information on the Home page, see the section called "Designating the Home page" later in this chapter.

Using the Site Diagram toolbar

When the site diagram editor displays a site diagram, the Site Diagram toolbar also appears (see Figure 5-4).

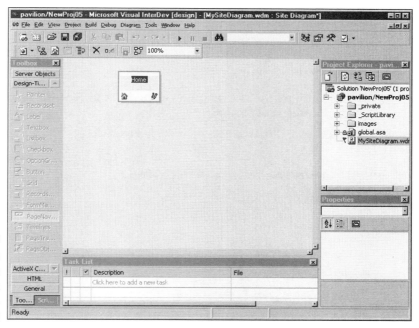

Figure 5-4:
The Site
Diagram
toolbar.

By default, this toolbar floats to the left of the editor. You may find it more convenient to dock the toolbar under the Standard toolbar at the top of the window. To do this, simply grab the Site Diagram toolbar by its title bar and drag up immediately under the primary toolbar. It docks automatically. After you move the toolbar, it will always appear in the new position unless you move it again.

I show you how to make use of the buttons in the Site Diagram toolbar in the coming sections.

Adding an existing page to a site diagram

If you've already begun creating your site and you want to go back and add a site diagram, you have already-existing pages that you want to add to the new site diagram. Visual InterDev offers an easy way for you to do that.

To add an existing page to a site diagram:

1. **While editing the site diagram, scroll through the Project Explorer window to find the page you want to add.**

2. **Drag the page from the Project Explorer window to the site diagram and drop it where you want it to appear (you can move it later, if you need to).**

   The page appears as a box with the name of the file in it.

Or you could do it another way:

1. **While editing the site diagram, click the Add Existing File button on the Site Diagram toolbar.**

   The Choose URL dialog appears (see Figure 5-5).

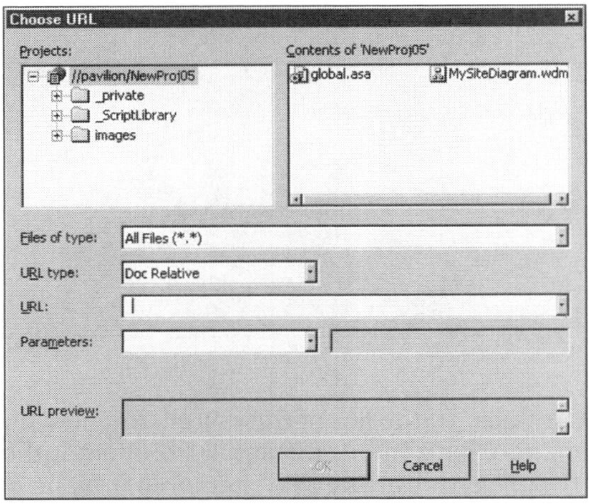

Figure 5-5:
The
Choose URL
dialog box.

2. **Navigate the folders in the tree-view list box on the right, if necessary. Find the file you want and click its icon on the right to select it.**

3. **Click OK.**

   The page appears in the middle of your diagram as a box with the name of the file in it.

Creating a new page in a site diagram

You can also create new pages in the site diagram that don't yet exist in your project.

To create a new page in a site diagram:

1. **Click the arrow beside the New Page drop-down toolbar button (the first button on the site diagram toolbar).**

   A menu appears with two options: New HTML Page and New ASP Page.

2. **Pick the option you want.**

   The new page appears in the center of your site diagram, and Visual InterDev automatically names it.

3. **Type a new name.**

   The name you enter replaces the default name.

4. **Drag the new page where you want it to appear on the diagram.**

Or you can do it another way:

1. **Click the diagram background to be sure that none of the pages are currently selected.**

2. **To add a new HTML page, press Ctrl+Shift+H. To add a new ASP page, press Ctrl+Shift+A.**

   The new page appears in the center of the diagram.

3. **Name it and move it where you like.**

Notice that the new page has a pencil icon on it (see Figure 5-6). This icon means that you have made changes to the page (in this case, you've created it) and that you have not yet saved these changes. When you save the site diagram, the new page is created in your project, and the pencil icon goes away.

Manipulating site diagram pages

The boxes that represent pages in a site diagram can be moved around, renamed, removed, and deleted. The following sections tell you how to manipulate your pages.

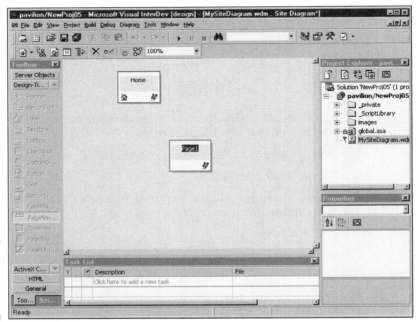

Figure 5-6:
The Pencil
icon on the
new page.

Moving a page

To move a page, simply drag the page where you want it placed and drop it. The physical location of a page on the diagram doesn't really affect anything. Organizing pages into groups that work together can be helpful, though.

Renaming a page

To rename a page, follow these steps:

1. **Right-click the page you want to rename.**

2. **Choose Property Pages from the pop-up menu.**

   The Property Pages dialog box appears (see Figure 5-7).

3. **Type the new name in the Title text box.**

4. **Click OK.**

In the Property Pages dialog box, you can also change the page filename that the current box on the diagram represents by changing the text in the URL text box.

Or you can rename a page another way:

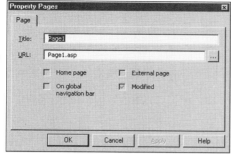

Figure 5-7:
The
Property
Pages
dialog box.

1. **Click to select a page.**

2. **Wait a moment, and then click directly on the name of the page.**

   Make sure you wait long enough before clicking the page again so that Visual InterDev knows you're not trying to double-click the page. (See the section called "Opening pages to edit" later in this chapter to see what happens when you double-click.)

3. **When the name is highlighted, type the new name.**

Removing a page

To remove a page from the diagram, you can do one of the following:

- ✔ Right-click the page you want to remove and choose Remove from the pop-up menu.
- ✔ Select the page and click the Remove button on the site diagram toolbar.

Removing a page does not delete it from your project. (See "Deleting a page" in the next section for information on that.)

You cannot remove a page that has changes that have not been saved (you can tell if the page contains unsaved changes because a pencil icon will be in the page). To save the page, you have to save the entire diagram by clicking the Save button on the Standard toolbar.

For information about how the Remove command works with parent/child relationships, see the section "Using the Remove and Delete commands with parents and children," later in this chapter.

Deleting a page

Deleting a page both removes the page from the diagram *and* deletes the page from the project entirely. Don't confuse the Delete and Remove commands!

If you want to delete a page, you have two options:

- ✔ Right-click the page you want to delete and choose Delete from the pop-up menu.
- ✔ Select the page and click the Delete button on the site diagram toolbar.

Either way, the page disappears from the diagram *and* from the Project Explorer window.

For information about how the Delete command works with parent/child relationships, see "Using the Remove and Delete commands with parents and children," later in this chapter.

Designating the Home page

One page on your diagram can be designated the Home page. You can tell that it is the Home page because of the little house icon (see Figure 5-8). This is the page that the user will likely come to first when he visits this site. Often the Home page is named default.asp or default.htm.

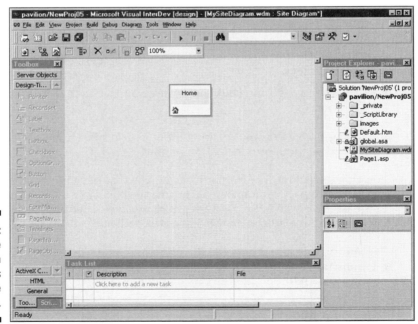

Figure 5-8:
The little house icon designates the Home page.

When you create your first site diagram for a site, Visual InterDev may put a Home page on the diagram automatically for you. If it doesn't, you can easily add a Home page to your diagram by using one of the following methods:

✔ Choose Diagram⇨Add Home Page from the menu bar.

✔ Click the Add Home Page button on the site diagram toolbar.

Either way, a new page with the house icon on it appears in the diagram.

By default, the Home page is always associated with a file called default.htm. If you already have a default.htm, it is automatically mapped to that one. If you don't, Visual InterDev creates a default.htm when you save the site diagram.

If you named your home page default.asp, you need to change the automatically created Home page so that it refers to default.asp, rather than default.htm.

To change the file associated with your Home page:

1. **Right-click the Home page and choose Property Pages from the pop-up menu.**

   The Property Pages dialog box appears.

2. **Change the page that this Home page is mapped to by entering the new name in the URL edit box.**

   For example, you may need to change default.htm to default.asp if your default page is an ASP page.

3. **Click OK.**

Opening pages to edit

The site diagram gives you a great high-level overview of your site and how the pages work together. Because of that, the site diagram is actually a good place to work from.

To edit one of the pages on the diagram, just double-click the page you want to edit. The editor launches with the page you just double-clicked. The site diagram is still open in its own window, and you can switch back to it by selecting it from the list of open windows in the Windows menu.

Saving a site diagram

To save a site diagram, choose File⇨Save from the menu bar.

All the new files created in the site diagram that didn't exist before are now created and appear in the Project Explorer window. The box representing those new pages in the site diagram lose their pencil icon after the page is actually created.

Nurturing the parent-child relationship

In the Visual InterDev site diagrams, pages can have only one type of relationship with each other — a *parent/child* relationship. You put pages together into trees in which a parent page links to one or more child pages and each child, in turn, is a parent to its own children. This organization can go as deep as you like. And you can have any number of separate trees in a site diagram as you want. You can even have pages that are completely separate and not a part of a tree at all.

Making babies

To make one page a child of another page:

1. **Select the child page and drag it under the parent page.**

   As you drag the box around, it appears as a dotted outline (see Figure 5-9).

   When you get close enough under the parent, a dotted line appears from the parent to the dotted outline of the child (see Figure 5-10).

2. **When you see the connecting line, you can drop the child.**

   The child appears under the parent with a solid line between them. The child lines up with any other children of that parent to make your diagram appear nice and neat.

You can add as many children to a single parent as you like.

 Also notice that there is a minus sign at the point where the lines from the children enter the parent. If you click the minus sign, all the children disappear, and a plus sign appears. Clicking the plus sign causes the children to reappear. Hiding the children can help save space when you are organizing a big site.

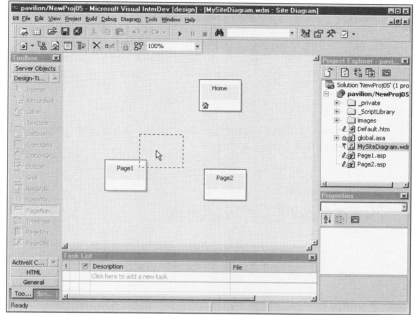

Figure 5-9:
The dragged page appears as a dotted-line box.

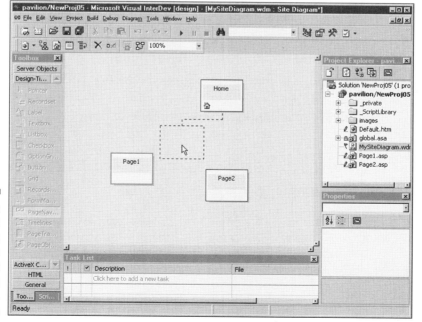

Figure 5-10:
The dotted line between the parent and the new child.

Divorcing your parents

It's easy to accidentally move one page too close to another and accidentally make it a child. In addition, sometimes you will need to break existing relationships in order to forge new ones when you reorganize your site.

To make a child page independent again:

1. **Drag the child far enough away from the parent that the dotted line between them disappears.**

2. **Drop the child.**

Breeding like rabbits

You can save some time by creating new pages that are immediately linked to a parent. This is helpful especially when you are creating a high-level page that has links to a lot of other pages.

To create a new child:

1. **Click to select the page that you want to be the parent.**

2. **Click the New Page drop-down toolbar button on the site diagram toolbar and choose New HTML Page or New ASP Page.**

   Alternately, you can use the keyboard shortcut Ctrl+Shift+H for an HTML page or Ctrl+Shift+A for an ASP page.

   The new page immediately appears under the parent as a child (see Figure 5-11).

3. **Now type the name you want the child to have.**

Using the Remove and Delete commands with parents and children

You cannot remove a page that has changes that have not been saved (the pencil icon indicates that a page includes unsaved changes). In addition, you can't remove a parent page that has children pages that include unsaved changes. You need to save all the changes in the tree before you can remove a parent page. To save changes, click the Save button on the Standard toolbar.

If both parent and children's changes are up-to-date and you try to remove the parent, all the children are removed too, automatically.

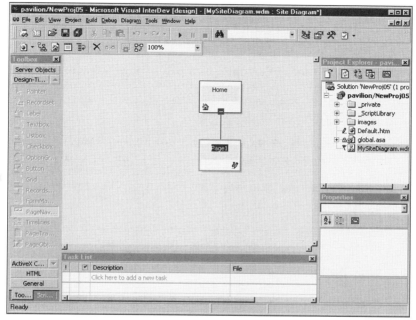

Figure 5-11:
The new
page
appears
as a child
of the
selected
parent.

If both parent and children's changes are up-to-date and you try to *delete* the parent, you see the dialog box that's shown in Figure 5-12.

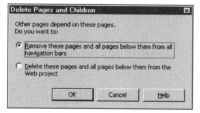

Figure 5-12:
The Delete
Pages and
Children
dialog box.

This dialog box allows you to choose whether you want to *remove* or *delete* the parent and all the pages under it.

Deleting the parent of many children and grandchildren is a good way to loose a lot of work very quickly. The pages are actually deleted from the project, so be careful!

The good new is that you will be warned before the pages are deleted, and the delete function won't actually take place until you save the site diagram.

You can go anywhere with the Global Navigation Bar

A Web page that's functioning as a parent page often includes links to all its children. And often a child page contains a link to its parent. Visual InterDev layouts (which are discussed later this chapter) make creating those links, based on your site diagrams, easy.

But aside from the links to parents and children, common links can often be found on almost every page of a site. They link to global pages that users will often want to jump to. For example, if you have a page that allows users to search your site, you may want to include a link to that page from all your pages.

To make identifying these pages easier, the site diagram editor has a feature that enables you to identify certain pages as a part of a *Global Navigation Bar*. This bar contains links to global pages (a search page is an example of a global page).

The Global Navigation Bar can be displayed along the top of your pages, along the side, along the bottom or really, anywhere you like. Where it appears (or if it appears at *all*) is determined by the layout you choose. For more information on Layouts see "Using Layouts to Create Consistent Site Navigation" later in this chapter.

A page that is a part of the Global Navigation Bar can be a parent of other pages, but it cannot be a child. It can also be completely off on its own and not attached to any other pages.

Adding a page to the Global Navigation Bar

To add a page to the Global Navigation Bar:

1. **In the site diagram, click to select the page you want to add.**

2. **Choose Diagram⇨Add to Global Navigation Bar or press Ctrl+Shift+G.**

   You can also click the Add to Global Navigation Bar button on the site diagram toolbar.

   The Global Navigation Bar icon appears in the box representing the page (see Figure 5-13).

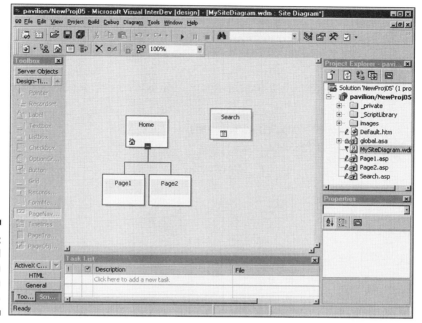

Removing a page from the Global Navigation Bar

To remove a page from the Global Navigation Bar, follow these steps:

1. **In the site diagram, click to select a page that is currently on the Global Navigation Bar (it has the icon pictured in Figure 5-13).**

2. **Choose Diagram⇨Remove from Global Navigation Bar or press Ctrl+Shift+G.**

   You can also click the Remove from Global Navigation Bar button on the site diagram toolbar.

   Both the keystroke and the toolbar button in this set of steps are the same ones you use to add a page. They both simply act as toggles.

Reordering the pages on the Global Navigation Bar

The order of the pages on the Global Navigation Bar is important. The links on your pages will appear in the same order. By default, the links appear in reverse order of how you added the pages. In other words, the last page you added appears first in the Global Navigation Bar.

To change the order of the pages on the Global Navigation Bar:

1. **Choose Diagram⇨Reorder Global Navigation Bar or click the Reorder Pages on Global Navigation Bar button on the Site Diagram toolbar.**

   The Reorder Global Navigation Bar window appears (see Figure 5-14).

2. **In the list box, click to select the page you want to move.**

3. **Click the Move Up or Move Down buttons to change the page's position on the Global Navigation Bar.**

4. **Select another page and use the Move Up and Move Down buttons to position it.**

5. **Repeat Step 5 until the pages are in the order that you like.**

6. **Click OK.**

Using Layouts to Create Consistent Site Navigation

A *layout* is a pre-defined page organization that specifies which navigational links will appear on your pages and where they will be placed. After you choose a layout, Visual InterDev automatically puts the links on your page to connect it with the appropriate pages. It does this via the one or more site diagrams you've already created for your site. (If you haven't already created them, check out the section titled "Creating a Site Diagram" earlier in this chapter for information on how to do it.)

If you have trouble with your layouts not showing the links that are supposed to appear, check to be sure you have Microsoft FrontPage Server extensions installed on both your workstation and the server.

Adding a layout when you create a new project

When you create a new project, you walk through the Web Project Wizard to give Visual InterDev all the information it needs to create the project (see Chapter 2 for more information on this process). If you've already created a project and you want to add a layout, jump down to the next section, "Adding a layout to an existing project."

To add a layout when you create a new project:

1. **Walk through the Web Project Wizard and provide all the information it requests.**

2. **In the third step in the wizard, choose a layout to be used in your new project (see Figure 5-15).**

   As you click different layouts, you can see how they look in the preview box on the left side of the window.

3. **When you find one you like, click it and then click Next.**

4. **In the fourth step of the wizard, pick which theme you want for your project.**

   For more information on themes, see Chapter 4.

5. **Click Finish.**

   Visual InterDev creates your project with the layout and theme you selected.

Now, each new HTML or ASP page you create in your project will make use of the layout and theme you just chose.

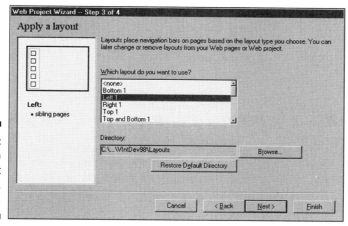

Figure 5-15:
The Web
Project
Wizard,
Step 3.

Adding a layout to an existing project

To add a layout to an existing project:

1. **Right-click the project itself in the Project Explorer window.**
2. **Choose Apply Theme and Layout from the pop-up menu.**

    The Apply Theme and Layout window appears.

3. **Click the Layout tab (see Figure 5-16).**

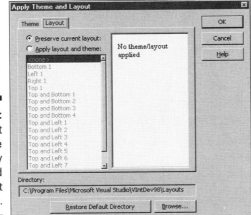

Figure 5-16:
The Layout tab of the Apply Theme and Layout window.

4. **Click the Apply Layout radio button above the list.**
5. **Click the various layouts to see them previewed along the right side of the window.**
6. **Click one of the layouts, and then click OK.**

    Visual InterDev applies the Layout to the project.

Now every time you create a new HTML or ASP page in an existing project, your newly chosen layout will be applied to it.

Adding a layout to the current page

One layout may not be appropriate for all your pages. Typically, for example, your Home page may have a different layout than the rest of your site. Other global pages, like your search page, are also likely to be different.

Adding a layout to a project doesn't force you to use that same layout for each page. Even if you haven't chosen a layout for a project, you can still add a layout to a specific page within that project.

To add a layout to the current page (regardless of whether one exists for the whole project):

1. **Open the page in the editor.**
2. **Choose Edit⇨Apply Theme and Layout.**

   The Apply Theme and Layout window appears.
3. **Click the Layout tab (refer to Figure 5-16).**
4. **Click the Apply Layout radio button above the list.**
5. **Click the various layouts to see them previewed along the right side of the window.**
6. **Click the one you want, and then click OK.**

   Visual InterDev applies the layout to your page.

   A dialog box appears that indicates that the page has been modified outside the editor (see Figure 5-17). It asks if you want to reload the modified page.
7. **Click Yes.**

   The current page is reloaded with the new layout.

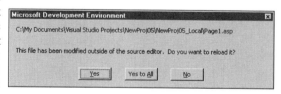

Using multiple layouts in a project

You can have as many layouts in use in a single project as you want. New pages are always given the last layout that you applied to the entire project.

Applying a new layout to your project causes all pages without a layout to take on the layout you are applying.

Using layouts with themes

You can use layouts and themes together to create a distinctive identity for your Web applications. Themes provide a look for the page and its text. Layouts provide a standard way of organizing the information and navigational links on the page. I discuss themes in Chapter 4.

Working with a page that has a layout

When you first begin working with a page that has a layout associated with it, you may be a bit confused by all the weird stuff that appears in the editor (see Figure 5-18).

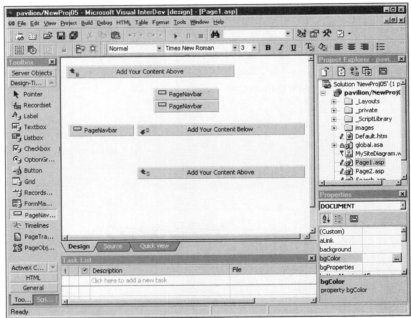

Figure 5-18:
A page that already has a layout in the editor.

You see two basic things in a page that has a layout applied. First, you see a PageNavbar control. This is the control that actually produces the links that you see on your final page.

The second feature is a gray bar that has the words Add Your Content Above or Add Your Content Below. These are not controls that actually do anything, they are simply guidelines for you as you add content to this page so that you know where you can add it.

To get a better feel for how this layout works, click the Visible Borders button on the Design toolbar (that's the short toolbar just under the Standard toolbar on the left). Clicking this button allows you to see the border of tables, even when the tables don't have visible borders that show up in the browser when the page is displayed. When you click Visible Borders, your page should look something like Figure 5-19.

The structure of the page should now make a little more sense to you and should, in fact, look a lot like the preview of the layout looked when you first chose it. Follow the guidelines of the gray bars when deciding where to place your content.

To preview how your page will look with the final layout navigation links in it, click the Start button on the Standard toolbar. A browser opens and displays the Start page for your site. (By the Start page, I mean the one you right-clicked when you chose "Set As Start." For more information on viewing your pages, see Chapter 3.) Navigate to the page you are working on, and you should see your content alongside the links produced by the PageNavbar controls.

You won't see the links produced by the PageNavbar control in the page editor's Quick View. PageNavbar is a *Design-Time Control* and must run on a Web server before it can produce the links.

Figure 5-19:
The same
page
that's in
Figure 5-18
with the
Visible
Borders
feature
turned on.

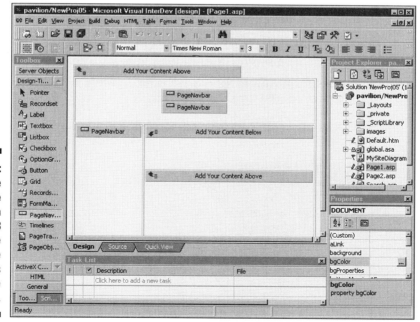

Using the PageNavbar Design Time Control

All layouts have one thing in common: the PageNavbar control. It is the Design Time Control that produces the links or buttons that provide navigation among your pages.

But you don't have to use the pre-defined layouts to make use of the PageNavbar control. You can use it in any page.

To add the PageNavbar control to your page:

1. **Click Design-Time Controls in the Toolbox.**

2. **Drag the PageNavbar control to your page and drop it where you want the bar placed.**

You can use a table to help you align it along the left or right or to keep it above or below your content, just as the layouts do. And remember, you can have as many PageNavbar controls on your page as you like, each in a different place providing access to a different set of pages.

To customize a PageNavbar control:

1. **Right-click the PageNavbar control.**

2. **Choose Properties from the pop-up menu.**

   The PageNavbar properties window appears (see Figure 5-20).

3. **Set the properties to specify what links you want on the page and how they should look.**

For more details on the options, see the following sections.

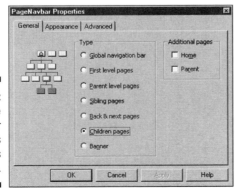

Figure 5-20:
The PageNavbar Properties dialog box's General tab.

PageNavbar Properties General tab

The General tab on the PageNavbar Properties dialog box (refer to Figure 5-20) allows you to specify exactly what navigation links you want to appear in your pages.

The Type radio buttons allow you to choose which navigation links you want this PageNavbar to produce. Here are the options:

- **Global Navigation Bar:** The Global Navigation Bar is specified in the site diagram. It provides links to pages that should be accessible throughout your project, such as a search page.

- **First level pages:** All the pages that are immediate children of the Home page designated in your site diagram. For more information on the Home page, see "Designating the Home page," earlier in this chapter.

- **Parent level pages:** All the pages at the same level as the parent of this page.

- **Sibling pages:** All the pages that are at the same level as this page.

- **Back and next pages:** The siblings immediately before and after this page. (Visual InterDev determines the order by the order that they appear in the site diagram.)

- **Children pages:** All the children of this page.

- **Banner:** Display the page banner graphic specified by the theme (if one is associated with this page).

You can also add the Home page and/or the parent of this page using the check boxes.

PageNavbar Properties Appearance tab

The PageNavbar Properties dialog box's Appearance tab (see Figure 5-21) allows you to specify how the links should appear on the page.

You can set the appearance of the links to be buttons or normal text links, or you can define your own custom HTML in the Link template and Current Page template edit boxes at the bottom of the dialog box.

You can also determine whether the links appear beside or on top of each other. Finally, the check boxes allow you to specify whether a table should be used around the links and whether the theme's definition for links should be adopted for this PageNavbar.

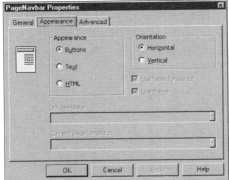

Figure 5-21: The PageNavbar Properties dialog box's Appearance tab.

PageNavbar Properties Advanced tab

The PageNavbar Properties dialog box's Advanced tab (see Figure 5-22) enables you to specify exactly what navigation links you want to appear.

This page allows you to enter the path to a page. If you do, the PageNavbar will use that page's navigation structure for this PageNavbar's links. For example, you could use the Home page's navigation structure on other pages throughout the site.

The path to the page specified in this dialog box should be project-relative. In other words, give the path as if you were starting in the root of the project, not starting from where this page is.

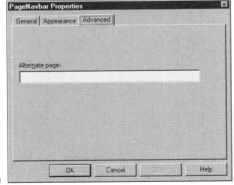

Figure 5-22: The PageNavbar Properties dialog box's Advanced tab.

Part II

Making Your Web Pages Smarter with Scripts

The 5th Wave   By Rich Tennant

"It's a letter from the company that
installed our in-ground sprinkler system.
They're offering Internet access now."

In this part . . .

*W*eb pages based on HTML can only take you so far. In order to turn your Web site into an interactive Web application, you need a real programming language. In this part, you see how Visual InterDev aids you in scripting for the client and the server. You also explore the world of object-oriented development and discover the power that these objects bring to you.

Chapter 6

Using Scripts

In This Chapter

▶ Discovering how different types of Web applications execute

▶ Adding different kinds of scripts to your Visual InterDev pages

▶ Exploring ASP scripting on the server

*I*n the previous chapters, I show you how to use Visual InterDev to create traditional Web pages and Web sites. In this chapter, you begin to exploit the real power of Visual InterDev to create Web applications.

Web applications are like any software application — they do calculations, massage data, and move data around to help make someone's life easier. But if you want to move from creating normal Web pages to true Web applications, you need more than HTML alone can offer. That's where *scripting* comes in.

The Anatomy of a Web Application

To understand how all the pieces of a Web application come together, I need to describe how a typical HTML page works before I show you how client scripting and ActiveX controls change things. Then I need to introduce you to the wonders of server-side script with Active Server Pages (ASP).

Although some of this might be review for you, walking through the process can help clarify when and where all the different pieces execute.

Mind your language!

In this chapter, I introduce you to the concepts of client and server scripting and show you how to add script to your pages. What I won't be doing is teaching you a scripting language. I am going to assume that you are already familiar with VBScript. If you are not familiar with VBScript, see Appendix A in the back of this book. It provides a quick introduction to the language and should give you enough information to get started. For more information on using VBScript to create Active Server Pages, see *Active Server Pages For Dummies*, written by yours truly and published by IDG Books Worldwide, Inc.

Understanding the life of a static HTML page

Here's the process that occurs when you browse the Web looking at normal, static HTML pages:

1. The user types a Web address in the URL line of his browser or clicks a site in his Favorites menu.

2. The browser locates the Web server and sends a request for the specific page.

3. The server receives the request, locates the page, and sends it out to the browser.

4. The browser receives the page, goes through the HTML and renders it, so the page looks just as it should look. If additional graphics appear on the page, the browser requests the graphics and displays them as it receives them.

5. If the user clicks a link in that page, the process repeats.

This process is the foundation for the World Wide Web. This simple idea has created the tremendous diversity of sites that you see today on the Web.

Although this simple concept is very powerful, it doesn't provide all the capabilities you need to create applications. HTML is limited — it describes the *look* of a page, not what the page should *do*. It lacks many of the basic capabilities expected in even the simplest programming language. Clearly something more has to be added. That "something" is *scripting languages*.

Learning to speak a scripting language

To make HTML more powerful, scripting languages were added. The most popular scripting languages are JavaScript and VBScript. Because VBScript isn't supported by the Netscape browser, programmers do most client scripting using JavaScript.

But what does a script do? It adds a real computer language to the basic HTML, enabling you to add intelligence to your pages.

Here's the typical scenario for client script:

1. The user types a Web address in the URL line of his browser or clicks a site in his Favorites menu.
2. The browser locates the Web server and sends a request for the specific page.
3. The server receives the request, locates the page, and sends it out to the browser.
4. The browser receives the page, goes through the HTML, and renders it. In addition, if it finds script, the browser may execute that script when the page is first rendered, or the browser may wait until the user does something (like click a button) before executing the script.

Notice that the script runs in the *browser* on the *client,* just as the HTML does. Scripts are just extensions of the capabilities of HTML.

Incorporating ActiveX controls

ActiveX controls are small programs written and compiled in a traditional programming language such as Visual Basic or Visual C++. They are automatically downloaded, executed on the client, and displayed in a page in the browser. From within a script, you can access these controls and manipulate them so that they can interact with each other and with the user to create a complete user interface for your Web application.

For more information on adding ActiveX controls, see Chapter 3.

The problem with the client

With the combination of client scripting and ActiveX controls, you'd think you'd have everything you need to create cool Web applications.

There's just one problem. As I mentioned previously, Netscape doesn't support VBScript. It also doesn't support ActiveX controls. Many other browsers don't support any client scripting at all. When you are working in a culture as diverse as the World Wide Web, you can't make a lot of assumptions about what kind of browser, machine, or operating system the user has. If you do, you may be cutting off a huge portion of your audience.

The solution: Moving the smarts to the server

Trusting the client to do all the complex tricks you need to perform to create Web applications isn't always practical. You don't have control over which browser people are using. So one solution is to bring all that intelligence to the server — a platform you *do* have some control over.

Using Active Server Pages

The server-side corollary to scripting is Active Server Pages (ASP), which enable you to write script inside your HTML page, just as you did with client-side script. The difference is that this script is executed by the Web server before it sends the page out. It works something like this:

1. The user requests a page.

2. The Web server finds the page and looks at it. If the page's filename has an .htm or .html extension, the server sends it out just like any normal HTML page.

3. If the page's filename has an .asp extension, the server handles it differently. First, the server walks through the page and executes all the server-side script in the page. When it is finished, the server strips out all the script, leaving only pure HTML. Then, the server sends the pure HTML page to the client.

4. The client renders the HTML and displays it to the user.

Using ActiveX server components

Just as you can create ActiveX controls to be automatically downloaded and accessed from client script, you can also create ActiveX *server* components that can be accessed from ASP script.

However, these server components are different from ActiveX controls in one important way: Server components do *not* have a user interface. They are just engines that can do calculations, retrieve data, or process information for your ASP scripts.

All together now

I can think of a number of advantages to using server script and server components instead of client script and ActiveX controls:

- ✔ The user can't look at your code by simply choosing View⇨Source from her browser menu, as she could with client-side script.

- ✔ Because the server sends out only pure HTML, your page is compatible with any browser.

- ✔ You have more control with server script because all the Web server resources are at your disposal.

- ✔ You can write your script in any language that your server understands. VBScript is the most commonly used for server scripting.

But one big disadvantage exists: performance. When you write client-side code, all the execution happens right on the user's machine and is very fast. With server-side script, the page has to go back to the server every time code is executed. This process can take time and can slow down the overall performance of the Web application.

Here's the good news: You are not forced to use only client-side scripts or sever-side scripts. You can use both! Even in the same page, you can have both client and server script.

The key to scripting is knowing your audience and deciding what browser capabilities you want to support.

Browser Capabilities versus Broad Reach: Three Common Solutions

In case you skipped over the last few sections, I'll summarize them for you: The more client-side features you use, the stiffer the restrictions on what type of browser your users must have. This dilemma has lead to three common solutions:

- ✔ The pure intranet
- ✔ The Microsoft/Netscape compromise
- ✔ The broad-reach plan

I cover the pros and cons of each of these solutions in the following sections.

The pure intranet

The pure intranet is the best of all possible worlds. This solution can be applied only when you are developing internal applications for a company's intranet and the company has standardized on one browser, say Microsoft Internet Explorer. If you are in this situation, you are free to use all the exciting client-side features of Internet Explorer, including:

- ✔ ActiveX controls
- ✔ Client scripting in either VBScript or JavaScript
- ✔ Dynamic HTML
- ✔ Cascading Style Sheets

You can choose to do processing on the server when it makes sense (for security reasons, for instance), but, more than likely, you'll want to maximize performance by putting as much code on the client as possible.

The Microsoft/Netscape compromise

Perhaps you are developing applications for worldwide use on the Internet. Or perhaps you have a more diverse intranet for a company that either hasn't completely standardized on one browser or has multiple operating systems that require the support of multiple browsers.

In either case, you can't depend on all the nifty Internet Explorer features being there for you. However, if you choose to support either Microsoft Internet Explorer or Netscape Navigator, then you can still assume that you have a strong client that supports:

- ✔ Advanced HTML 3.2 tags
- ✔ JavaScript client scripting
- ✔ More limited support for Cascading Style Sheets than the pure intranet solution offers

The broad-reach plan

If you want to reach the broadest possible audience, then the safest bet is to assume only standard HTML support. This doesn't mean that you can't write Web applications, but it does mean that *all* your processing should be done on the server and that only pure HTML should be sent to the client. This solution doesn't give you the greatest performance, but it can provide very complete applications.

Adding Scripts to Your Application

If you want to add script to your Web pages, you must use an HTML tag that separates the script from the rest of the page. That tag is <SCRIPT>, and it has several attributes. For example, LANGUAGE determines what scripting language you are writing in. RUNAT determines where the script will execute — on the client or the server.

Adding a client script to your page

To add client script to your HTML or ASP page:

1. **Place the cursor where you want to place the script within your code.**

2. **Choose HTML⇨Script Block⇨Client.**

   Visual InterDev adds the <SCRIPT> tag to your code (see Listing 6-1).

Listing 6-1	**Everything between <SCRIPT> and </SCRIPT> Is Added to Your Code Automatically**

```
<HTML>
<HEAD>
<META NAME="GENERATOR"
Content="Microsoft Visual Studio 6.0">
<TITLE></TITLE>
<SCRIPT LANGUAGE=javascript>
<!--

//-->
</SCRIPT>
</HEAD>
<BODY>

<P> </P>

</BODY>
</HTML>
```

The code inside the <SCRIPT> tag is surrounded by HTML comments so that older browsers that don't support client scripting will ignore it.

In this example, the RUNAT attribute is omitted. By default, the client is assumed. To see the RUNAT attribute used to specify server script, see Listing 6-2 in the next section.

Notice here that the client scripting language is assumed to be JavaScript.

You should place your scripts in the `<HEAD>` portion of your document unless you have a specific reason to place them elsewhere.

Adding a server script to your page

Client script can be added to either HTML pages or ASP pages. Server script can be added only to ASP pages. The page must have an .asp extension so that the Web server knows to process the script and strip the script out before it sends the rest of the HTML on to the browser.

To add server script to an ASP page:

1. **Place the cursor where you want to place the script within your code.**

2. **Choose HTML⇨Script Block⇨Server.**

   Visual InterDev adds the `<SCRIPT>` tag to your code (see Listing 6-2).

Listing 6-2   The <SCRIPT> Tag Is Added to Your Code

```
<%@ Language=VBScript %>
<HTML>
<HEAD>
<META NAME="GENERATOR"
Content="Microsoft Visual Studio 6.0">
<SCRIPT LANGUAGE=vbscript RUNAT=Server>


</SCRIPT>
</HEAD>
<BODY>

<P> </P>

</BODY>
</HTML>
```

As you can see in Listing 6-2, the default language for server scripting is VBScript. The `RUNAT` attribute is specified as `Server`. Notice that you don't need to include the HTML comments because the server will strip out the script before it sends the page back to the browser.

Remember where you are! Client or server?

Client and server scripting can seem very similar. You use the same tag for both, and you may even be using the same language for both. And you can easily do both kinds of scripting in the same page.

But it is essential that you remember which is which. Not only do you need to remember where your code is executing — on the server before it sends the page or on the client machine in the user's browser — but also what *environment* that platform provides for you. You can do things on the client that are impossible on the server, and vice-versa.

For example, in client script, you can sometimes modify the browser window itself and specify how it should look. This is impossible to do from the server. Likewise, in server

script, you can access files on the server's hard drive. You certainly can't do that in a client script.

Throughout the rest of this chapter and in Chapter 7, I introduce you to many of the features and capabilities of both client and server script. And I let you know which techniques work in which environment.

In Chapter 8, I introduce you to a technology that is built into Visual InterDev called the Scripting Object Model (SOM). SOM provides a way of doing many common scripting tasks in exactly the same way, regardless of whether you're using client or server scripts. But for now, be sure to keep client and server scripts separate in your mind!

Scripting the Client

In this section, I discuss some of the issues and techniques for using client-side scripting. The topics I cover here apply to *client-side* scripting only.

Unless you are in a pure intranet environment in which Microsoft Internet Explorer 4.0 or later is installed and used by all your users, you are probably not going to be able to take advantage of the cool, advanced features of Dynamic HTML (DHTML).

So what can you rely on? The consensus seems to have settled on HTML 3.2, which is a standard that is supported by Netscape Navigator 3.0 and Internet Explorer 3.0. Navigator and Internet Explorer have, by far, the largest market share of all the browsers. And because both Netscape and Microsoft have come out with at least one newer version of their browser since Version 3.0, you can rest assured that most people, even if they haven't upgraded in a while, have browsers that support HTML 3.2.

For specific information on what is a part of the HTML 3.2 standard, check out the official specification at: www.w3.org/TR/REC-html32.html.

In addition, Internet Explorer 3.0 and Netscape Navigator 2.0 both support client scripting in JavaScript. No version of Netscape Navigator supports client scripting in VBScript, so if you want to do client scripting with as broad a reach as possible, JavaScript is the only way to go.

Scripting the Server with ASP

In this section, I show you how server-side ASP scripting works and how you can begin using it to create powerful Web applications. All the topics I discuss in this section apply only to *server-side* scripting in Active Server Pages.

Using server script delimiters

In addition to the `<SCRIPT>` tag, you can set off ASP script with a unique set of delimiters: `<%` and `%>`. Listing 6-3 shows an example.

Listing 6-3 Using the <% and %> Delimiters to Set Off ASP Script

```
<HTML>
<HEAD>
<META NAME="GENERATOR"
Content="Microsoft Visual Studio 6.0">
</HEAD>
<BODY>
You have arrived at...
<% For I = 1 to 3 %>
<center><h2>The EdgeQuest ASP Zone</h2></center>
<% Next %>

</BODY>
</HTML>
```

The code in Listing 6-3 produces a page that looks like Figure 6-1.

The HTML inside the loop is displayed three times. Notice how the `<%` and `%>` delimiters are easier to open and close when your ASP code is intermingled with HTML.

In general, when you are writing a lot of code, like a subroutine or function, you can use the `<SCRIPT>` tag. But when your code is intermingled with HTML, you'll find the delimiters much handier.

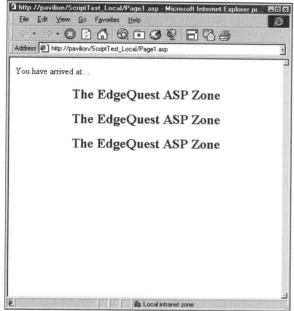

Figure 6-1:
The
EdgeQuest
ASP Zone
page.

Remember that ASP pages must be executed by a Web server in order to work. If you preview them in the script editor's Quick View or open them directly from the browser, the ASP script does not go through the Web server and doesn't get a chance to execute. The best way to test your ASP pages is to work in local mode and click the Start button on the Standard toolbar. Doing so runs the pages through the local Web server so that they can be processed correctly.

You can tell if you're in Local mode by choosing Project⇨Web Project⇨ Working Mode. The pop-up menu indicates whether Local or Master is chosen. You can also use that same menu to change your mode. Just click the one you want.

Conditionally displaying HTML

In Listing 6-3, you can see how you can use VBScript to display the same HTML text again and again using a loop. You can also use VBScript to conditionally display or not display certain HTML. Or to display one line of HTML in some circumstances and another line in other circumstances. Listing 6-4 demonstrates this flexibility.

Listing 6-4	Conditionally Displaying HTML

```
<HTML>
<HEAD>
<META NAME="GENERATOR"
Content="Microsoft Visual Studio 6.0">
</HEAD>
<BODY>
<% If Time < #6:00 PM# Then %>
<h3>Good Day!</h3>
<% Else %>
<h3>Good Evening!</h3>
<% End If %>
</BODY>
</HTML>
```

Even if you are familiar with VBScript, you may not be familiar with using the # (pound sign) around dates and times. You use # around dates and times just like you use quotes around strings.

If the time is before 6:00 PM, Good Day! is displayed. Otherwise, Good Evening! is displayed.

Displaying a value with server script

You can use a special shorthand way to display information using the server script delimiters. Listing 6-5 demonstrates how this works.

Listing 6-5 Using the <% and %> Delimiters to Set Off ASP Script

```
<%@ Language=VBScript %>
<HTML>
<HEAD>
<META NAME="GENERATOR"
Content="Microsoft Visual Studio 6.0">
</HEAD>
<BODY>
<%
Rent = 900
LeaseLength = 12
LeaseAmount = Rent * LeaseLength
%>
```

```
With a rent amount of <% =Rent %> and a lease
length of <% =LeaseLength %>, you'll end up
paying <% =LeaseAmount %>.<p>
</BODY>
</HTML>
```

The code in Listing 6-4 produces a page that looks like Figure 6-2.

By including the variable alone with an equal sign in front of it within delimiters, the Web server knows to strip out the variable name and replace it with the variable value in each place. This is a very handy technique.

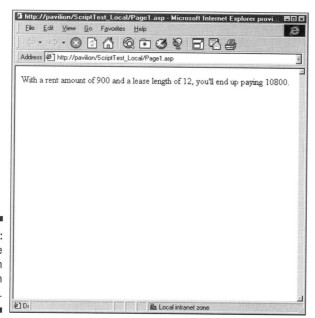

Figure 6-2:
The lease
calculation
from
Listing 6-4.

Chapter 7

Discovering Objects

*A*dding scripts to your pages is pretty straightforward. But you can only pull so many tricks with script alone. The real power is in using *objects*.

In this chapter, I introduce you to the concept of an object and all the stuff that makes up an object. I also show you some of the basics for putting objects to use in your scripts. (In Chapters 8 and 9, I show you a bunch of specific objects you can use to beef up your scripts.)

What's an Object?

If you are familiar with object-oriented concepts such as properties, methods, and events, you may want to simply skim over these few pages in this chapter to make sure we're talking the same language. Even if you are inclined to skip this chapter, at least check out the "Using Objects" and "Responding to Events" sections because they show the more practical side of making this stuff work in Visual InterDev.

But if objects, properties, and methods are unfamiliar or fuzzy for you, read on! You'll be manipulating objects with the best of them in no time!

Before I explain a bunch of stuff you don't know about, let me talk about something you *do* know about. When you are writing a program and you find a few lines that you are using over and over again throughout your code, you can probably take those lines of code and create a function or subroutine. Then you can call that function or subroutine from many different places. Sometimes, you end up with a collection of subroutines that go together, and you may collect them together into a library of subroutines.

An *object* is another way of collecting subroutines together into groups. But in addition to subroutines, you can also create variables that are associated directly with the object. So you bring together common subroutines and data into one unit, or object.

For example, if you were writing a Human Resources system, you might need to create an `Employee` object. This object might have a `CalculateSalary` subroutine, an `AssignVacation` subroutine, and many others. It may also have variables associated with it such as `Name`, `HireDate`, and `CurrentStatus`. By combining variables and subroutines together into common objects, you can create systems that are more intuitive.

So what's an object? It's nothing more than a bunch of variables and subroutines pulled together under one roof and given a name.

Talk the Talk

But, of course, like any field of study, object-oriented programming has a bunch of weird words for simple things in order to keep everyone confused. Here are the words you need to know:

- ✔ **Property (or Attribute):** The name of a variable that is associated with an object. People often say that a property *describes* an object or provides information about an object. In the example in the last section, `HireDate` is a *property* of the `Employee` object.

- ✔ **Method:** The name of a subroutine or function that is associated with an object. A method is something that the object has the ability to *do*. In the example in the last section, `CalculateSalary` is a *method* of the `Employee` object.

- ✔ **Object:** You already know this one — an object is a collection of properties and methods!

One More Thing — An Event

You need to know one more thing about objects. In addition to properties and methods, objects can also contain one other type of thing: *events*. An event is something that can happen *to* an object.

Often, user-interface elements are represented as objects. Imagine a button. A button may have a property called `Caption` that would determine what text would appear on the button. It might also have an event: `Click`. This is something that can happen *to* the button — the user could click the button.

What good is an event? Well, if an object has an event, you can write a script that will execute in *response to* that event. So you could write a script for the Click event of a button. Then, every time someone clicks that button, your script gets executed.

Most of the client and server scripting you write in Visual InterDev is in response to different events. This is a very powerful and simple way of organizing the code for your Web applications.

In summary, then, objects contain properties, which are variables; methods, which are subroutines; and finally, events, which you can write code to respond to (see Figure 7-1).

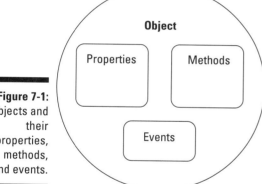

Figure 7-1:
Objects and their properties, methods, and events.

Using Objects

You use objects along with their properties and methods in both VBScript and JavaScript by using *dot-notation*. It's really simple.

To assign a value to a property, you write:

```
Object.Property = value
```

Replace *Object* with the name of the object, *Property* with the name of the property, and *value* with what you want to assign.

All the examples in this chapter are in VBScript, but they are nearly identical to the corresponding JavaScript.

To check the value of a property, you write

```
If Object.Property > value Then
```

And finally, to call a method, you write

```
Object.Method(arg1, arg2)
```

where *Method* is the name of the method to call, and *arg1* and *arg2* represent any arguments sent to the subroutine or function.

Basically, you use the properties as you would any variable, and you call the methods as you would any function or subroutine. The only difference is that you have to put the name of the object before the property or method, separated by a period.

In Chapter 8, you see how to start putting real objects to work for you in your scripts.

Responding to Events

After you understand dot-notation, you see that properties and methods work just like any other variable or subroutine.

Writing code to respond to events, however, is a little different. To respond to an event, you need to know three things:

- ✔ **Client or Server?** Do you want to write code that runs on the client or server? Are you responding to an event that was triggered on the client or the server?

- ✔ **What object, what event?** Exactly what object and what event of that object do you want to respond to? Any number of objects can exist in your project, and each object can have many different events that you could respond to.

- ✔ **What's the name?** How are you going to name your function that responds to the event, and how will you make it clear what object and event it goes with?

Fortunately, Visual InterDev has a tool that makes answering all these questions at once pretty easy. The tool is called the *Script Outline,* which is covered in the next section.

Using the Script Outline

The Script Outline window appears only when the script editor is in Source view. It appears in the same space that the Toolbox appears in. The tabs at the bottom of the Toolbox let you switch back and forth (see Figure 7-2).

If you don't see the Script Outline tab, the window may not be visible yet.

To display the Script Outline window, choose View⇨Other Windows⇨ Script Outline, or press Ctrl+Alt+S. The Script Outline window contains four folders:

- ✔ **Client Objects & Events:** Contains the document and window objects along with any other ActiveX controls you have on the page. You can open each object to display all the events associated with it.

- ✔ **Client Scripts:** Contains an icon for each client script that appears in your code. Double-clicking one scrolls the editor to that script.

- ✔ **Server Objects & Events:** Contains all the server objects and any server components on the page. Objects that have events may be opened to view them.

- ✔ **Server Scripts:** Contains an icon for each server script that appears in your code. Double-clicking one scrolls the editor to that script.

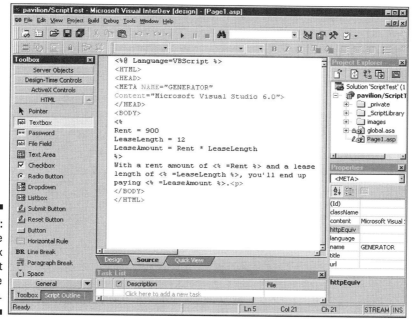

Figure 7-2:
The
Toolbox
and Script
Outline
tabs.

Creating an event response

To begin writing code that will execute in response to an event, follow these steps:

1. **Decide whether you want to write client code to respond to a client event or server code to respond to a server event. If you decide on client code, open the Client Objects & Events; otherwise, open Server Objects & Events.**

2. **Look through the objects and pick the one you want. Open it to view its events.**

3. **Pick the event you want to respond to.**

4. **Double-click the event.**

5. **Visual InterDev adds code to the editor, and your cursor is placed in the function or subroutine that will be executed in response to the event (see Figure 7-3).**

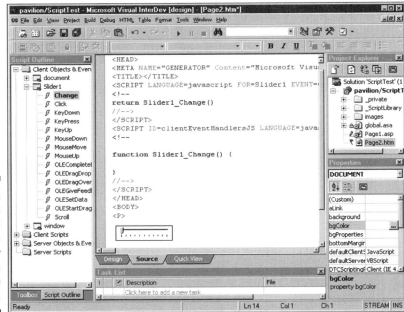

Figure 7-3: The page is changed to execute the new function in response to the event.

The code in Figure 7-3 was added when a Slider ActiveX control was added and its `Change` event was double-clicked in the Script Outline. This is the code that was added:

```
<SCRIPT LANGUAGE=javascript FOR=Slider1 EVENT=Change>
<!--
return Slider1_Change()
//-->
</SCRIPT>
<SCRIPT ID=clientEventHandlersJS LANGUAGE=javascript>
<!--

function Slider1_Change() {

}

//-->
</SCRIPT>
```

Notice that the first `<SCRIPT>` tag identifies the object and event using the `FOR` and `EVENT` attributes. The code then simply calls the `Slider1_Change` function and returns the result.

The second `<SCRIPT>` tag is where all the event handlers will be placed. The first one is the `Slider1_Change` that was just created.

This is how it works for an ActiveX control in client script. Other objects on the client and server objects all work differently in how they prepare the page to respond to the event.

But you don't have to worry about any of that! Simply double-click the event that you want to respond to in the Script Outline, and it's all done for you. And, later, if you want to come back and modify the code for an event, just double-click the event in the Script Outline again, and the editor automatically scrolls to the code you wrote.

Chapter 8
Exploring Client Script Objects

· ·

· ·

*I*n this chapter, I explore some of the objects that you can access and manipulate from your client scripts. (See Chapter 7 if you need a refresher course on objects.) Remember that these can only be accessed on the *client* from client-side script.

In Chapter 9, I describe a different set of objects that you can access from *server* script.

Rounding Up the Suspects

In client scripting, you can access five basic objects or types of objects from your scripts. They are:

- ✔ The window object
- ✔ The document object
- ✔ The history object
- ✔ Various form and element objects
- ✔ ActiveX controls

I discuss each of these in the next few sections.

When you write client script that takes advantage of a particular object's properties or methods, always be sure to test out your page on a wide variety of browsers. For example, a browser may support the window object, and it may support several common methods, but not all of them. The only way you can know for sure is by testing.

The Window Object

The window object represents the physical window of the Web browser that holds your HTML page. The window object provides access to many of the capabilities of the browser itself.

Manipulating the window

Because the window object represents the browser window itself, the methods for manipulating, opening, and closing windows reside in the window object.

Open sesame!

The open method allows you to open a new browser window and to even specify its size and location and how it looks. Here's an example:

```
<SCRIPT LANGUAGE=javascript>
<!--
window.open("Page2.htm",null,
    "height=100,width=300,status=no,toolbar=no," +
    "menubar=no,location=no,top=200,left=400");
//-->
</SCRIPT>
```

This code produces a small window that sits just to the right of the main window (see Figure 8-1). You could use this type of window to provide additional instructions on how to fill out a form, for example.

For the specifics on the individual arguments for the open method or any of the other methods discussed, check the online Help system that comes with Visual InterDev. These client-side objects are documented there in the Internet Explorer Platform SDK.

Close sesame!

The close method allows you to close the current window. It takes no arguments and works very simply.

```
<SCRIPT LANGUAGE=javascript>
<!--
window.close();
//-->
</SCRIPT>
```

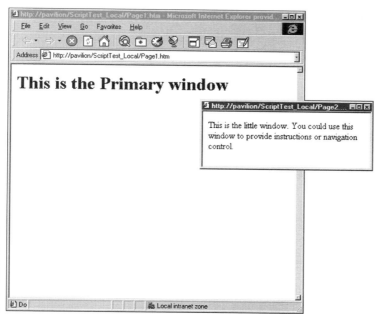

Figure 8-1:
Displaying
a second
window.

Depending on your security settings and on your browser, you may see a dialog box like the one in Figure 8-2 when you use this method. This gives the user the option to override your JavaScript code, if he wants to.

Figure 8-2:
Giving the
user the
option not
to close.

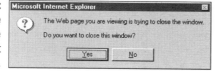

What's yer status?

Using the `status` property is a nifty way you can manipulate the window using the window object. You can assign a string to the status property and see that string displayed on the status bar at the bottom of your browser.

```
<SCRIPT LANGUAGE=javascript>
<!--
window.status = "*** Hello and Welcome to EdgeQuest ***";
//-->
</SCRIPT>
```

Whatever you assign to status appears in the gray bar along the bottom of your browser window (see Figure 8-3).

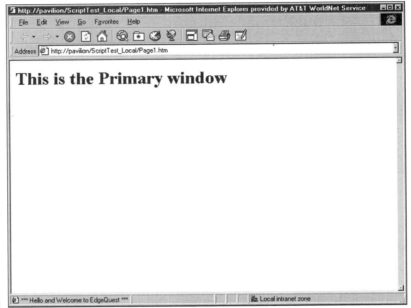

Figure 8-3:
Putting a
message
in the
status bar.

Whenever the status bar is not being used for anything else, it usually simply displays nothing. You can change that with defaultStatus. Whatever you assign as defaultStatus is what appears when the status bar isn't being used for anything else.

Opening a dialog box

The window object has three methods that enable you to display three different kinds of dialog boxes to the user. I cover these dialog boxes in the next few sections.

Be alert. The world needs more lerts.

The first dialog box is called an alert. It simply provides information to the user and asks her to read it and click OK.

```
<SCRIPT LANGUAGE=javascript>
<!--
window.alert("Your hard drive is on fire.");
//-->
</SCRIPT>
```

The alert is displayed in a simple dialog box (see Figure 8-4).

Figure 8-4:
The alert
dialog box.

I cannot confirm or deny. . . .

The next dialog box is called `confirm`. As its name implies, `confirm` gives the user a bit more interaction by allowing him to choose between the OK and Cancel buttons.

```
<SCRIPT LANGUAGE=javascript>
<!--
var ques;
ques = window.confirm("Are you sure you want to do this?");
if(ques) {
    window.alert("OK, Doing it!"); }
else {
    window.alert("Canceling the whole thing!"); }
//-->
</SCRIPT>
```

This code uses `confirm` to ask the user a question (see Figure 8-5). The result (either True or False) is returned into the `ques` variable. Then, based on the user's choice, different alerts are displayed (see Figure 8-6).

Figure 8-5:
The confirm
dialog box.

Figure 8-6:
The alert
dialog box,
identifying
which
option the
user chose.

Prompt and courteous

The last dialog box method in the window object is `prompt`. The `prompt` method allows you to ask the user for information and then receive that information into a variable.

```
<SCRIPT LANGUAGE=javascript>
<!--
var name;
name = window.prompt("What's your name?");
window.alert("Hello there, " + name);
//-->
</SCRIPT>
```

The string you send to prompt is displayed in the dialog box above the edit box (see Figure 8-7). After you enter your name in the code above, the alert box greets you (see Figure 8-8).

Figure 8-7:
The prompt
dialog box.

Figure 8-8:
The alert
dialog box
greeting.

These dialog boxes can be handy when you are debugging your application. Use them liberally to be sure a certain segment of code is being executed or that the value of a variable is what you expect it to be. (See Chapter 16 for more information on debugging.)

On the other hand, you're probably better off not using these methods much in your *final* code. Seeing a dialog box pop up when surfing the Web in a browser can be a jarring experience for the user.

Window events: onLoad and onUnload

In addition to all its properties and methods, the window object has two events:

- **onLoad:** Fires immediately after the browser loads the page.
- **onUnload:** Fires immediately before the browser unloads the page.

The code that is executed when these events occur looks like this:

```
<SCRIPT LANGUAGE=javascript>
<!--
function window_onload() {

}
//-->
</SCRIPT>
```

The Document Object

The document object represents the Web page displayed inside the browser. It provides access to the document and allows you to get information about it and even change it.

Writing to the page

The document object includes a method to make it easy to write HTML text to a page: `write`.

```
<SCRIPT LANGUAGE=javascript>
<!--
var name
name = window.prompt("Enter your name:");
document.write(
    "<h1>Welcome to " + name + "'s Home Page</h1>");
//-->
</SCRIPT>
```

The page asks the user for the user's name (see Figure 8-9) and then uses that name in the header for the page (see Figure 8-10).

Figure 8-9:
The prompt
dialog box.

Figure 8-10:
The new
Home page.

A page of a different color

Within your script, you can dynamically change the colors that are used for text, background, and links on a page. You can do all this by changing properties of the document object with code that looks like the following:

```
<HTML>
<HEAD>
<META NAME="GENERATOR"
Content="Microsoft Visual Studio 6.0">
<TITLE></TITLE>
</HEAD>
<SCRIPT LANGUAGE=javascript>
<!--
document.bgColor = "#FFDEAD"
document.fgColor = "#C71585"
document.linkColor = "#000000"
//-->
```

```
</SCRIPT>
<h1>This Is My Colorful Page</h1>
Hope you like it!<p>
If you do, click <a href=Page2.htm>here</a>.
<P> </P>

</BODY>
</HTML>
```

This code produces an unusually colored page. The shades of gray in Figure 8-11 don't really communicate the true weirdness of the colors, so you'll have to trust me on this one.

Figure 8-11:
An unusually colored page (Trust me!).

Here's a list of all the properties of the document object that enable you to set page colors:

- ✔ **bgColor:** Controls the color of the background. You won't notice a change if you have a picture as the background of your page.
- ✔ **fgColor:** Controls the color of the text and headings on the page.
- ✔ **linkColor:** Controls the color of unvisited links on the page.
- ✔ **alinkColor:** Controls the color of the active link on the page.
- ✔ **vlinkColor:** Controls the color of the visited links on the page.

Other document information

A few document properties give you information about various aspects of the document itself. Here's a list of the important ones:

- **title:** Contains the information within the title tags of the document
- **lastModified:** Provides the date the page was last changed
- **URL:** Has the URL of the current document

The History Object

The history object represents the list of all the places the browser has been. It enables you to access three common browser capabilities:

- **back:** Just like the Back button on your browser, this method takes you to the page you most recently visited (the one just before this one in your history list).
- **forward:** Like the Forward button on your browser, this method takes you to the next page in your history list.
- **go:** If you pass a positive or negative number, this method moves you that many places forward or backward in the history list.

Various Form and Element Objects

Traditionally, Web pages use forms to allow users to enter information. You create forms using the <FORM> tag. Within the <FORM> tag, a number of varieties of the <INPUT> tag end up producing edit boxes, option buttons, drop-down list boxes, and command buttons. After the user enters information into these fields, your client script accesses them using form objects and object within the forms to represent the controls where the user actually entered her information.

In Visual InterDev, you don't need to do any of this. You can handle all the user interaction in Visual InterDev using the much more convenient Scripting Object Model (SOM), which is covered in Chapter 9.

ActiveX Controls

ActiveX controls are small programs that are downloaded and automatically installed on the user's machine when she goes to a page that uses them. They are generally small, specialized controls such as a slider or tree view that enhance the user interface of your pages.

ActiveX controls are also objects. They are different from the other objects I mention earlier in this chapter. Unlike the document and the window that are always there in every page, you must add ActiveX controls to your page as you need them. But after they are on your page, you can access their properties and call their methods just like any other object.

ActiveX controls do *not* work in Netscape Navigator unless you have a plug-in that enables you to use them.

Adding an ActiveX control to a page

To add an ActiveX control to your page:

1. **Click the ActiveX Controls tab in the Toolbox (see Figure 8-12).**

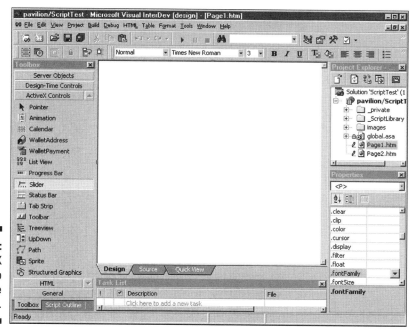

Figure 8-12:
The ActiveX Controls tab in the Toolbox.

2. **Drag the control you want from the Toolbox to the place where you want it to appear on the page and drop it.**

   A control appears where you dropped it (see Figure 8-13).

Notice that the ActiveX control appears much as it will look on the final page, even in the Source view of the script editor.

Changing an ActiveX control's properties

ActiveX controls don't always look and act like you want them to right out of the box. To enable you to customize them, they have properties that you can set when you are creating your page. These properties allow you to coax the control into working just right.

To change the properties of an ActiveX control:

1. **Right-click the ActiveX control in the script editor's Source or Design view.**

2. **Choose Properties from the pop-up menu.**

   The ActiveX control's Properties window appears (see Figure 8-14). This Properties window is different for each ActiveX control.

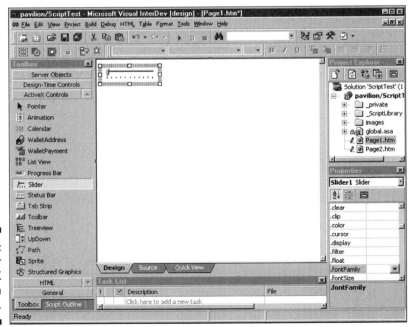

Figure 8-13: The Slider ActiveX control on a page.

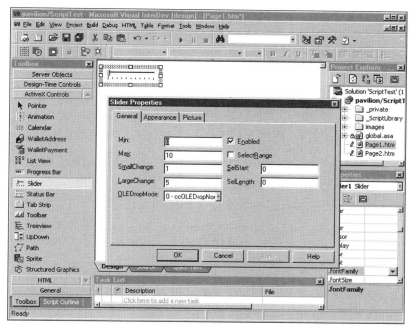

Figure 8-14:
The Slider
Properties
dialog box.

Some ActiveX controls don't have a custom properties dialog box, and you have to use the standard Properties window that's always in the lower-right corner of your window to change their properties.

Writing code for ActiveX control events

In addition to properties and methods, ActiveX controls have events. You can write code for these events using the Script Outline. For an introduction to the Script Outline window, see Chapter 7.

To write code for an ActiveX control event:

1. **Add the ActiveX control to your page (see the previous section, "Adding an ActiveX control to a page" for details). Name it appropriately.**

2. **Go to the script editor's Source view and click to view the Script Outline.**

3. **Click Client Objects & Events.**

4. **Find the ActiveX control in the list. Click it to open it.**

5. **Find the event you want to respond to. Double-click it.**

   Visual InterDev makes the necessary changes to your source code. It creates a new function that will be executed in response to the event you double-clicked. Your cursor appears inside the function.

6. **Write the code you want to execute when the event is triggered.**

Exploring an ActiveX control example

Here's a small example that should give you a feel of how you can use events and properties to get ActiveX controls to work together:

1. **Create a new project and a default.htm page.**

2. **Add text and drag the Slider and Progress Bar ActiveX controls to the page so that it looks like Figure 8-15 in the script editor's Design view.**

3. **Switch over to Source view and open the Client Objects & Events folder and the Slider1 object to reveal the Slider1 events (see Figure 8-16).**

4. **Double-click the Change event.**

   The code in Source view changes to look like Figure 8-17.

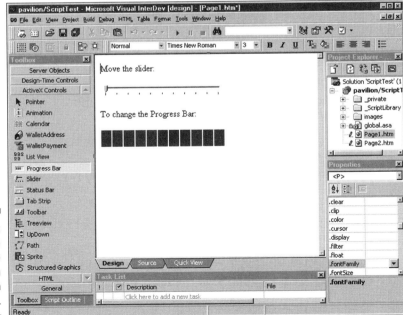

Figure 8-15:
The example page in Design view.

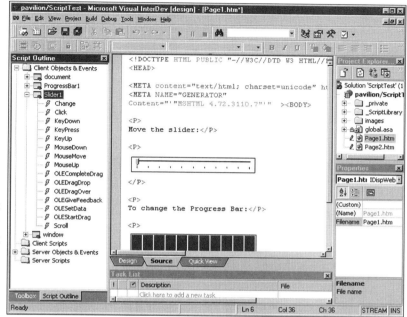

Figure 8-16:
The Script
Outline
showing the
Slider1
events.

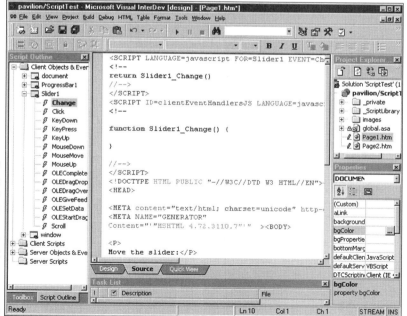

Figure 8-17:
The newly
created
Slider1
Change
event
function in
Source
view.

5. Enter this line:

```
ProgressBar1.Value = Slider1.Value * 10
```

6. Either run the page or click over to Quick View.

Your page works either way.

7. Move the slider bar halfway and release it. Then move it three-quarters of the way and release it.

The Progress Bar changes in response (see Figure 8-18).

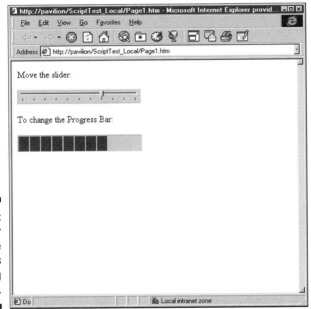

Figure 8-18:
The Slider and the Progress Bar working together.

How does it work? The `Change` event of the slider is triggered every time you change the slider bar and release it. Because the slider tracks its changes on a scale of 0 to 10 and the Progress Bar has a scale of 0 to 100, I simply multiply the current value of the slider bar by 10 and set the Progress Bar's value to the result. The Progress Bar is then immediately updated to keep up with the status bar every time it changes.

Chapter 9

Exploring Server Script Objects

· ·

· ·

*I*n Chapter 8, I discuss different kinds of objects and controls that you can access and manipulate from client script. In this chapter, I focus on server objects and server components that you can access and manipulate using server script in ASP pages.

Server objects offer a lot of power over your environment. You can pass arguments from one page to another, manipulate users' cookies and create variables that hold their value from one page to the next.

But if all that isn't enough for you, then server components are sure to meet your needs! You can create or buy server components to do almost anything you can imagine. In this chapter, I not only show you how to use them, I tell you all about a few really useful ones that you can get for free from Microsoft.

What Are Server Objects?

When you create ASP pages, you have access to a set of objects called the *server objects*. These objects provide access to the Web server itself and to a lot of other useful information.

In the following sections, I show you the highlights of the server object properties, methods, and even a couple of events. You can find details and additional, less common properties and methods in the Visual InterDev online Help system.

Using the Request and Response Objects

The Request and Response objects are the input and output objects for the Web server. You use Request to receive information passed from the Web browser in to the Web server (input), and the Response object sends information from the Web server out to the browser (output).

You can do a number of important things with this pair of objects. I talk about a few of the most important ones here: cookies, queryString, and the buffer.

Adding to a page with Response.Write

Write is a method of the Response object and it can be used to write HTML to the page at the current position.

In Chapter 6, I show you a page that looks, in part, like this:

```
<BODY>
<% If Time < #6:00 PM# Then %>
<h3>Good Day!</h3>
<% Else %>
<h3>Good Evening!</h3>
<% End If %>
</BODY>
```

You can rewrite this code using Response.Write to look like this:

```
<BODY>
<%
If Time < #6:00 PM# Then
    Response.Write "<h3>Good Day!</h3>"
Else
    Response.Write "<h3>Good Evening!</h3>"
End If
%>
</BODY>
```

As you can see, using Response.Write cleans up the code quite a bit. Instead of switching back and forth from script to HTML, the whole thing is transformed into script. Often, as in this example, you can write it either way, and it will work fine. But sometimes, when the HTML is long or complex, it may be easier just to close off the script and do the HTML separately.

Bakin' cookies

Cookies are small text files that are created by a Web site and saved on the client's machine. When the user returns later, the site can retrieve the text file and get whatever information was saved last time. Cookies can be used for a variety of things. They can be used to simply identify a person and keep track of the number of times he's visited, or it can hold the user's preferences that he specified when he first came to the site. This allows a site to customize itself based on what the user wants to see.

For example, the first time you visit a site that sells CDs, it may ask you to fill in a questionnaire describing your musical tastes. It can then save the information you entered in your cookie and, when you return, it can specifically show you music selections that you'd be most interested in.

The address of the site is saved with the cookie, so when a site retrieves a cookie, it can always be assured it's the same cookie that it saved for that person before, not one saved by another site.

You can make use of cookies through the Request and Response objects.

Creating and saving cookie information

Cookies are structured something like Windows INI files. Each person can have multiple cookies. Each cookie has a name. And within each cookie, a bunch of *key* names exist that are assigned values. You create those keys and give them values when you create the cookie, and then you access those keys to retrieve the values later when you want them.

To create a key and assign it a value, you use the Response object.

```
<% Response.cookie("Music")("Style") = "Alternative" %>
```

The first string inside parentheses is the name of the cookie you are creating or modifying. The second string inside parentheses is the name of the key that you want to give a value. Finally, the value after the equal sign is assigned to the key. You can have as many keys inside the cookie as you want.

```
<%
Response.cookie("Music")("FavoriteArtist") = _
    "Crash Test Dummies"
Response.cookie("Music")("FavoriteCD") = _
    "God Shuffled His Feet"
%>
```

You can also have as many different cookies for each visitor as you like.

```
<% Response.cookie("Books")("FavoriteAuthor") = _
   "Douglas Adams" %>
```

Retrieving cookie information

You can use the Request object to get information back out of cookies. And it works just like the Response object.

```
<% If Request.cookie("Music")("Style") = _
   "Alternative" Then %>
<h1>Today's Alternative Selection: Nirvana</h1>
<% ElseIf Request.cookie("Music")("Style") = "Rock" Then %>
...
```

Communicating with queryString

Sometimes, it's convenient to pass information from one page to the next. Using the URL is an easy way of doing this. For example, if you wanted to link to a page and pass the user's name, you could use code like this.

```
<a  href="greet.asp?Name=<%  =UserName  %>">
```

Assuming the variable UserName contained the value Fred, the HTML that's actually sent to the browser would look like this.

```
<a href="greet.asp?Name=Fred">
```

But when you are in the greet.asp page, how do you retrieve that information that was sent on the URL? You use Request.queryString.

```
<h1>Good To See You, <%=Request.queryString("Name")%></h1>
```

The HTML the server sends to the browser ends up looking like this.

```
<h1>Good To See You, Fred</h1>
```

You can pass as many arguments on the URL as you like. Just give them each different names and separate them with an &.

```
<a href="greet.asp?Name=Fred&Spouse=Mary>
```

Then you can reference each by its name.

```
<h1>Good To See You, <%=Request.queryString("Name")%> and
<%=Request.queryString("Spouse")%></h1>
```

Control buffering with the Response.buffer property

Normally, when the Web server processes your ASP page, the server sends it out *as it is processed.* That is, the first part of the page may already be sent off while the last part is being executed. This helps keep things going and gives the user more immediate feedback, even when the later part of your page is doing something that takes time.

Sometimes, though, you don't want to send the page out until it is completely processed. For example, if your page is manipulating cookies, you'll almost always need to include this line at the very top of your page:

```
<% Response.buffer = True %>
```

This causes the page to completely finish all its processing before any of it is sent out to the browser. This is necessary when you are working with cookies because cookies are stored in the HTTP headers that are at the very top of the page and are the first thing sent out.

Other things are stored in the HTTP headers, too, that can affect you. But instead of going through all the possible stuff that could go wrong, let me put it this way. If you ever get this error:

```
The HTTP headers are already written to the client browser.
Any HTTP header  modifications must be made before writing
page content.
```

if you add the line I mentioned previously that sets the buffer property to true to the top of your page, the error goes away.

Using forms (or not!)

You can create and respond to HTML forms using ASP. The `Request` object contains all the information you need to access the information the user entered, and after you have it in your server script, you can do whatever you like with it — save it to a database, store it in a file, or display it on another page.

But Visual InterDev has created a much better way of dealing with user input — it's a part of the Visual InterDev Scripting Object Model (SOM). I discuss SOM in Chapter 10.

Using the Application and Session Objects

The application object and the session object work in a similar way. The application object holds information about the ASP application itself. The session object holds information about each individual person who opens and uses your application.

An example could make this a little clearer. Imagine that you have a used car catalog application. Users can look through lists of used cars, calculate their down payment and monthly payments, and even place a hold on a car. Only one copy of this application exists on the server, but many people can access the application on the Web and use it.

The application object holds information about the application — the used car catalog. When the first person accesses the application, it is started. The application continues working and working as a variety of people access it. The application ends only after everyone leaves and no one is accessing it anymore.

The session is different. A session begins when an individual person accesses the application and continues until that *same* person leaves. A new session begins for every new person accessing the application. If two people access the application at once, there are two separate sessions — but still only one application.

Session variables

As you work with ASP, you find yourself often needing to share information between different pages in your application. The problem is that when you create a variable in this page, it exists only for this page, and then the variable's gone.

To create a variable that lasts across all pages, you need a session variable.

```
<% Session("UserName") = "Amber" %>
```

This line of code creates the variable UserName if it didn't exist before now and assigns the value Amber to it. If UserName had existed before now, this code would simply change its value.

After UserName is created, it can be accessed from any page in the application as long as this user continues using the application.

How does it know?

If you know something about HTML and how it works, you may know that the server doesn't actually keep track of users and who is accessing which page. It gets a request and sends out a page. It gets another request and sends out another page. It doesn't keep track of who it is sending to now or who it has sent pages to in the past.

So how can you refer to a session beginning and ending in VBScript? Well, as it turns out, Internet Information Server (IIS) *does* try to

keep track of who's who. It does this with cookies. If a browser with the same cookie makes a request, IIS assumes that it is the same person who made the request in the past. And if that person doesn't make a request for 20 minutes or so, IIS assumes the person left.

Of course, this only works if the user's browser supports cookies and if she has cookie support turned on. Fortunately, most users do.

In addition, remember that the session variable is associated with the user who is using the application. If two people are using this page at the same time, *two* UserName variables will exist, each with its own value — one for each session (see Figure 9-1).

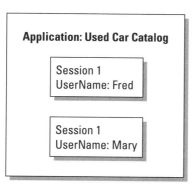

Figure 9-1:
Two sessions, each with its own copy of the session variable.

Application: Used Car Catalog

Session 1
UserName: Fred

Session 1
UserName: Mary

Application variables

Just as you can create session variables that last for the life of the *session,* you can create application variables that last for the life of the *application.*

```
<% Application("NumHits") = 0 %>
```

But remember: An application variable lasts for as long as the application is running. And when you create an application variable, only one exists for all the users on the system.

In fact, that's something you have to consider. Because it's global to all the users, an application variable could be accessed by two or more users at the same time. When this happens, the results are unpredictable. To keep this from happening two application methods exist — Lock and Unlock.

```
<%
Application.Lock
Application("NumHits") = 0
Application.Unlock
%>
```

Lock stops anyone else from accessing the application object until Unlock is executed. Never keep the application object locked for more than an instant while you change an application variable.

But be sure to always use it when you do change an application variable. Otherwise you could end up with weird things happening every now and then.

Because application variables have such a broad scope, you don't use them nearly as often as you use session variables. Whenever you simply want to share data among different pages in your application, session variables are the way to go. Application variables are good for holding truly global things like the number of hits a page gets or information that you want to share among multiple users of your application.

Application and session object events

Both the application and session objects have two events — a start event and an end event.

`Application_OnStart` happens when the application is first accessed. `Application_OnEnd` happens when the last person has left the application.

`Session_OnStart` happens every time a new user begins using the application. `Session_OnEnd` happens every time a user leaves.

But how do you write code that gets executed when these events happen? The answer is the global.asa file.

The global.asa file is created automatically when you create a project in Visual InterDev. It holds the code for the application and session events. Just create a subroutine with one of the names I listed previously in this section, and write the code in the subroutine you want executed when that event is triggered. Then save your new global.asa file.

The most commonly used of these events is probably `Session_OnStart`. It's a good place to set up session variables or anything else you think the user will need as he uses the application.

The Server object

Server provides access to information about the Web server itself. There's not a lot of really interesting stuff here, but you may find three methods useful:

- ✔ **CreateObject:** Allows you to create an ActiveX server component to use from within your scripts. This one is actually *very* useful, but I discuss it later in this chapter in the section titled "Server Components."

- ✔ **HTMLEncode:** Accepts a string and creates the HTML to display that string. For example, if you pass the string "<->" to HTMLEncode, it produces this string: "<->". This would be rendered on a Web page to look like the original string: "<->".

- ✔ **URLEncode:** When you pass arguments on the URL line, you find that some characters aren't legal in a URL. So they have to converted to legal characters so you can send them that way. For example, the ">" sign is translated to "%3E". You can use the URLEncode method to make these translations.

Server Components

Server objects and *server components,* despite their similar names, are two completely different things:

- ✔ **Server objects** refer to a very specific set of objects that are built into the IIS Web server and are always available to your scripts. These include the Response object, the Server object, and so on.

- ✔ **Server components** are the server-side equivalent to ActiveX controls. They are engines that your script can interact with to do various things. You can create and use any number of server components in your scripts.

First, I show you how to use a server component, and then I give you some examples of some of the cool components that are either already on your Web server or can be easily downloaded from the Microsoft Web site.

Instantia-What?

All server components must be *instantiated* before they can be used. That is, you must make an *instance* of the component before you can access its properties and methods. You can do this using one of two ways:

✔ The `Server.CreateObject` method

✔ The `<OBJECT>` tag

I cover both of these methods in the following sections.

Instantiating with Server.CreateObject

If you instantiate an object with the `CreateObject` method, you must receive the object sent back from this method into a variable, like so:

```
<%
Dim browser
Set browser = Server.CreateObject("MSWC.BrowserType")
%>
```

Notice that you must use the VBScript `Set` keyword, as you always do when you assign an *object* to a variable (rather than a value).

If you want to use this object in other pages, too, you can assign it to a session variable.

```
<%
Set Session("browser") = _
    Server.CreateObject("MSWC.BrowserType")
%>
```

Instantiating with the <OBJECT> tag

If you want to access the component on multiple pages, using the `<OBJECT>` tag is a good way to instantiate a server component. The `<OBJECT>` tag allows you to instantiate a server component for the life of the session or even the life of the entire application.

If you are going to use the `<OBJECT>` tag, the best place to put it is in the global.asa file. You can place it anywhere *outside* the `<SCRIPT>` tags.

CreateObject versus <OBJECT> tag — which is better?

So, if you can do the instantiation thing in two ways, which way is best? The answer is that it depends. (Doesn't it always?)

If you are going to use the server component throughout a session or the whole application, it is best to use the <OBJECT> tag in the global.asa file. This way is more efficient because IIS doesn't actually go out and create the object until it's used. If you don't end up needing it, the object is never created.

On the other hand, if you are using the component on only one page, then the CreateObject method is a great way to go.

In the following code, I instantiate the same object I instantiate in the last section with CreateObject.

```
<OBJECT RUNAT=Server SCOPE=Session ID=browser
PROGID="MSWC.BrowserType">
```

To change the scope, all you have to do is change the value of the SCOPE attribute to Application.

After the server component is instantiated in the global.asa file, you can use it in any of the pages throughout the application by simply referring to the name you gave the ID attribute (in this case, browser).

The Browser Capabilities Component: Peeking at Your User's Browser

The component I use as an example in the last two sections is the Browser Capabilities component. It's very cool.

The Browser Capabilities component allows you to check to see if the browser the user is using has specific capabilities so that you can change how you present your content to accommodate it. For example, you could check to see if the browser supports tables using the Tables property and then present the data using some alternate means, if the browser doesn't support it.

```
<%
Dim browser
Set browser = Server.CreateObject("MSWC.BrowserType")
If browser.Tables = True Then
%>
Table Version<p>
<% Else %>
Non-Table Version<p>
<% End If %>
```

You can use quite a number of other interesting properties to check for the existence of specific features. All these properties contain either True or False.

- Frames
- BackgroundSounds
- ActiveXControls
- JavaApplets
- VBScript
- JavaScript

In addition, the Browser property provides the browser name, and the `Version` property tells you exactly what version of the browser they are using.

If you are going to use this component throughout your site, it is an excellent one to instantiate in the global.asa file using the `<OBJECT>` tag. Use the Session scope, not Application, because every user's browser will be different.

The Content Rotator — Like an Air Freshener for Your Site!

The Content Rotator component has many uses. You give this component a list of HTML segments, and it automatically chooses one of those segments at random to display every time the user comes to your page. So, for example, you could display a quote of the day taken from a long list of quotes. Or, because each of the segments can contain any valid HTML, you could display different pictures or links each time the user comes to your page. You could even randomly choose different background music for your visitor to listen to each time she comes to your site.

The Content Rotator component is not actually included with IIS. It's included in the IIS Resource Kit. You can also freely download it at the Microsoft Web site: www.microsoft.com/iis.

Creating the Content Schedule file

How does the Content Rotator work? It is really pretty simple. First you create a special Content Schedule file. This is the file that contains the list of HTML segments. Here's an example:

```
%% #2 // This one is Irish
May the road <b>rise</b> <p>
to meet your feet.<p>
%% #1 // A public service announcement
Friends don't let friends<p>
drive drunk.<p>
%% #1
He who laughs last...<p>
I forget the rest.<p>
```

Each segment begins with %%. Then a # comes just before the *weight*. The weight is a number between 1 and 65535 that indicates how often this segment should appear, relative to the others. The higher the number, the more often it will appear. If you want to figure it up exactly, just add up all the numbers for all the segments in your file and then divide the specific number by the total number. For example, in this file, the total for the file is 4. The last two will each come up one-fourth of the time, and the top one will come up two-fourths, or half, the time.

After the weight, you can optionally add a comment that is preceded by a //.

The rest of the lines are the HTML segment, until you get to another %%.

Using the component

To put the Content Schedule file to use, you must first create the component.

```
<% Set Quote = Server.CreateObject("MSWC.ContentRotator") %>
```

Then you can use one of the components two methods:

- ✔ ChooseContent: Randomly pick one of the segments from the Content Schedule file, according to the weights, and display it.
- ✔ GetAllContent: Get all the content from the Content Schedule file and display it all at once.

You are more likely to use `ChooseContent` most often, of course.

```
<BODY>
<h1>Welcome To My Homepage</h1>
Now here's your quote for the day:<p>
<%
Dim Quote
Set Quote = Server.CreateObject("MSWC.ContentRotator")
Quote.ChooseContent("Content.txt")
%>
</BODY>
```

The Page Counter — It's Not Easy Counting Hits

The Page Counter component enables you to easily keep track of the number of hits each of your pages gets.

The Page Counter component is not actually included with IIS. It's included in the IIS Resource Kit. You can also freely download it at the Microsoft Web site: www.microsoft.com/iis.

To count the number of hits a page receives, create the Page Counter component and call the `PageHit` method.

```
<%
Dim counter
Set counter = Server.CreateObject("MSWC.PageCounter")
counter.PageHit
%>
```

The `Hits` method returns the number of hits this page has received.

```
Hits so far: <% =counter.Hits %>
```

Other Free Server Stuff

I picked three common server components to give you a feel for the scope and capabilities that server component can provide to your scripts. A number of others are included with your Web server or are available for easy download. Among them are:

- **Ad Rotator:** Works like the Content Rotator but is optimized for rotating advertising banners on your site.

- **File Access:** Is actually comprised of a number of objects that give you full access to the server's hard drive folders and files.

- **Collaboration Data Objects:** Is a set of objects that enable you to send e-mail or interact in other ways with Microsoft Exchange Server.

- **Permission Checker:** Allows you to exercise the IIS password authentication to verify appropriate access to files.

But in addition to those that came with your Web server, you can get many more available from a variety of sources:

- Freeware and shareware components are available for free download on the Internet. You can also find demos of commercial server components so you can try before you buy.

- Commercial components are available to purchase on the Web or through catalogs.

- You can even create your own server components using Microsoft Visual C++ or Microsoft Visual Basic.

Chapter 10

Using the Scripting Object Model

*T*he Scripting Object Model (SOM) is a technology that is unique to Visual InterDev. It provides an easy way to add controls like text boxes, check boxes, and list boxes to a page and allow users to enter data. After controls are added to the page, you can respond to events that happen to the controls. You can also change the control's properties and call the control's methods.

SOM completely replaces the HTML forms and makes the whole process of user interaction much smoother and easier to understand.

Enabling the Scripting Object Model

Before you can use SOM on a page, you must enable SOM.

To enable SOM for your page:

1. **First, be sure you are using an ASP page.**

   Although you can use SOM on the client-side in HTML pages, you must then require everyone who views your pages to use Internet Explorer 4.0 or above. Because of this sever restriction on client SOM, I focus my attention on server SOM, which can be accessed with any browser.

2. **Right-click anywhere on the page away from any controls.**

3. **Choose Properties from the pop-up menu.**

   Be sure you are looking at the General tab (see Figure 10-1).

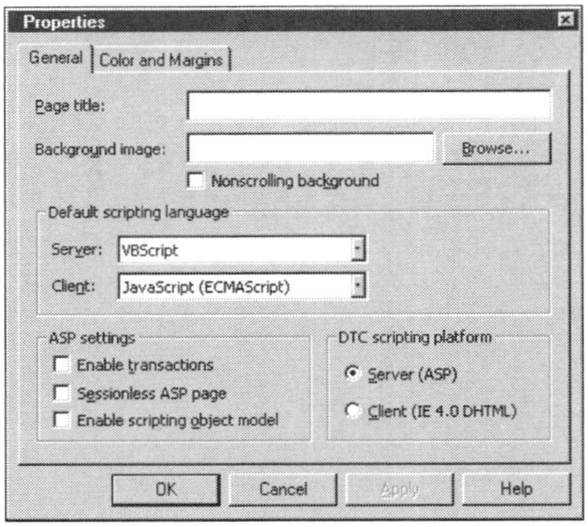

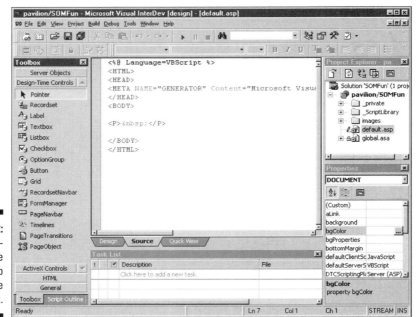

Figure 10-1:
The general
tab of the
page
Properties
dialog box.

4. **Under ASP settings, click the Enable Scripting Object Model check box.**

Design-Time Controls (DTCs)

After you have SOM enabled for your page, you are ready to start building a page with Design-Time Controls (DTCs). You can find them, oddly enough, in the Design-Time Control tab of the Toolbox (see Figure 10-2).

Figure 10-2:
The Design-
Time
Control tab
of the
Toolbox.

DTCs — What the heck are they?

What exactly is a Design-Time Control? Is it an ActiveX control? Is it just a fancy way of adding forms to a page?

Actually, DTCs are *server components* (for more information on server components, see Chapter 9). That is, they are ActiveX engines that run on the server and provide a service to server scripts. When your page is retrieved, a server component actually generates script and HTML to produce the appropriate HTML

forms control and sets it up to correspond to all the properties you've set for it.

Because they are simple HTML form controls when they appear in the browser, you can use DTCs with any browser that supports forms. And yet, because a DTC is a server component, you can use its properties and methods and respond to its events just as you could if you were programming in an environment like Visual Basic or Access.

These controls can be divided into three categories:

✓ **Standard controls:** Label, Listbox, Checkbox, OptionGroup, and Button

✓ **Database-specific controls:** Recordset, Grid, RecordsetNavbar, and FormManager

✓ **Other controls:** PageNavbar, Timelines, PageTransitions, and the PageObject

In this chapter, I focus on the Standard controls. I show you all the wonders the Database controls can perform in Chapter 13. I discuss the PageNavbar in Chapter 5, and I discuss the PageObject later in this chapter (in the section "Welcome to thisPage") and in Chapter 11. The others are thoroughly covered in the online Help.

Adding a DTC to a Page

DTCs work just like all the other components in the Toolbox.

To add a DTC to a page:

1. **Locate the DTC you want.**

2. **Put the editor into Design view or Source view.**

   Design view offers a better look at how the DTC will appear on the final page.

3. **Drag it to the page at the location where you want it to appear.**

4. **Drop it on the page.**

   If you forgot to enable SOM for this page and you are dropping your first DTC on the page, you'll see the error message in Figure 10-3. Clicking Yes on this dialog box enables SOM for you automatically.

   The DTC appears on the page.

Figure 10-3:
The error
you see
when you
add a DTC
before
enabling
SOM.

Resizing, Moving, and Changing a DTC's Properties

When you place a DTC on a page, it appears at a default size.

To change the size of a DTC:

1. **Click to select the DTC.**

   Small square resizing handles appear (see Figure 10-4).

2. **Move to one of the handles and drag it in or out to decrease or increase the size of the control.**

If you accidentally drop a DTC in the wrong place, you can easily move it.

To move a DTC:

1. **Click to select the DTC.**

2. **Move your mouse pointer over the gray outline that surrounds the DTC.**

   The mouse pointer turns into a four-way arrow.

3. **Drag the DTC to its new location and drop it.**

   The DTC moves to the new location.

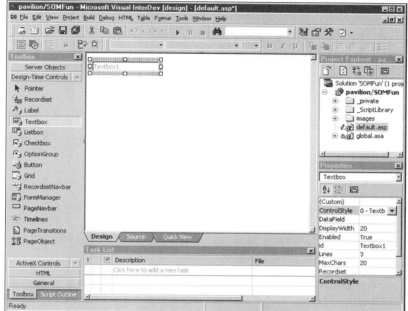

Each DTC has its own set of properties that defines how it looks and acts.

To change a DTC's properties:

1. **Right-click the DTC.**

2. **Choose Properties from the pop-up menu.**

   The Properties dialog box appears (see Figure 10-5).

Each DTC has a different set of properties and a different Properties dialog box. Some may not even have a custom Properties dialog box, and you have to change its properties using the Properties window.

Coding for DTC Events

With the basic DTC controls provided, you should be able to create virtually any type of user interface you want. But once you have the information, then what?

The answer is in coding events. With SOM and DTCs, you don't have to worry about creating a submit button and sending the information to the server and then handling them on the server and sending back a response. Visual InterDev handles all that passing of data back and forth for you automatically. That way you can write code as if everything were happening on the server.

So, if you want to do something when the user clicks a button, all you have to do is write server script for the button's Click event.

To write code for an event, you use the Script Outline window while the editor is in Source view. For an introduction to the Script Outline window, see Chapter 7.

To write code for a DTC event:

1. **Switch to Source view in the editor and click the tab below the Toolbox to display the Script Outline.**

   If you don't see any tabs below the Toolbox, then the Script Outline window isn't open. Choose View⇨Other Windows⇨Script Outline from the menu bar to open it, or simply press Ctrl+Alt+S.

2. **Open the Server Objects & Events folder.**

   All the server objects and the DTCs you've added to the page appear (see Figure 10-6).

   You see a plus sign beside some of the DTCs, which means that you can open them to display all the events that they support.

3. **Open the DTC you want to write an event for.**

   All the events that the DTC supports appear (see Figure 10-7).

4. **Double-click the event you want to write code for.**

Figure 10-6:
The server objects and DTCs on the page.

Figure 10-7:
The event(s) that the DTC supports.

Visual InterDev automatically generates the code in the editor (see Figure 10-8).

Your cursor appears inside the subroutine that will be executed when the event happens.

5. Write the code you want to execute.

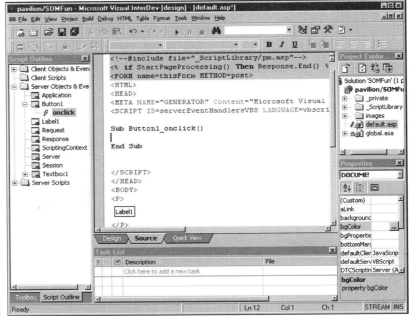

Figure 10-8:
The editor
generates
code for
you.

When you write event code for DTCs, you are usually writing *server-side* code. You can use the server objects and server components that exist on the Web server, and you can refer to any of the DTCs on the page by name to access their properties or methods.

When referring to properties and methods of a DTC in your scripts, be sure you enter their names exactly as they appear in the documentation or online Help, including correct upper- and lowercase. Although VBScript isn't usually case sensitive, it often *is* when referring to SOM objects, properties, and methods because SOM is written largely in JavaScript, which is case sensitive.

Welcome to thisPage

The Scripting Object Model offers another object to simplify your script: thisPage. As you may guess, thisPage refers to the Web page where your script is being executed. The thisPage object is a very handy object and has properties, methods, and events.

You can use the `thisPage` object directly without creating it or placing it on the page, but not all of its properties, methods, and events are easily accessible. To make them more accessible, a DTC can help: PageObject.

PageObject appears in the Design-Time Control Toolbar, and you add it to your page just as you would any other DTC. But the PageObject is different from other DTCs in that you won't see it on the final page. It shows up in Design mode, but not when you run the page.

Even though you don't end up seeing the PageObject itself when you look at the page, using it makes your script coding simpler by offering easy access to `thisPage`'s properties, methods, and events. It is a good idea to get in the habit of adding the PageObject to each of your ASP pages where you do any significant scripting.

Because the PageObject DTC doesn't show up when you view the page in a browser, you can put it anywhere on the page you like. Some people prefer to put it at the top of the page and some like it at the bottom. Either option is better than mixing it in with the rest of your page's content because that could get confusing

An Example: A Number Guess Game

In order to demonstrate the use of `thisPage` and the other DTCs, I'm going to walk you through the process of creating a simple Web page game.

In the Number Guess game, the computer picks a number between 1 and 100. Then you have to guess what the number is. If you guess wrong, the computer says Higher or Lower to guide you until you finally get it right.

To place the controls for the game on the page:

1. **Create a new project and a default.asp page for that project.**

   Be sure you are creating an ASP page!

2. **Type this text at the top of the page:**

   ```
   Number Guess
   I'm thinking of a number between 1 and 100. See if you
   can guess what it is.
   ```

3. **Select Number Guess and make it a Header 1.**

4. **Add a label, a text box, a button, and a PageObject on the page, one after the other, each on its own separate line (see Figure 10-9).**

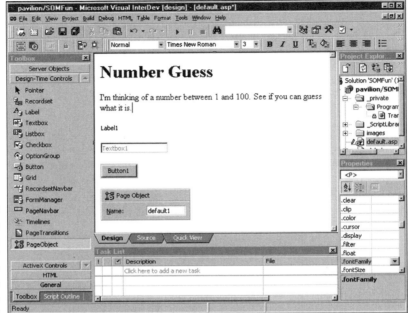

Figure 10-9:
Design
view, after
all the
controls are
added.

5. **Set the properties for the label. Name:** `lblResponse`. **Field:** `Enter Your Guess:`.

6. **Set the properties for the text box. Name:** `txtGuess`. **Display Width:** `15`.

7. **Set the properties for the button. Name:** `btnGuess`. **Caption:** `Guess!`.

After all the controls are on the page and their properties are set, your editor should look like Figure 10-10.

The user interface for this game is complete. Now all you have to do is write the code to make it work!

To write the code for the game:

1. **Click the tab at the bottom of the editor window to switch to Source view.**

   The page looks like Figure 10-11.

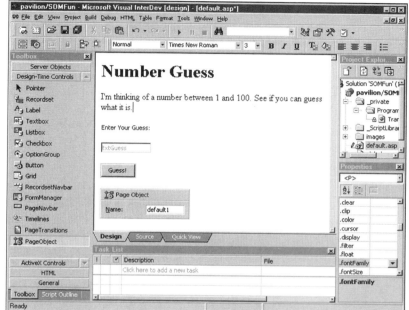

Figure 10-10: Design view, after the properties are set.

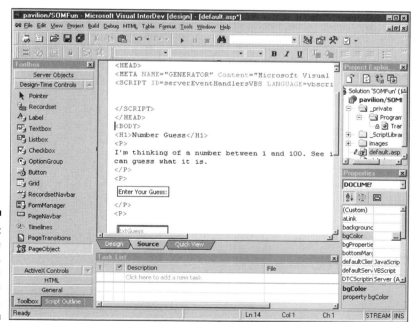

Figure 10-11: Source view, before the code is added.

Why lblResponse and btnGuess?

Why did I ask you to name your controls with three funny little letters on the beginning? In Visual Basic, people commonly name controls this way, and it's a good idea to do it here, too. The letters at the beginning are a prefix to make it clear what *kind* of DTC you are naming. Here are some suggested prefixes.

DTC	Prefix
Recordset	rs
Label	lbl
Check box	cbx
OptionGroup	opt
Button	btn
Grid	grd
RecordsetNavbar	rsn
FormManager	fmg
PageNavbar	pgn
Timelines	tln
PageTransitions	pgt

Note that PageObjects don't actually have a name. They provide a name for the page, but that name should *not* have a prefix.

It doesn't really matter exactly what prefix you use, as long as you are consistent.

2. **Click the tab below the Toolbox window to display the Script Outline.**

3. **Open the Server Objects & Events folder.**

   You see all the server objects and the DTCs you added to the page listed in alphabetical order (see Figure 10-12).

Figure 10-12:
The Script Outline's Server Objects.

4. **Click the plus sign beside** thisPage.

   Three events appear under thisPage — onenter, onexit, and onshow.

5. **Double-click** onenter.

   The page in Source view changes to look like Figure 10-13.

6. **Enter this code for the** thisPage_onenter **subroutine:**

```
session("TheNumber") = int(rnd * 100) + 1
```

7. **Now open the** btnGuess **object in the Script Outline.**

   You see only one event: onclick.

8. **Double-click it (see Figure 10-14).**

9. **Enter this code for the** btnGuess_onclick **subroutine:**

```
If CInt(txtGuess.value) > session("TheNumber") Then
    lblResponse.setCaption("Lower! Guess again...")
ElseIf CInt(txtGuess.value) < session("TheNumber") Then
    lblResponse.setCaption("Higher! Guess again...")
Else
    lblResponse.setCaption("Right! You win!")
End If
```

That's all there is to it!

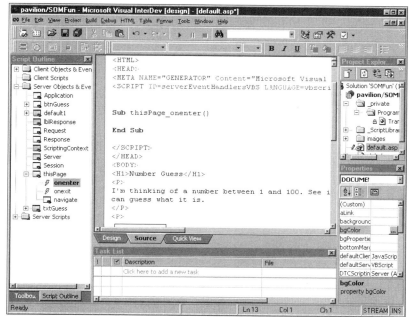

Figure 10-13:
After the
thisPage_
onenter
event
subroutine
is added.

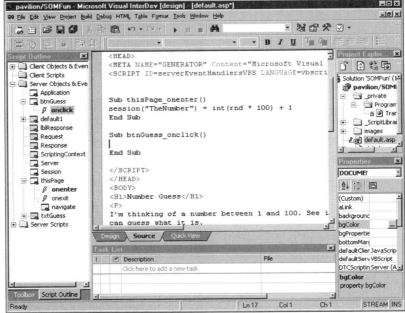

Figure 10-14:
After the
`btnGuess_`
`onclick`
event
subroutine
is added.

How Does It Work?

When the page is first opened, a new session variable called TheNumber is created and assigned a random number.

If you haven't worked with basic much in the past, the little formula there may be a bit bewildering. The `rnd` function returns a random floating point number between 0 and 1. By multiplying that number by 100 and converting it to an integer, you get a random number between 0 and 99. The +1 makes the number fall in the range 1 to 100.

Now that the number is established, the user interface is presented to the user, who enters a number and clicks the Guess! button. When he does, the value of txtGuess is converted to an integer and compared with TheNumber. Based on the result, lblResponse's Caption set to let the user know how he did. The Label DTC doesn't have a value property. To set its caption, you always have to use the setCaption method.

After the user is informed, he can guess again by typing a new number and clicking the Guess! button again.

Try It!

When you execute the page, it looks like Figure 10-15.

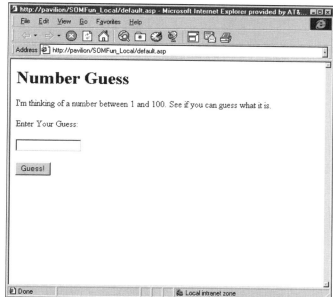

Figure 10-15:
Running the
Number
Guess
page.

Type in a number and click Guess! Try again. Keep going until you find the number the computer is thinking about. Pretty simple!

Things to Notice about DTCs

As you execute this page and work with it, you may notice several important things about the way DTCs work.

First, every time script needs to be executed, the page goes to the server to do it. This causes the page to flash and can sometime even take time, depending on the server's load and the Internet/intranet traffic.

However, you may also notice that when the page goes to the server to execute code and then comes back, the *state* of the page remains the same. By that, I mean that if you entered information into a text box, that same information is still there when the page comes back. Everything is just as it was, except the code was executed on the server. All the details of shuttling information back and forth between the client and the server and keeping track of what the page looks like is all handled for you automatically by SOM.

This provides a solid platform that works seamlessly between the client and the server. It provides the best of both worlds — broad reach and easy, object-oriented development.

Chapter 11

Scripting Tips and Tricks

. . . .

In This Chapter

▶ Strategies for sharing common code

▶ Trapping events

▶ Navigating the online Help

▶ Using pages as objects

. . . .

*V*isual InterDev provides a whole lot of options for you when you create Web applications — so many options that it's often difficult to wade through them all and find out which one works best.

I don't claim to have all the answers, but I do have some tips and tricks that may help you along the way. In this chapter, I don't stick to one topic as I try to do in other chapters. Instead you find a variety of ideas on a broad range of topics related to scripting, ASP, SOM, DTCs, and other topics.

Sharing Common Code

One common question new Visual InterDev developers have is how to share commonly used subroutines and functions that are used in more than one page.

You should know about a couple of sharing techniques:

✔ Toolbox code fragments
✔ #include

Toolbox code fragments

You can actually use the Toolbox itself as a place to park common code fragments or bits of HTML that you need to use again and again. This is a very handy extension of the traditional cut and paste commands.

Adding a fragment to the Toolbox

To add a fragment of code or HTML to the Toolbox:

1. **Click the Toolbox tab to make sure the Toolbox is showing.**

2. **Within the Toolbox, click the tab where you want to add your fragment.**

   You can add your code fragment to any tab you like. The General tab is a good choice because it's mostly blank. Or you can create your own tab, which I show you how to do later in this section.

3. **Select the code or HTML in the Source view of the editor that you want to save.**

4. **Drag the selection to an empty spot on the Toolbox and drop it.**

   The fragment appears on the Toolbox (see Figure 11-1).

Renaming the fragment

Of course, unless you want a bunch of fragments with the name HTML Fragment, you'll want to rename the fragments to something useful.

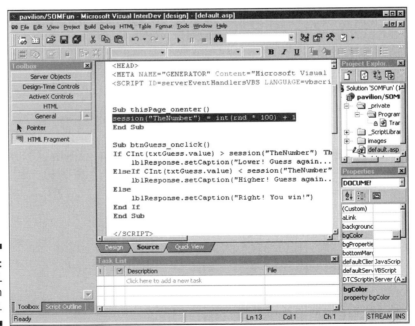

Figure 11-1:
The HTML fragment in the Toolbox.

To rename a fragment:

1. **Right-click the fragment and choose Rename Item from the pop-up menu.**

   The text appears selected in the Toolbox (see Figure 11-2).

Figure 11-2:
Renaming
an HTML
fragment.

2. **Type a new name.**

   Feel free to use spaces and punctuation marks in the name. But keep it to around 20 characters. Otherwise, you won't be able to read it all unless it's selected.

3. **Press Enter.**

Creating your own Toolbox tab

If you begin using fragments a lot, one tab may not be enough. You may find it easier to create several tabs for several different categories of fragments.

To create a tab:

1. **Right-click any open area in the Toolbox (not on a Toolbox item) and choose Add Tab from the pop-up menu.**

   A white box appears as the lowest tab in the Toolbox (see Figure 11-3).

2. **Type the name you want to give this tab and press Enter.**

3. **Click the tab to bring it up (see Figure 11-4).**

   You can begin saving new fragments to it.

Figure 11-3:
A new
Toolbox tab
is created.

Figure 11-4:
Using the
new
Toolbox tab.

Moving fragments from one tab to another

If you need to reorganize your fragments, Visual InterDev makes it easy to move fragments from one Toolbox tab to another.

To move a fragment from one Toolbox tab to another:

1. **Click the tab where the fragment is now.**

2. **Drag the fragment to the tab name either above or below this tab.**

3. **Drop the fragment on the tab name.**

   The fragment disappears from this tab.

4. **Click the new tab.**

   The fragment is listed there.

Using the fragment

After you save and organize your fragments, you are ready to put them to use. They work like any other object in the Toolbox.

To use a fragment:

1. **In the editor's Source view, scroll to the place where you want to add the fragment in the code.**

2. **Click the tab in the Toolbox where the fragment is located.**

3. **Drag the fragment from the Toolbox to the place where you want the fragment to appear.**

4. **Drop the fragment.**

   The fragment appears in the editor.

This process does not remove the fragment from the Toolbox tab. So you can keep your commonly used fragments there and drop them into your code whenever you need them.

A warning about fragments

Placing fragments in the Toolbox is a very handy way of dealing with portions of code or HTML that you use again and again within a page or across many pages.

There's only one problem with fragments. The process of creating a fragment and then dropping it into your code is exactly the same as a copy and paste operation. Imagine that you create a fragment and then paste it into your pages in a dozen different places. Then you decide that the code in the fragment isn't quite right, and you want to change it. In order to make the change, you are going to have to revisit all the different places where you've dropped in the fragment and change each one individually.

Does this mean that you shouldn't use fragments? No. Fragments are a very handy extension of the old cut and paste for saving small portions of HTML or code. But keep them small! After you start creating fragments that are 10 or 20 lines long, then you run a much greater risk of finding something that needs to be changed later.

If you have a large portion of HTML or code that you want to use in a number of different pages, then #include is a much better way to go.

#include

The #include command can be used to include the contents of a file as a part of the contents of the current page.

For example, if your site has a standard header that provides the name of the site and links to key pages on the site, you could save the header to its own file called header.inc and use #include to make it a part of each of your other pages.

```
<%@ Language=VBScript %>
<HTML>
<HEAD>
<META NAME="GENERATOR"
Content="Microsoft Visual Studio 6.0">
</HEAD>
<BODY>
<!-- #include file="header.inc" -->
...
</BODY>
</HTML>
```

The contents of the file physically replace the #include line when the page is processed by the Web server. The file can include *anything* that you could have entered there in the page by hand.

It's a great idea to use #include for common headers, navigation bars, logos, or any other features that appear on a lot of pages.

But it is *also* a good way to include common script subroutines and functions. If you have a library of script functions that you use all the time, you can keep the entire library in a file and then include it in any page where you are scripting. Or you can divide your library up into different files and only include the ones you need.

The #include command has several benefits. It saves you having to enter the HTML/code again and again and it is even easier than cutting and pasting. But the biggest benefit is that if the HTML or code ever needs to change, you can go to the file and change it once. From that point on, all the pages will begin including the corrected file.

Trapping Events: onBeforeServerEvent

Sometimes when you are writing scripts and using DTCs, it's handy to catch execution on the client right before it goes to the server to run some script.

The most common example is when you ask the user to fill in some information, and you want to make sure it is all filled in and looks good before you send it off to the server.

Fortunately, SOM has provided an event to make this possible: thisPage's onBeforeServerEvent.

To write script that runs before execution returns to the server:

1. **Add a PageObject DTC to your page if you haven't already.**
2. **Click over to the Source view of the editor.**
3. **In the Script Outline, open the Client Objects & Events.**
4. **Open** thisPage.
5. **Double-click the event** onbeforeserverevent.

    Code is added to the page to execute the event. Your cursor appears in the thisPage_onbeforeserverevent function (see Figure 11-5).

6. **Write the code you want to execute.**

Remember that this event is executed every time execution returns to the server for any reason. You probably don't want to execute the code you put in this event every time. Because of this, two arguments are passed to the onBeforeServerEvent: object and event. These let you know exactly what object and what event were just triggered.

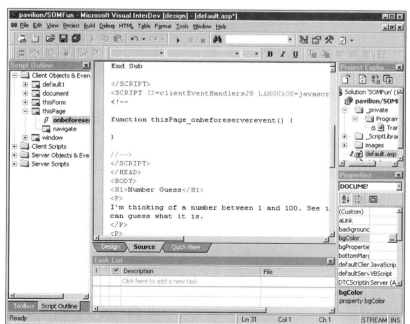

Figure 11-5:
The onbefore serverevent is added.

So usually, the first thing you'll want to do inside the `onBeforeServerEvent` is check to see which object and event were triggered. Then you can write different code to respond to different events.

```
<SCRIPT ID=clientEventHandlersJS LANGUAGE=javascript>
<!--
function thisPage_onbeforeserverevent(obj, event) {
if(obj=="btnOK" && event=="onclick") {
   if(thisForm.txtName.value == "") {
      alert("You must fill in the Name text box");
      thisPage.cancelEvent = true;
   }
}
}
//-->
</SCRIPT>
```

After verifying that the right object and event have been triggered, I check to see if the txtName DTC textbox contains any text.

Notice that when you refer to a DTC in this event you *must* prefix it with `thisForm`. If you don't, the name won't be recognized.

If the name isn't filled in, an alert dialog box is displayed (see Figure 11-6).

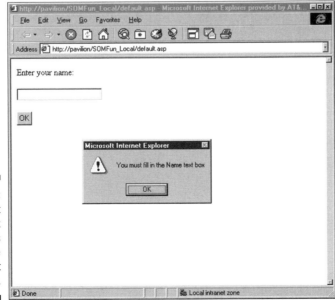

Figure 11-6:
An alert dialog box appears when the textbox isn't filled in.

Finally, the `cancelEvent` property of `thisPage` is set to true. You might already be guessing what this does. It stops the execution from going back to the server.

The code above will *only* be triggered if there is server-side script written for the btnOK button's Click event. If you haven't written server script for that event, then the page won't return to the server when the user clicks the button, and the `onBeforeServerEvent` won't get executed.

It's a good idea to use the `onBeforeServerEvent` liberally any time you have DTCs on a page to collect information from the user. By checking to make sure necessary fields are filled in and that they are filled in with the right number and type of characters, you can save unnecessary trips to the server. This reduces the load on the server *and* increases your application's performance.

Navigating to Another Page

Suppose you want to tell the browser to navigate to another page from your script. How do you do it?

The preferred way to do it is by using one of a couple of methods of the `thisPage` object.

```
thisPage.NavigateURL "http://www.microsoft.com"
```

This takes you to whatever URL is passed as an argument to the `NavigateURL` method.

This method can be called from either client or server script.

Finding Your Way Through the Online Help

Sometimes the online Help isn't even worth your time trying to navigate. It is either really poorly organized, astonishingly shy on content, or provides help on only the most obvious parts of the program.

Not so with Microsoft's Visual InterDev Help. With Version 6 of Visual InterDev, Microsoft has integrated *all* the Visual Studio tools' Help into the Microsoft Developer Network (MSDN) Library. It is well organized and absolutely packed with useful information. The only downside is finding your way through the sheer quantity of it!

Narrowing your options

Because this Help system supports all the Visual Studio development products, you can find a lot of information there that doesn't directly apply to you in Visual InterDev. However, a number of technologies are shared among the different development environments, including Visual InterDev.

To narrow down your choices a bit, you can ask the Help system to show you only the stuff that applies to Visual InterDev.

To show only the Help files that apply to Visual InterDev:

1. **Choose Help⇨Contents from the Visual InterDev menu bar.**

   The MSDN Library Visual Studio 6.0 release appears (see Figure 11-7).

   On the left, you see a number of tabs that include selections for Contents, Index, Search, and Favorites. Directly above these tabs is a drop-down list box labeled Active Subset.

2. **Click to drop down the Active Subset list.**

3. **Find and select the entry labeled Visual InterDev Documentation.**

   Now the Contents will show only the topics that are related to Visual InterDev. In addition, the Index grays out any items that are not a part of the Visual InterDev sphere.

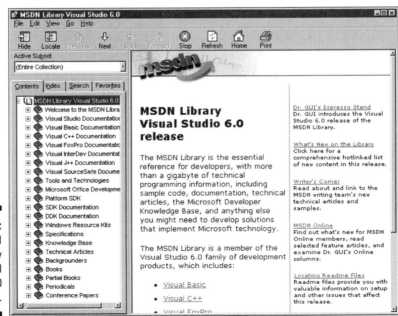

Figure 11-7:
MSDN
Library
Visual
Studio 6.0
release.

There may be times when you are searching in the index for a particular topic that you'll find that the item you want is there, it is just grayed out. If that happens, just go through the previous set of steps and switch the Active Subset to (Entire Collection) and then choose the item you want. Although all the core documentation is included as a part of the Visual InterDev Documentation, you can certainly find topics you may need to know about that fall outside that arena.

Finding what you need

To help you wade through all the stuff in the online Help, the following list shows some of the key topics you may be interested in finding more information about and where to find the information in the MSDN Library's sometimes-confusing tree:

✔ **Tutorial and reference for JavaScript and VBScript:**

MSDN Library Visual Studio 6.0➪Platform SDK➪Internet/Intranet/Extranet Services➪Scripting

✔ **Introductory Active Server Pages topics:**

MSDN Library Visual Studio 6.0➪Tools and Technologies➪Active Server Pages

✔ **More advanced ASP topics:**

MSDN Library Visual Studio 6.0➪Platform SDK➪Internet/Intranet/Extranet Services➪Active Server Pages

✔ **An HTML Reference:**

MSDN Library Visual Studio 6.0➪Platform SDK➪Internet/Intranet/Extranet Services➪Dynamic HTML➪DHTML References➪HTML References

✔ **Dynamic HTML:**

MSDN Library Visual Studio 6.0➪Platform SDK➪Internet/Intranet/Extranet Services➪Dynamic HTML

✔ **Server Components:**

MSDN Library Visual Studio 6.0➪Platform SDK➪Internet/Intranet/Extranet Services➪Active Server Pages➪Installable Components for ASP

Avoiding outdated development approaches

Visual InterDev 6 provides a number of new, easier ways of doing things that were not possible before Visual InterDev 6. Some of these older approaches are still in the online Help because they still work and many people may have older applications that use those techniques. The techniques just aren't the *preferred* way anymore.

If you aren't aware that those sections refer to outdated techniques, they can be very confusing and seem contradictory to this book and other sections of the online Help.

Here's a list of some of those sections to watch out for. This is not an exhaustive list, but it should give you an idea of the kinds of things to be aware of.

> MSDN Library Visual Studio 6.0⇨Platform SDK⇨Database and Messaging Services⇨Microsoft Data Access SDK⇨Microsoft ActiveX Data Objects

This documentation describes ActiveX Data Objects (ADO). ADO is the underlying structure that supports the SOM data-bound DTCs and Recordset DTCs in Visual InterDev (these topics are discussed in Chapter 13). All the ADO objects and methods still exist and can still be used, but many of the procedures described are no longer necessary because of SOM.

> MSDN Library Visual Studio 6.0⇨Platform SDK⇨Internet/Intranet/ Extranet Services⇨Active Server Pages⇨Built-in ASP Objects Reference⇨Request Object⇨Request Collections⇨Form

Although this method of accessing data sent to the server from HTML forms still works, it is unnecessary if you use SOM. This and other references to handling HTML forms are no longer the best way to write applications in Visual InterDev.

> MSDN Library Visual Studio 6.0⇨Platform SDK⇨Internet/Intranet/ Extranet Services⇨Active Server Pages⇨Built-in ASP Objects Reference⇨Response Object⇨Response Methods⇨Redirect

The Response.Redirect method works in server-side script to cause the browser to load a new page. However, the preferred method, when using SOM, is to use `thisPage.navigateURL` in both client *and* server scripts. For more information on `navigateURL`, see "Navigating to Another Page," earlier in this chapter.

MSDN Library Visual Studio 6.0⇨Platform SDK⇨Internet/Intranet/
Extranet Services⇨Active Server Pages⇨Installable Components for
ASP⇨Content Linking Component

The Content Linking component works just as it always has to help auto-
mate the process of creating links for your site. However, the Visual InterDev
site diagram and PageNavbar component provide a much higher level of
control and flexibility than this simple linking component. Because of this,
the site diagram/PageNavbar solution is definitely preferred.

Copying and pasting examples

When you look at examples in the online Help, you can easily just copy the
example code and paste it right into your own page and then make changes
to it there for your own needs.

If you've tried to do this in Visual InterDev, you may have noticed a particularly annoying problem. Figure 11-8 shows what the code looks like in the online Help, and Figure 11-9 shows what it looks like after it is pasted into a page.

Notice that the quotes have been replaced by `&quot;` and the greater than
sign is replaced by `&gt;`, among other changes. If you have to go through
and fix all these problems by hand, you're better off just typing the code in
by hand to begin with!

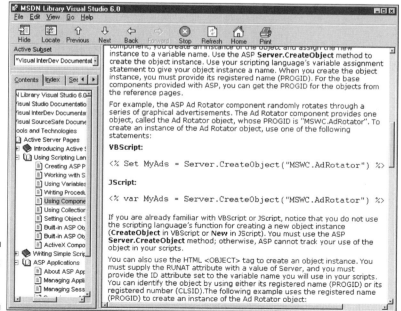

Figure 11-8:
The code in
online Help.

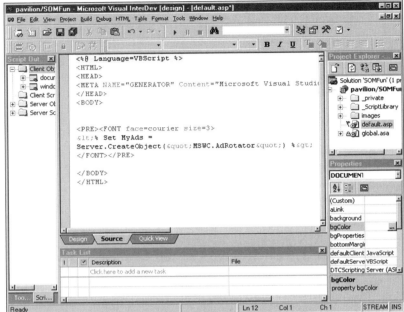

Figure 11-9:
The code
pasted into
the editor.

Fortunately there's an answer — Paste as HTML. Instead of using Edit⇨ Paste, use Edit⇨Paste as HTML from the menu bar. Or right-click in the Source view and choose Paste as HTML from the pop-up menu. This command pastes the code in just as you expect it (see Figure 11-10).

Pages as Objects

In Chapter 10, I introduce the `thisPage` object and the PageObject DTC. The `thisPage` object represents the current page in the browser as if it were an object and exposes certain properties, methods, and events.

But these properties, methods, and events are not easily accessible unless you add a PageObject DTC to your page. After it's on your page, the `thisPage` object appears in your Script Outline, and you can work with it as you do any other object on the page.

Giving the page a name

However, you can also refer to a page from another page using the PageObject. When you place a PageObject DTC on a page, notice that it gives the page a name (see Figure 11-11).

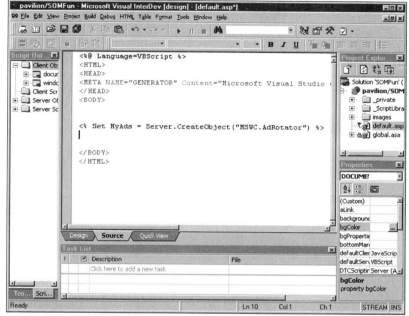

Figure 11-10:
The code in
the editor
when you
use Paste
as HTML.

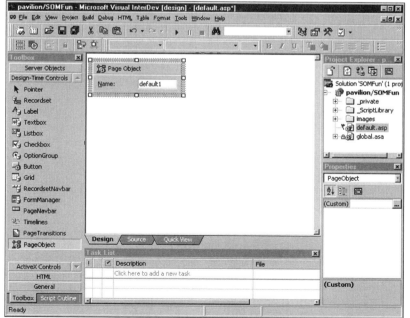

Figure 11-11:
The
PageObject
DTC gives
the page a
name.

You can change that name by clicking inside the PageObject and typing a new name there. This is the name that this page's object will have when *other* pages refer to it.

It's a good idea to name your page something similar to its filename or the title you've given it.

Exposing page methods

If a page is an object, then it should be able to have methods. In Visual InterDev, you can identify certain subroutines and functions as methods of the page and then call those methods from another page. Not all the functions and subroutines you create in the script on a page are automatically considered methods of the page object. Only those that you *expose* or make available can be called as methods of this page.

To expose a function or subroutine as a method of this page:

1. **Write the function or subroutine using server-side script.**

2. **Add a PageObject DTC to the page if it doesn't have one already.**

3. **Give this page an appropriate name in the PageObject DTC (see the previous section for details on how to do this).**

4. **Right-click the PageObject DTC. Choose Properties from the pop-up menu.**

   The PageObject Property dialog box appears (see Figure 11-12).

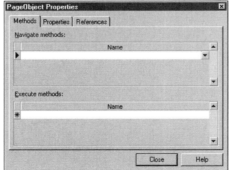

Figure 11-12: The PageObject Properties dialog box.

5. **In the top grid under Navigate methods, click the drop-down button to the far right of the first line.**

   You should see all the functions and subroutines on this page listed there (see Figure 11-13).

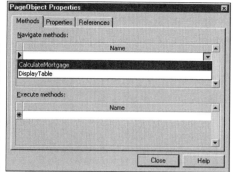

Figure 11-13:
All the
functions
and
subroutines
on the page
are listed.

6. **Choose the one you want to expose as a method.**

   It now appears in the first line (see Figure 11-14).

7. **If you want to expose another one, click the drop-down button in the next line and repeat the process.**

8. **When you are done, click Close.**

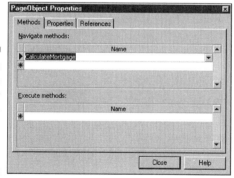

Figure 11-14:
The
function or
subroutine
you chose
appears in
the first line.

Specifying references

If you are writing script in page A and you want for that script to have access to the methods and properties of pages B and C, you have to inform page A ahead of time that you'll be using pages B and C. This process is called *specifying page references*. In other words, *what other pages will you be referencing from this page?*

To specify references for a page:

1. **Add a PageObject DTC to the page if it doesn't have one already.**

2. **Give this page an appropriate name in the PageObject DTC (see the previous section for details on how to do this).**

3. **Right-click the PageObject DTC. Choose Properties from the pop-up menu.**

   The PageObject Property dialog box appears.

4. **Click the References tab (see Figure 11-15).**

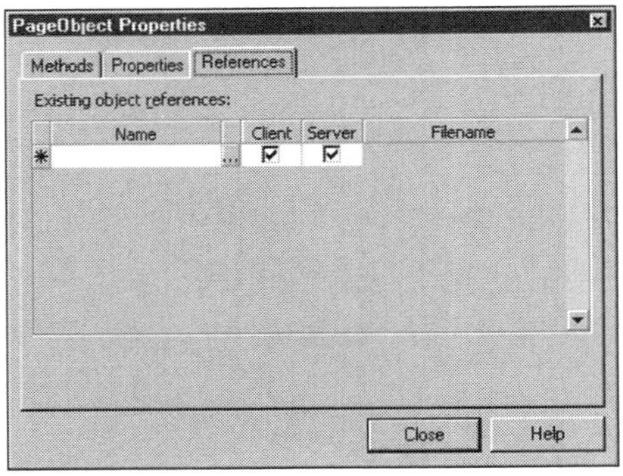

Figure 11-15:
The
PageObject
Properties
dialog box,
References
tab.

5. **Under name, type the name of the page.**

   You can click the button with three dots to browse for it.

6. **Check off the boxes to indicate whether you want to access this page from client script, server script, or both.**

7. **Repeat these steps until you specify all the pages that you want to access from this page.**

8. **Click Close when you are done.**

Calling page methods

After you have exposed one or more methods of a page and you've specified a reference to that page in *another* page, then you are ready to call methods.

```
CustList.navigate.ShowCustomers(State)
```

This line refers to a page object named CustList. Then comes navigate, and finally, the method name that was exposed on that page. If the method takes arguments, you can pass those arguments after the method name.

This line causes the browser to load the CustList page and immediately execute the ShowCustomers subroutine.

Be aware that after the ShowCustomers subroutine is executed, control does *not* return to the page that called it. The CustList page is displayed and executed. This does *not* work like calls to subroutines and functions that you are used to. Instead, you can think of it as more like a way to navigate to a page and control that is the first subroutine or function executed when the page is loaded. This can be a handy feature, as long as you remember that it doesn't work like a traditional function call.

Exposing page properties

If pages can have methods, then they should also be able to have properties. Adding a property to a page is as easy as exposing a method.

To add a property to a page:

1. **Add a PageObject DTC to the page if it doesn't have one already.**

2. **Give this page an appropriate name in the PageObject DTC.**

Finishing the job . . .

So if a page is treated like an object and you can expose methods of a page, why can't you call a method and have it *return to* the original page, just as a normal function or subroutine call?

The answer is not simple. There *is* another way to call a method of a page. It looks like this:

```
CustList.execute.ShowCustomers(State)
```

Execute *does* work like a normal function call. It goes to the page, runs the subroutine, and returns to the current page.

The only problem is that you can't execute a method from a server script. You can only use execute to call a server script *from the client*. This is a very interesting feature. It

enables you to call a server subroutine while you are on a page and return to that page without loosing your context.

Although this is very handy, it's confusing why the folks at Microsoft didn't just go ahead and allow you to also call a method from a server script, too. It seems like that would have been the easier one to implement because both scripts are on the server already.

My guess is that you'll see this capability added in a future version of Visual InterDev. If you can call methods of any page from any page on either the client or the server, you end up with a very clean object-oriented development environment.

---

3. **Right-click the PageObject DTC. Choose Properties from the pop-up menu.**

   The PageObject Property dialog box appears.

4. **Click the Properties tab (see Figure 11-16).**

5. **In the grid under Defined properties, click the first line under Name. Type the name you want to give your property.**

6. **Under Lifetime, choose the life of your property.**

   If you choose Page, this property will only exist while this page is displayed and will cease to exist when a new page is loaded. If you choose Session, the page property will live as long as the user is visiting this site. Choosing Application causes the property to exist for the life of the entire application from the time the first user logs in until the last user logs out. It also means that only one application property will be shared among all users.

7. **Under Client and Server, choose the type of access you want your client script and server script to have.**

   The options are Read, Read and Write, or no access.

8. **When you are done, click Close.**

Accessing page properties

To access a property of one page from another, you must first specify a reference to the page with the property on this page. See "Specifying References" earlier in this chapter for more information on that.

After you have exposed a property and made a reference to the page from the current page, it is easy to access the property. If your property's name was `ColorPref`, the code to set the value would look like this:

```
PrefPage.navigate.SetColorPref(0)
```

`PrefPage` is the name of the page that has exposed the property. Notice that I didn't change the property directly. When you create a property on a page, Visual InterDev automatically creates `Set` and `Get` functions that allow access to the variable. They are always named `Set`*Name* and `Get`*Name,* where *Name* is the name you gave the property. To retrieve the value of a property, you use the `Get` method.

```
Color = PrefPage.navigate.GetColorPref()
```

Changing the SOM Target Platform

When you create a project that will use SOM, you have a choice to make. You can choose to implement SOM on the server or on the client. Throughout this book, when I discuss SOM and the DTCs, I use the default — implementing SOM on the server.

If you want to implement SOM on the client, you must specify that when you first enable SOM for a page.

To specify that you want to implement SOM on the client:

1. **Right-click any empty spot on the page and choose Properties.**

   The page's Properties dialog box appears (see Figure 11-17).

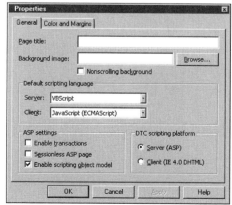

Figure 11-17: The page's Properties dialog box.

2. **Under DTC scripting platform, choose Client (IE 4.0 DHTML).**

3. **Click to check the Enable Scripting Object model check box.**

4. **Click OK.**

Now when you write script to respond to DTC events, they will all be executed on the client using client script. This solution executes much faster because it doesn't have to continually be returning to the server every time script needs to be executed. And it allows you to create a much richer user interface experience.

However, there is just one problem with targeting the client-side with SOM. It only works when the people who are browsing your site use Internet Explorer 4.0 or higher. If you can't depend on that always being the case, then you are better off targeting the server for SOM.

Part III
Accessing the Database

The 5th Wave   By Rich Tennant

"I guess you could say this is the hub of our network."

In this part . . .

Make the database part of your Web application. You can retrieve and display data from the database. You can create pages that enable the user to easily change the database by adding new records or updating data. And it's all as easy as drag-and-drop — well, almost that simple!

In this part, you not only discover all the features for accessing and updating the database, you also uncover a complete Web application — an Internet Auction. You'll have users bidding and buying stuff from you and from each other before you can say "Going, going, GONE!"

Chapter 12

Creating and Managing Your Database

In This Chapter

▶ Selecting the right database for your needs

▶ Getting connected to a database

▶ Creating and using database diagrams

▶ Creating, changing, and deleting tables in a database

*W*eb applications, like other types of computer applications come in all shapes and sizes. They do everything from simply presenting information to doing complex calculations to providing an interesting experience so that the visitor will want to come back. But because the Web is all about sharing information, and because the most common way of storing large volumes of information is a database, it's inevitable that the Web application and database worlds would collide.

Fortunately, database access is one of Visual InterDev's specialties. Visual InterDev makes accessing, displaying, and modifying data easy. But, beyond that, it gives you the ability to directly create, modify, and delete database structures like tables graphically, from right within the environment itself. No need for extra database utilities.

In this chapter, you discover how to choose a database to meet your needs and how to use database diagrams to create and maintain those databases. Visual InterDev puts all the capabilities you need right at your fingertips.

DB rookies — beware!

This chapter assumes that you have a basic understanding of relational database concepts and terms. You should be familiar with databases, tables, rows (or records), and columns (or fields). You should know what a primary key is. You should also know how a foreign key in one table relates to the primary key in another table.

If any of these concepts are unfamiliar to you, I suggest you brush up on basic database concepts before moving on in these chapters. You can find a discussion of these topics in the online Help for Microsoft Access and in the online Help for Microsoft SQL Server.

So Many Choices!

Before you start creating database diagrams, you have to first get connected to a database. And before that, you have to decide what database you are going to connect to. Sometimes this is already decided for you by the Powers That Be. In that case, you must simply make it work the best you can.

Other times, you might have the option to choose a database based on budget and project needs. In the next few sections, I discuss common databases you should consider and give you some idea of the strengths and weaknesses of each.

Microsoft Access

Microsoft Access is a great choice for small projects because, well, it's cheap! It's much less expensive than Microsoft SQL Server or Oracle and even within the price range of a lowly Web developer.

In addition, it is easy to install, set up, and maintain. In fact, you don't need to have Access itself installed on your Web server. Just put the file out there and create a Data Source Name (for more on this, see "Getting Connected" later this chapter). Then you can access and use databases from your Web applications. Easy!

There's one more important consideration. Microsoft, as you might guess, created Microsoft Access. And using Microsoft development tools with Microsoft databases is a *very* good idea. In fact, the more you can integrate Microsoft technologies and avoid non-Microsoft technologies, the smoother your development will go.

- New project
- Visual studio
  - database project

www

l_m_lawson@yahoo.com

Cybe

Comin,

r café

g Soon

1. Select project in project explorer
2. From project menu choose add data connection
3. On the File Data Source Tab choose new
4. Select database driver you want and select NEXT
5. type in name of the connection file and choose NEXT. (adds extension DSN to filename)
6. Choose finish
7. Fill in driver specific info such as name of database

Then you return to SDS dialog box, the file data source name will be displayed

ADD DATACONNECTION

On- File data source tab of the select data source box

Data connection is displayed under DataEnvironment Folder in your project, underneath the global.asa folder. you can browse and edit the data from this database in the data view window.

Why do I say that? It's not because Microsoft tools are necessarily better than everyone else's. It's also not because I'm a tool of the power of Gates' empire. It's because, believe it or not, Microsoft makes their tools integrate better with *each other* than with anyone else's tools. You can always bet that they'll do more development and testing on integrating their development environments with Microsoft databases than with others. It's just a fact of life.

Now for the not-so-good news. Microsoft Access is a *desktop* database. Access stores all its database information in files on the hard drive. Desktop databases, like Access, are created to be used by a single user. Although it is possible for multiple users to access the database file over a network or the Internet, it is not terribly efficient and once the number of users and level of activity get high enough, performance can suffer considerably. It can get slow. Very slow.

In addition, Access doesn't have a lot of built-in capabilities to assure that the data stored in the database is secure from prying eyes or that only correct data is entered into the database.

Finally, Access lacks stored procedures and triggers which are capabilities provided by other databases that allow you to write code that is stored in the database and helps perform tasks on the data. Stored procedures and triggers provide an extra level of flexibility in your development and relieve you of some coding drudgery.

To summarize, here are the advantages of Microsoft Access:

- ✔ It's cheap.
- ✔ It's easy to set up and maintain.
- ✔ It's made by Microsoft.

And here are the disadvantages of Microsoft Access:

- ✔ It can get slow with large number of users.
- ✔ It doesn't have strong security or integrity capabilities.
- ✔ It doesn't support stored procedures or triggers.

Microsoft SQL Server

Microsoft SQL Server is Microsoft's high-end *client/server* database. Client/ server databases are different from desktop databases like Access in that they are designed from the beginning to work with many users at the same time. As you add more users, their performance continues to be good.

In addition, SQL Server provides user-level security with passwords that allow access to only the portions of the database that the administrator allows. It also has capabilities to help ensure data integrity (that is, the data is in the correct format and corresponds with other data throughout the database).

SQL Server supports stored procedures and triggers offering a way to attach code to the database tables themselves and do actions when activities like table adds, updates, and deletes are performed.

Finally, like Access, SQL Server is created by Microsoft and integrates very, very well with Visual InterDev.

On the down side, SQL Server is definitely not cheap. And it is also not as easy to set up and maintain as Microsoft Access.

In short, here are the advantages of Microsoft SQL Server:

- ✔ It continues to perform well, even with many users.
- ✔ It provides strong security or integrity capabilities.
- ✔ It supports stored procedures or triggers.
- ✔ It's made by Microsoft.

And here are the disadvantages of Microsoft SQL Server:

- ✔ It's not cheap.
- ✔ It's not as easy to set up and maintain.

Oracle

Oracle is another client/server database that supports all the same important features as SQL Server: it supports many users, has strong security and integrity capabilities, and it allows you to create stored procedures and triggers. It also has many of the same disadvantages — it isn't cheap and it isn't easy to set up or maintain.

In fact, Oracle is a direct competitor of Microsoft SQL Server. So what's the difference?

Oracle has a very large piece of the client/server database pie. Many large corporations have set Oracle as their corporate standard for enterprise-level database storage. So it is both very common and often a requirement when creating any information system. And, with its capabilities, it is up to the task.

There's one more downside. It's not a Microsoft product. Although Microsoft has made a point of saying that they are working very hard to fully support Oracle, I believe it will always be a second priority to making sure that they fully support their own SQL Server database.

In summary, the advantages of Oracle are:

- ✔ It continues to perform well, even with many users.
- ✔ It provides strong security or integrity capabilities.
- ✔ It supports stored procedures or triggers.
- ✔ It is broadly used and is the standard for many companies.

And here are the disadvantages of Oracle:

- ✔ It's not cheap.
- ✔ It's not as easy to set up and maintain.
- ✔ It's *not* made by Microsoft.

Making a decision

So which database should you use? Here's what I recommend.

Take a look at the number of users you expect to be accessing your Web site. If you are only talking about a few hundred users viewing or occasionally updating data, you can probably get by with Microsoft Access. Its cost and ease-of-use are too compelling to ignore in these low-volume settings.

If you expect more on the order of thousands or tens-of-thousands of users hitting the database hard with complex reports and updates, then you definitely should be looking at Microsoft SQL Server. Serious problems require serious tools.

If you are working with a company that has already standardized on Oracle or there's already a significant investment of time, data and resources in Oracle, then don't fight the system. Visual InterDev works perfectly well with Oracle and the existing investment far outweighs the benefits of staying pure Microsoft.

Finally, if your company has standardized on a completely different database like Sybase SQL Server, Informix, or DB/2 (just to name a few), you'll have to weigh the investment in these versus the accessibility and capabilities provided for accessing these databases from Visual InterDev. I doubt if you'll find a common commercially available database that Visual InterDev can't access, one way or another. The difference will be in the ease of access and the capabilities Visual InterDev provides for working with the database structures and data.

Getting Connected

The process of getting your Web server and Visual InterDev set up to access a database differs greatly from one database to another. See your database documentation and readme files for details on the process involved.

In this section, I cover some of the issues that are important for all databases.

ODBC Drivers

ODBC stands for Open DataBase Connectivity. It is a standard created by Microsoft to allow easy access to almost any database. However, in order for you to access a database from Visual InterDev, an ODBC driver specifically designed for your database must be installed. There are ODBC drivers for almost every common commercially available database out there.

See your database's documentation for information on installing its ODBC driver. You must have the driver installed on your workstation and on the workstation of anyone else who will be creating Web pages that access the database. You also need for the ODBC driver to be installed on the Web server.

The Data Source Name (DSN)

Normally when you connect to a database, there's a whole bunch of arguments you have to specify to get the connection going. It is tedious to spell out this information again and again every time you connect to the database. Especially because the information never changes. That's why Data Source Names (DSNs) were created. A DSN allows you to store all the connection information in one place and give it a name — the Data Source Name. Then, whenever you want to connect to a database, instead of spelling out all that stuff, you simply use the DSN.

There are two types of DSNs. There are Machine DSNs which are stored in a computer's registry and made available to anyone who uses the computer where the DSN is defined. There are also File DSNs that are created as an independent file that can easily be moved from one system to the next.

When you set up a DSN for your Web applications, I recommend you create a File DSN. If it is created correctly, the same File DSN can be used on all workstations and on the Web server itself, thus saving you from having to re-create it on each machine, as you'd have to do with a Machine DSN.

When you Add a Data Connection to your project (discussed in the next section), you can choose an existing DSN or create a new File DSN as part of the process.

A Data Connection

A Data Connection is *not* part of the Windows 95/98 or Windows NT environment like ODBC drivers and DSNs. A Data Connection is specific to the Visual InterDev environment.

A Data Connection is the object in Visual InterDev that represents your connection to the database. Whenever you create a Recordset object, it is associated with a Data Connection. If you want to create database commands, they are associated with a Data Connection. All database activity in your application must happen through a Data Connection.

When you first create a Data Connection, you provide a DSN where the Data Connection can find the information it needs to connect to the database. Once the Data Connection has accessed a file DSN, all the DSN information is copied into the project and the File DSN itself is no longer needed.

You can create more than one Data Connection in a Visual InterDev project, if you need to access more than one database at a time. But usually you'll get by just fine with only one.

Adding a Data Connection

Every project that accesses the database has a DataEnvironment. The DataEnvironment is a part of the project where all the database-specific objects are housed. In the last section, I discuss one of the most important database objects in your DataEnvironment — the Data Connection. When you add a Data Connection to your project, a DataEnvironment is created for it automatically.

When you create a Data Connection, you must have a DSN available to tell the Data Connection how to get to the database. If you don't, you have to create a new DSN at the same time you create a Data Connection.

To create a Data Connection for an existing DSN:

1. **Look through your project in the Project Explorer window. Find the file named global.asa and right-click it.**

   A pop-up menu appears.

2. **Choose Add Data Connection from the pop-up menu.**

   A window appears with the title Select Data Source.

3. **Click the File Data Source tab (see Figure 12-1).**

   This is a list of all the File DSNs on this machine. The list of File DSNs on your machine list is likely to be different from the one in Figure 12-1.

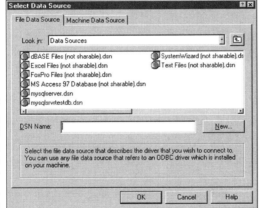

Figure 12-1:
The ODBC
Data
Source
Administrator
dialog box.

You have several options here. You can select one of the File DSNs listed to establish your connection to the database. Or you can click the Look in drop-down list box to find File DSNs in other locations on this machine or on the network.

4. **Locate and select the DSN you want to use.**

5. **Click OK.**

   A new dialog box appears called Connection1 Properties (see Figure 12-2).

6. **Enter a name for your connection in the Connection Name edit.**

   You may want to name this the same name you gave your DSN and/or your database. All the rest of the information should be correct.

7. **Click OK.**

   A new icon appears under global.asa — DataEnvironment. And under DataEnvironment, another icon with the name you just entered for your Data Connection.

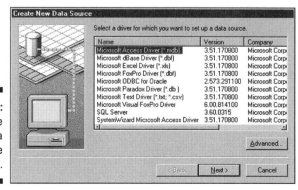

Figure 12-2:
The
Connection1
Properties
dialog box.

If you don't already have a DSN available, it's easy to create one as part of the process of creating a Data Connection.

To create a Data Connection and a DSN at the same time:

1. **In the Project Explorer window, find global.asa and right-click it. A pop-up menu appears.**

2. **Choose Add Data Connection from the pop-up menu. A window appears with the title Select Data Source.**

3. **Click the File Data Source tab (refer to Figure 12-1).**

4. **Click the New button. The Create New Data Source dialog box appears (see Figure 12-3).**

5. **Scroll down and click the name of the driver that goes with your database. If you don't see the driver for your database it is probably because you don't have the right ODBC driver installed on this machine. For more information on ODBC, see "ODBC Drivers" earlier in this chapter or check your database's documentation.**

Figure 12-3:
The Create
New Data
Source
dialog box.

6. **Click Next.** The next step of the Create New Data Source dialog box appears (see Figure 12-4).

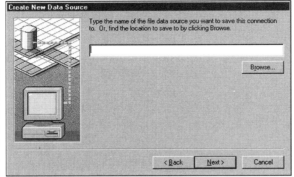

Figure 12-4:
The next step of the Create New Data Source dialog box.

7. **Type the name you want to give to this DSN. Often this is the same as the name of the database that this DSN will access.**

8. **Click Next.** The next step of the Create New Data Source dialog box appears (see Figure 12-5). Here you see a summary of the information you've entered so far.

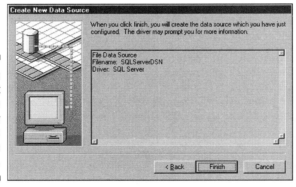

Figure 12-5:
The next step of the Create New Data Source dialog box.

9. **Click Finish.**

   A dialog box appropriate to your database appears. Each database's dialog box is different. For SQL Server, you'll see the Create a New Data Source wizard. For Access, you'll see the ODBC Microsoft Access 97 Setup dialog box.

10. **If you are using Access, click the Select button to browse and find the database file you want this DSN associated with.**

If you are using SQL Server, Oracle or another client/server database, you'll have to specify the name of the server where the database is installed, the name of the database, and your user ID and password.

11. **Walk through all the required steps of the database's dialog box.**

    When you are finished, you should be able to find the new DSN you just created in the list on the Select Data Source window (they're in alphabetical order).

12. **Click to select the newly created DSN.**

13. **Click OK.**

14. **At this point, you** *may* **see a login dialog box for your database. If you do, enter a valid user ID and password.**

    A new dialog box appears called Connection1 Properties (see Figure 12-6).

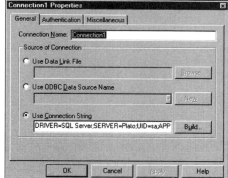

Figure 12-6:
The
Connection1
Properties
dialog box.

15. **Enter a name for your connection in the Connection Name edit. You may want to name this the same name you gave your DSN and/or your database. All the rest of the information should be correct.**

16. **Click OK.**

    A new icon appears under global.asa — DataEnvironment. And under DataEnvironment, another icon with the name you just entered for your Data Connection.

The default location where File DSNs are saved in this folder:

```
C:\Program Files\Common Files\ODBC\Data Sources
```

They all have the extension .dsn. After you create the file DSN, you can copy it to other machines and you won't have to re-create it there.

The DataEnvironment and Data View

The DataEnvironment is found under the global.asa file. The DataEnvironment houses all the database-specific objects that will be a part of your project. The first object, a Data Connection is already there (otherwise you wouldn't even have a DataEnvironment). You can add a second and third Data Connection to your DataEnvironment just by right-clicking the DataEnvironment and choosing Add Data Connection. Although you probably won't do this often, it's nice to know that you can connect to multiple databases at once in a single project.

After you have a DataEnvironment, a new window appears in your Visual InterDev development environment — the Data View. Look at the bottom of your Properties window in the lower right. You should see two tabs there — Properties and Data View. If you click Data View, you see the Data View window (see Figure 12-7).

This window looks like the Project Explorer window. The first item is the solution you are working on, and under it, the project. This window shows the database portions of the project, rather than the pages and files associated with the project. You see under your project an icon that represents the database you created a connection for. And under that, you see icons for Tables and Views. If you are connected to SQL Server, you also see icons for database diagrams and Stored Procedures.

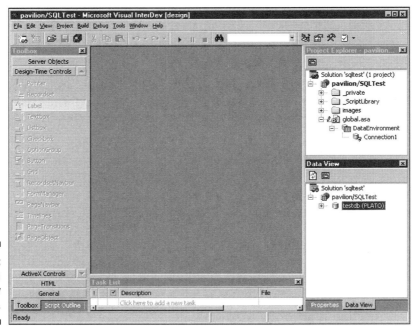

Figure 12-7:
The Data
View
window.

Requirements to use database diagrams

Database diagrams are a very handy feature. But they are only available in the Enterprise version of Visual InterDev. If you have Visual InterDev Pro, you'll have to get by making your database changes in a tool like SQL Enterprise Manager for SQL Server.

Also, database diagrams do not work in desktop databases like Microsoft Access or Microsoft FoxPro. If you are using an Access or FoxPro database, you'll have to use those respective tools to create tables and fill them with data, rather than Visual InterDev database diagrams.

The Tables icon can be further opened to see the columns in each table.

This Data View provides you with an equivalent to the Project Explorer on the database side. You can see what tables are out there and what they contain.

Database Diagrams

Visual InterDev allows you to work with the structure of your database through database diagrams. In Chapter 4, I demonstrate how site diagrams allow you to create new pages, delete pages that are no longer needed, and define the relationship among pages. In the same way, database diagrams allow you to create and delete tables and establish relationships among them.

Database diagrams share other characteristics in common with site diagrams. Among them:

✔ You can have as many database diagrams for a single database as you like.

✔ The same table can appear in more than one diagram.

✔ Changes you make to a table in one diagram can cause another diagram containing that table to change, too, since, ultimately, it is the same table represented in both places.

There is also an important *difference* between database diagrams and site diagrams. Database diagrams are stored in the database itself, not as a file that is part of any particular Visual InterDev project. This makes sense because you might very well want to access the same database from a number of different projects.

Creating a Database Diagram

To create a new database diagram:

1. **In the Data View window, open the solution, project, and database you want to work with.**

   Under the database you should see four icons — database diagrams, Tables, Views, and Stored Procedures (see Figure 12-8).

2. **Right-click the database diagrams icon.**

3. **Choose New Diagram from the pop-up menu.**

   A blank window appears (see Figure 12-9).

You fill this diagram with meaningful stuff in the next few sections.

Adding an Existing Table to a Diagram

A database diagram does not automatically include all the tables from the database on it. In fact, when a database diagram is created, it is blank.

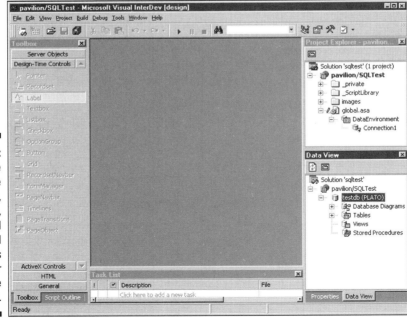

Figure 12-8:
The database diagrams, Tables, Views, and Stored Procedures icons under the database.

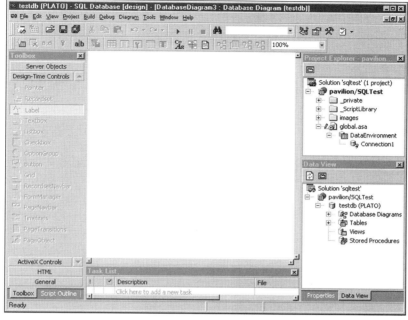

Figure 12-9:
The new,
blank
database
diagram
window.

To add an existing table to a database diagram:

1. **In the Data View window, find the Tables icon under the database you are using.**

2. **Open the Tables icon. All the tables in the database appear under it (see Figure 12-10).**

3. **Locate the table you want to add to the diagram, and drag it from the Data View window out onto your diagram.**

   A new window appears on your diagram to represent the table (see Figure 12-11).

Changing How You View the Table

By default, you see only the column names for the table in the window that appears in your diagram. But you can change that.

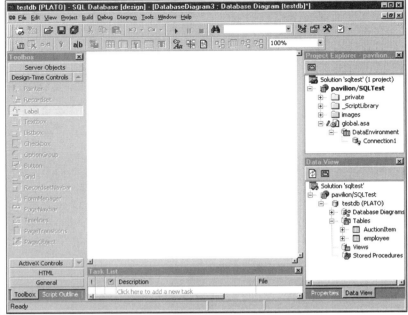

Figure 12-10:
All the tables in the database appear under the table icon.

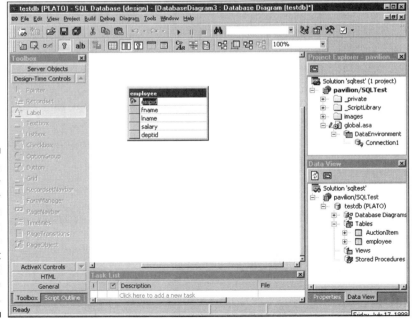

Figure 12-11:
A new window appears representing the table you just dragged onto the diagram.

To change how you view a table in your diagram:

1. **Right-click the title bar of the window, where the table's name appears.**

2. **Choose from one of these options: Column Properties, Column Names, Keys, Name Only, Custom.**

   The window changes to reflect your selection.

The common views

Each of the options shows a different amount of detail. In order, from least detail to most, here are the options:

✔ **Name Only** — Only the title bar of the window appears, showing the table's name (see Figure 12-12). This is useful when you have a whole lot of tables on the diagram and you don't need the details.

✔ **Keys** — The table's name, primary key columns, and foreign key columns appear in the window (see Figure 12-13). Provides a bit more detail at the expense of additional room on the diagram.

✔ **Column Names** — This is the default. The table name and all columns are listed (see Figure 12-14).

✔ **Column Properties** — Not only the column names, but also all the details about each column are displayed (see Figure 12-15). This is the view to use when you want to make changes to a table.

Figure 12-12:
Name Only.

Figure 12-13:
Keys.

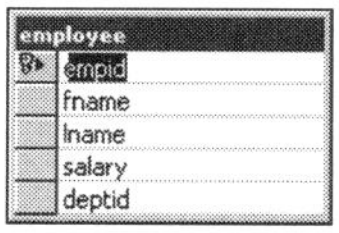

Figure 12-14:
Column
Names.

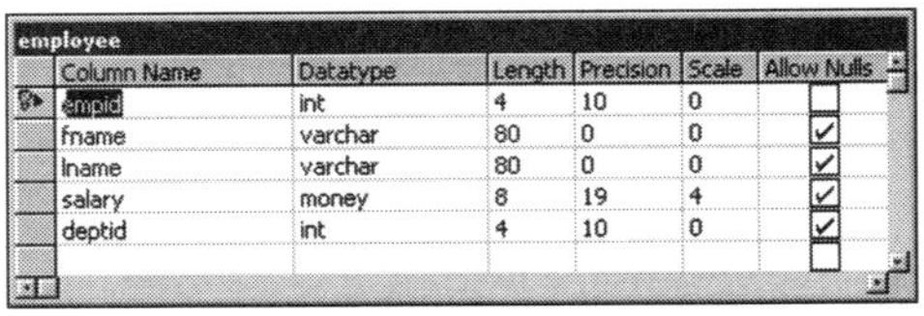

Figure 12-15:
Column
Properties.

Custom views

In addition to Name Only, Keys, Column Names, and Column Properties, there is one more view to choose from — Custom. If you select Modify Custom View... from the pop-up menu, you will see the Custom Selection window (see Figure 12-16).

Figure 12-16:
Custom
Selection
window.

Here you can move columns from the Available Columns list to the Selected Columns list to indicate which columns you want to appear in the Custom view. After you've specified which should appear, you can choose Custom from the pop-up menu to change the table to appear as you specified.

Creating and Modifying Tables

The ability to create tables from right inside Visual InterDev is very handy. It makes quickly developing Web database applications a snap!

One word of warning, though. The changes I show you how to make in this section actually *modify the database itself.* You are not simply changing a diagram. When you finally save the diagram all the changes you made to it are made to the database. So, be very careful.

Creating a table and adding columns

To create a new table:

1. **Right-click in a blank part of the database diagram.**

2. **Choose New Table from the pop-up menu.**

    The Choose Name dialog box appears (see Figure 12-17).

Figure 12-17:
The Choose
Name
dialog box.

3. **Enter a name for the table.**

    The table design window appears (see Figure 12-18).

4. **Enter the column name, data type, length, precision, and scale (if necessary) and whether or not Nulls are allowed for this column.**

    You can also enter a default value for the columns and identity information (see the nearby sidebar "Identity confirmed!" for more information).

5. **Repeat Step 4 for each of the columns in your table.**

Specifying a primary key

To specify the primary key for a table:

1. **Right-click the column name of the column you want to make a primary key.**

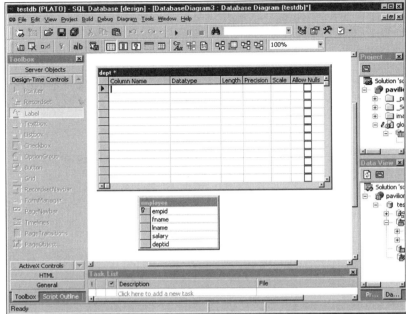

Figure 12-18:
The table
design
window.

Identity confirmed!

When you are creating a new table in Microsoft SQL Server, you can specify whether a column is or is not an *Identity* column. If it is, you can specify an Identity Seed and an Identity Increment. What does all this mean?

A column labeled as an Identity column is one that has a value that is *automatically* generated when a new row is added. For example, if you have an Employee table, you might include as your first column an EmployeeID. This ID is the primary key for the table and you just want for it to be a unique number.

So you specify that EmployeeID is an integer data type and an Identity column. When you do, the first Employee record entered will be automatically assigned the EmployeeID 1. The second will be assigned 2 and so forth. Each

number generated for that column is guaranteed to be unique.

Identity *Seed* provides the number to start with, if you don't want to start at one. Identity *Increment* determines what is added to the number each time a new record is added. For example, if the Identity Seed is 10000 and the Identity Increment is 10, the first row inserted would have the value 10000, the second would be 10010 and the third 10020, and so on.

It's a great idea to use Identity columns as the primary key for most, if not all, of your tables. You don't have to show these columns to your users and they certainly don't have to enter values in these columns, but they provide you with a handy way to refer to rows uniquely using only one column.

2. **Choose Set Primary Key from the pop-up menu.**

   A small key icon appears beside the column name (see Figure 12-19).

3. **To add another column to the primary key, repeat the process.**

Inserting and deleting columns

To insert a new column:

1. **Right-click the first column you want to appear after the newly inserted column.**

2. **Choose Insert Column from the pop-up menu.**

   A new line is inserted, and you can enter a column name and all the rest of the information about the column.

To delete a column:

1. **Right-click the column you want to delete.**

2. **Choose Delete Column from the pop-up menu.**

   The column disappears.

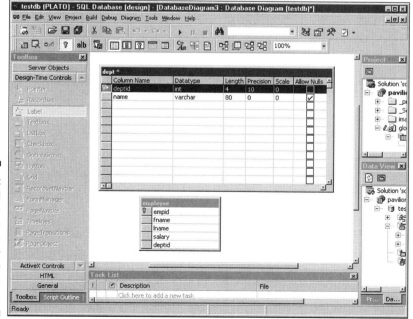

Figure 12-19:
A small key icon appears beside the new primary key column name.

Adding and deleting an index

Indexes can be applied to any column or set of columns in a table to make it quick and easy to sort or search on those columns. In SQL Server, an index is automatically created for your primary key column(s).

To add an index to a column on a table:

1. **Right-click anywhere on the table window.**

2. **Choose Property Pages from the pop-up menu.**

   The Property Pages dialog box appears (see Figure 12-20).

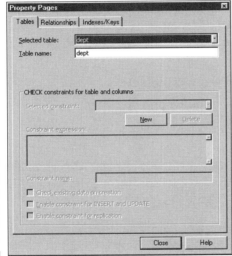

Figure 12-20: The Property Pages dialog box.

3. **Click the Indexes/Keys tab (see Figure 12-21).**

4. **Click the New button.**

5. **Under Column name, use the drop-down list box to choose what column you want to index on.**

   If you want to index on multiple columns, use the second and third line.

6. **Enter the name you want to give this index in the Index name edit.**

7. **Choose whether you want this to be a Unique index.**

   A unique index forces each row to have a unique value for the column(s) that are a part of this index, just like a primary key.

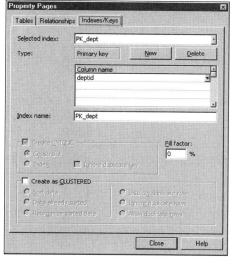

Figure 12-21:
The
Indexes/
Keys tab.

8. **Choose whether you want this to be a Clustered index.**

   When an index is clustered, all the rows in the table are actually stored in the table as if they were sorted on this index. Because this option affects the physical storage of the rows, only one index in each table can be clustered. By default, the table's primary key index is the one that is clustered. Unless you have a good reason to change it, it is best to leave the table clustered on the primary key only.

9. **Don't worry about Fill Factor.**

   It can be used for fine-tuning performance, but its default setting is usually fine.

10. **Click Close.**

To delete an index:

1. **Right-click anywhere on the table window.**

2. **Choose Property Pages from the pop-up menu.**

   The Property Pages dialog box appears.

3. **Click the Indexes/Keys tab (refer to Figure 12-21).**

4. **Choose the index you want to delete from the Selected index drop-down list box at the top of the dialog box.**

5. **Click Delete.**

   The index is deleted.

Saving Your Changes

As you are working with your database, you should save your changes often to be sure you don't lose them.

You can always tell which tables have had changes made to them since the last save — a * appears after the table name in the title bar.

To save your changes:

1. **Choose File⇨Save from the menu bar or click the Save button on the Standard toolbar.**

   The Save dialog box appears (see Figure 12-22). It tells you what tables have been changed before it makes those changes in the database.

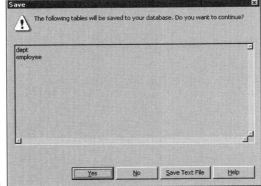

Figure 12-22:
The Save
dialog box.

2. **Click Yes.**

   If there are errors, you see a Save Incomplete dialog box.

   You can save these messages to a text file by clicking the Save Text File button or you can select the text and hit Ctrl+C to copy the text to the Clipboard. Click OK.

   Whether there were errors or not, you'll next see the Save Change Script dialog box (see Figure 12-23). This dialog box allows you to save the changes that were made to the database in the form of SQL statements in a text file. This allows you to see exactly what Visual InterDev did and allows you to make these changes again in the future, if necessary.

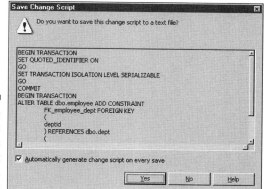

Figure 12-23:
The Save
Change
Script
dialog box.

3. Click Yes or No.

The database changes are made and the database diagram is saved.

Creating Table Constraints

A constraint is a rule that must be followed by the data that is entered into a table. If data is entered that does not follow the rule, the data is rejected. Constraints help maintain data integrity. That is, they help assure that the data that is put into the table is as correct as it can be.

To add a constraint to a table:

1. **Right-click anywhere on the table and choose Property Pages from the pop-up menu.**

2. **Click the Tables tab (see Figure 12-24).**

3. **In the CHECK constraints for tables and columns group box, click the New button.**

4. **Enter an expression in the Constraint expression edit box.**

The constraint expression can be as complex as you like. Use the same syntax that you would use in the WHERE clause of a SQL SELECT statement. You can use AND, OR, NOT, LIKE, equalities, and inequalities.

Here are some examples:

```
Salary > 10000
(PassNum > 100) AND (PassNum <= 999)
InventoryNum LIKE '[A-Z][A-Z][1-9][1-9]'
```

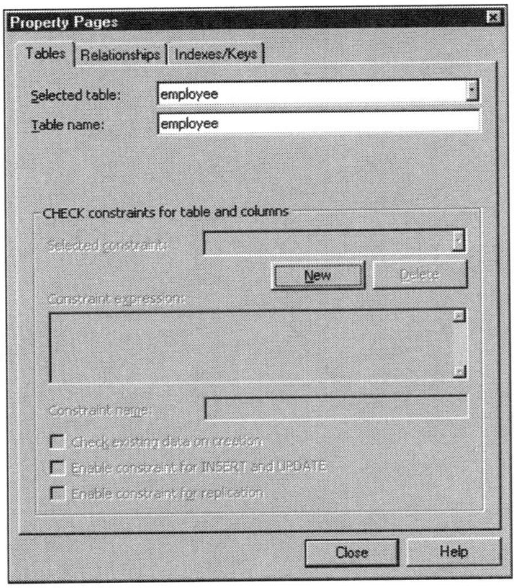

Figure 12-24:
The Tables
tab of the
Property
Pages
dialog box.

5. **Enter a name for the constraint in the Constraint name edit box.**

6. **Click Close.**

To delete a constraint:

1. **Right-click anywhere on the table and choose Property Pages from the pop-up menu.**

2. **Click the Tables tab (refer to Figure 12-24).**

3. **Choose the constraint you want to delete from the Selected constraint drop-down list box.**

4. **Click Delete.**

   The constraint is deleted.

Table Matchmakers: Creating Relationships Between Tables

Relationships between tables in a relational database are created with foreign keys. A foreign key is simply a column or set of columns in one table that corresponds to the primary key column(s) in another table.

To create a relationship between two tables:

1. **Select the column(s) that make up the foreign key.**

2. **Drag the selected columns to the table whose primary key the foreign key is associated with.**

3. **Drop the columns.**

   The Create Relationship window appears (see Figure 12-25).

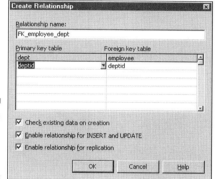

Figure 12-25:
The Create
Relationship
window.

4. **Change the name assigned to the key in the Relationship name edit box as you see fit.**

5. **Make sure the column(s) of the foreign key table correspond to the appropriate column(s) of the primary key table.**

6. **Click OK.**

   A line appears between the tables labeled with the name of the foreign key (see Figure 12-26).

To delete a relationship between two tables:

1. **Right-click the line in the diagram that represents the foreign key you want to delete.**

2. **Choose Delete Relationship from Database from the pop-up menu.**

   The line disappears.

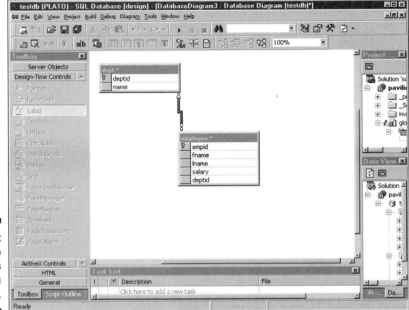

Figure 12-26:
The two
tables
joined by a
foreign key.

Deleting (Dropping) a Table from the Database

Deleting a table from the database actually drops the table structure *and all its data* from the database. Be very careful when you do this.

If you do delete a table accidentally, remember, like all the other changes made to a database diagram, the delete won't actually happen until you save the diagram. If you close the diagram without saving, the delete won't happen. Of course none of the other changes you've made to the diagram will happen either!

To delete a table from the database:

1. **Right-click the table.**

2. **Choose Delete Table from Database.**

   A dialog box asks if you are sure you want to permanently delete the table from the database.

3. **Click Yes.**

   The table disappears.

Changing the Database Diagram

The database diagram provides a very convenient place for you to make changes to your database. However, the diagram itself can also be very useful in getting an high-level look at you tables and how they are related.

In this section, I introduce you to database diagram features that don't modify the database structure but do make it easier for you to see how it all fits together.

Removing a table from the diagram

If you don't want to see a table on the diagram anymore, you can remove it from the diagram without deleting it from the database.

To remove a table from the database diagram:

1. **Right-click the table.**

2. **Choose Remove Table from Diagram from the pop-up menu.**

   The table disappears from the diagram (but remains in the database).

Adding text annotations

Text annotations are simply labels where you can type any text you like to act as a headline, label, descriptive text, or whatever. This text has no effect on the database itself but exists in the diagram to help others who read the diagram understand it better.

To add a Text Annotation:

1. **Right-click in a blank area of the database diagram.**

2. **Choose New Text Annotation from the pop-up menu.**

   A box with a flashing cursor appears on the diagram.

3. **You can type any text you want in the box.**

To change the font and size of the text:

1. **Right-click inside the box.**

2. **Choose Set Text Annotation Font from the pop-up menu.**

   The standard Font dialog box appears.

3. **Set it as you like and click OK.**

You can change the font size of each annotation independently.

To resize the Text Annotation box:

1. **Click to select the annotation.**
2. **Move the mouse pointer over the small, white, square resize boxes.**
3. **Drag the mouse pointer to the size you like.**

To move the Text Annotation:

1. **Click to select the box.**
2. **Click directly on the gray outline and drag the text where you like it.**

Adding related tables

Sometimes you want a primary table and all the tables that are related to it added to a diagram. To make it easy on you, the makers of Visual InterDev added an option to do it automatically.

To add related tables to a database diagram:

1. **Right-click a table.**
2. **Choose Add Related Tables from the pop-up menu.**

   All tables that have foreign key relationships to the selected table are added to the diagram.

Relationship labels

The lines that represent foreign key relationships between tables are usually labeled with the name of the relationship.

To toggle relationship labels on or off:

1. **Right-click a blank spot in the diagram.**
2. **Choose Show Relationship Labels.**

Zooming

When you create a large diagram, it's sometimes hard to see the whole thing at once. You can always scroll around, but sometimes you need to get a bird's-eye view.

To zoom in or out of your diagram:

1. **Right-click a blank spot in the database diagram.**

2. **Choose Zoom from the pop-up menu.**

   A cascading menu appears.

3. **Choose the zoom level from the cascading menu — from 10% up to 200%.**

Page breaks

On a large diagram, printing may become a problem. The traditional solution is to print the diagram out on multiple pages and then tape them all together. To make this process easier, Visual InterDev can show you where the page breaks are so that you can best organize your tables around them.

To view page breaks:

1. **Zoom out to the level where you can see the entire diagram at once.**

2. **Right-click a blank part of the diagram and choose View Page Breaks from the pop-up menu.**

   Blue lines appear where the page breaks would be.

3. **Selectively zoom in and move tables around as appropriate.**

Printing your diagram

After you have your tables aligned well with the page breaks, it's time to print your masterpiece.

To print a database diagram:

1. **Choose File➪Print from the menu bar.**

   The diagram is printed.

2. **Start taping pages together as described on the diagram (use the page numbers at the bottom of each page to figure out where it belongs).**

Accessing Table Data

Database diagrams allow you to get a look at your tables and how they work together. They also allow you to modify the structure of tables, primary keys, foreign keys, and indexes in the database. What they don't allow you to do is enter and update the data *in* the tables.

Fortunately, there's another way to do that in Visual InterDev.

Viewing the data

To look at the data in a table:

1. **In the Data View window, open the solution, project, and database you want to work with.**

2. **Open the Tables icon under the database.**

3. **Double-click the table you want to view.**

   A grid with the data appears (see Figure 12-27).

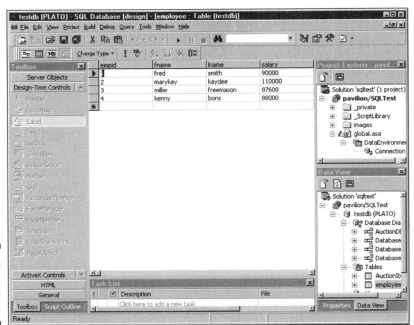

Figure 12-27:
The grid with the table data.

A Query toolbar also appears. You can use the Query toolbar to build queries (SQL Select statements). I explore this topic in Chapter 7.

But you don't need the Query toolbar to change the data, add rows, and delete rows. See "Editing data," "Deleting rows" and "Adding rows" in the next few sections to see how that's done.

Moving around

When you have only a few rows in a table, you can view them all on the screen at once, and you can easily click whatever row you want to work with.

However when you have a lot of rows, the navigation controls can help.

To navigate a long set of rows:

1. **Right-click anywhere in the set of rows.**

2. **Choose one of the navigation options: First, Last, Next, Previous, or Row.**

First and Last take you to the very first and very last row. Next and Previous move forward or backward one row from your current row. Row allows you to type in a row number and the cursor immediately jumps to that row.

Editing data

To edit the data:

1. **Scroll to find the row you want to change.**

2. **Make changes to as many columns as you like.**

3. **Move your cursor to a different row.**

    The changes are automatically saved when you move to a different row.

Deleting rows

To delete a row in a table:

1. **Click the gray box on the left side of the row you want to delete.**

    This selects the row.

2. **Press the Delete key on your keyboard.**

   You are warned that you are about to delete a row.

3. **Click Yes to continue.**

   The row is deleted from the table.

You can also click a gray box beside a row and then drag your cursor up or down to select multiple rows at once. Then when you press the Delete key, they are all deleted.

Adding rows

To add a new row to a table:

1. **Simply click the bottom, blank row. Or press the Insert key on your keyboard.**

   The cursor immediately moves down to the bottom, blank row.

2. **Enter the data you want for each column of the new row.**

3. **Move the cursor to a different row.**

   When you do, the new record is inserted and the information is saved.

Chapter 13

Creating Web Database Applications

*T*he Scripting Object Model and all the database tools in Visual InterDev, as cool as they are, are not enough to put Visual InterDev in the same league as Visual Basic or PowerBuilder for creating database applications.

For that, you need some way to easily display data that is returned from the database. Actually, you need a way to not only display but also edit the data and then update the database with those changes without having to write a lot of complicated SQL statements.

Fortunately, Visual InterDev offers these features and a whole lot more. That's what I show you in this chapter. As you read through the steps for accomplishing the different tasks described in this chapter, go ahead and follow along and actually create your own project. It always makes more sense when you actually do it!

The Linchpin: The Recordset DTC

The Recordset DTC is a non-visual control. Like the PageObject, the Recordset is visible at design time, in both the Design and Source views of the editor, but it isn't visible at runtime. It exists to interact with the database and to represent a collection of data that is retrieved. If you need to work with more than one set of data on a page, you can drop as many Recordset DTCs on the page as you like.

To add a Recordset DTC to your page:

1. **Create a Data Connection.**

   For information on how to do this, see Chapter 12.

   A DataEnvironment is automatically created to hold the new connection object.

2. **Click the Design-Time Controls tab of the Toolbox.**

3. **Drag a Recordset DTC to your page.**

4. **If you haven't turned on the Scripting Object Model for this page, you see a dialog box that asks you if you want to. Click Yes.**

   The Recordset appears as a big gray box in either Design view or Source view (see Figure 13-1).

The Recordset DTC has several fields that you can fill in right on its face. But if you want to fill in all the information for a Recordset, you need to look at its properties dialog box.

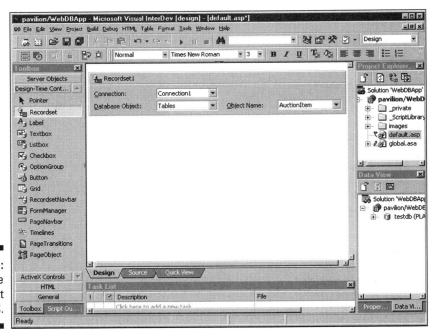

Figure 13-1: The Recordset DTC.

To access a Recordset's properties:

1. **Right-click the Recordset DTC.**

2. **Choose Properties from the pop-up menu.**

   The Recordset Properties dialog box appears (see Figure 13-2).

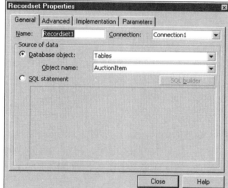

Figure 13-2:
The
Recordset
Properties
dialog box.

The most important properties are on the General tab of the Recordset Properties dialog box. The Recordset represents a set of data on your page. This tab enables you to specify exactly where the Recordset is to find the data it represents.

Here's a rundown describing what each of them does:

- ✔ **Name:** The name of the Recordset object. It's a good idea to give it a meaningful name, especially if you have more than one Recordset on a page.

- ✔ **Connection:** The name of the connection object that you want to use to get to the database. Remember that you can have more than one connection object in a project.

- ✔ **Database object:** This is an important one. It determines how you are going to get the information from the database. Four possibilities exist:

   - **Tables:** Simply pull all the information out of a specific table.

   - **Stored Procedures:** Call a stored procedure (which is like a subroutine that's stored in the database) and get the result set that it returns.

- **Views:** Pull all the information from a view that is defined in the database.

- **DE Commands:** Use a command that has been created and stored in your project as a separate object.

✔ **Object name:** This field allows you to pick the specific table, stored procedure view, or DE command that you want to receive data from.

✔ **SQL statement:** The Database object and SQL statement are each associated with option buttons, meaning that you can choose only one or the other. If you choose not to associate this Recordset with any specific Database object, you can, instead, write a SQL Select statement to retrieve exactly the information you want from the database.

This single tab provides a simple interface for creating Recordsets from an incredibly broad variety of sources.

After you specify how the data is to be retrieved, the Recordset, by default, automatically retrieves the data it needs when this page is first displayed. With the data identified and retrieved, you are ready to display it to the world.

Using Data-Bound DTCs to Display and Update Data

In Chapter 10, I describe how to add Design-Time Controls to your page, create events, call methods, and set properties. If you want to review any of those topics, that's the place to look.

In this section, I show you how to use those same DTCs along with the Recordset DTC to display and update data from a database.

Displaying database data

To display data from a Recordset using DTCs:

1. **Create a Data Connection to the appropriate database.**

2. **Drop a Recordset DTC on your page and set its properties so that it retrieves data from one or more tables in the database.**

   See the last section for details about how to do this.

3. **Begin dropping Textbox DTCs on your page for each of the columns in the Recordset, and type text beside them so the user will know what they're seeing (see Figure 13-3).**

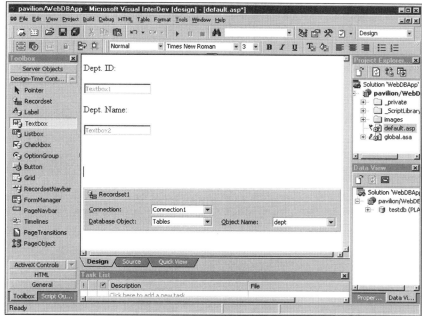

Figure 13-3:
Dropping
Textboxes
on the page
in Design
view.

4. **Right-click the first Textbox DTC and choose Properties from the pop-up menu.**

   The Textbox Properties dialog box appears (see Figure 13-4).

5. **Select the name of your Recordset DTC from the Recordset drop-down list box in the Data group box.**

6. **Select the field that you want this particular Textbox to show from the Field drop-down list box in the Data group box.**

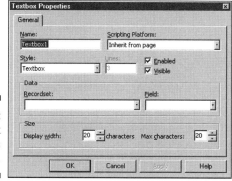

Figure 13-4:
The Textbox
Properties
dialog box.

7. **Check to make sure the Display width and Max characters are appropriate for that field.**

8. **Click OK.**

9. **Repeat this process starting at Step 4 for each Textbox on your page until all the fields you want to display from the Recordset are each assigned to a Textbox.**

10. **Finally, add a RecordsetNavbar to your page (see Figure 13-5).**

11. **Right-click the RecordsetNavbar and choose Properties from the pop-up menu.**

    The RecordsetNavbar Properties dialog box appears (see Figure 13-6).

12. **Click the Recordset drop-down list box and choose the same Recordset you've chosen for all the rest of the DTCs.**

13. **Click OK.**

Now, if you run the page, you see data appear in the Textboxes when the page first appears (see Figure 13-7).

And you can click the First, Previous, Next, and Last buttons on the RecordsetNavbar to move to other records in the Recordset.

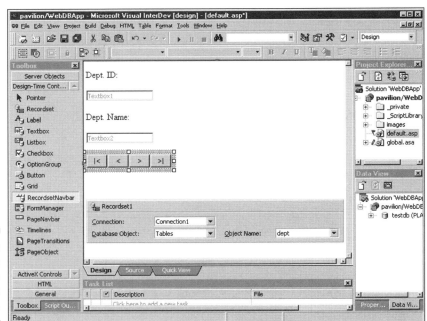

Figure 13-5:
Add a
Recordset-
Navbar to
your page.

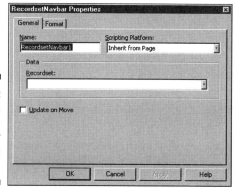

Figure 13-6:
The
Recordset-
Navbar
Properties
dialog box.

Figure 13-7:
Data
appears
when the
page first
comes up.

When you use SOM, all the intelligence for retrieving and handling the rows from the database is handled in the Recordset DTC. Then, you can use the normal DTC controls, including the Textbox as well as all the other DTCs you're familiar with to display the data. The RecordsetNavbar just provides a convenient way to navigate the data.

Using Visual InterDev, displaying data in a Web page is just that easy!

Updating database data

To make your data updatable:

1. **Add a button to your page. Set the button's Caption to Update and the name to btnUpdate.**

   (For information on adding DTCs to your page and setting their properties, see Chapter 10.)

2. **Write a script for the click event that includes the following code:**

   ```
   Recordset1.updateRecord
   ```

Replace Recordset1 with your Recordset DTCs name, if the name is different.

When you run the application, you can make changes to the data and click the Update button to save changes to the database.

You can easily update capabilities that happen automatically to your page.

To make your page automatically updatable:

1. **Right-click the Recordset Navbar.**

2. **Choose Properties from the pop-up menu.**

   The RecordsetNavbar Properties dialog box appears (see Figure 13-8).

3. **Click to select the Update on Move check box.**

4. **Click OK.**

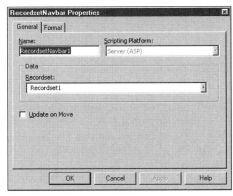

Figure 13-8:
The Recordset-Navbar Properties dialog box.

Sorry, no batch updates . . .

Is there a way you can make changes to two or more records and then send all the updates at once to the database? Unfortunately the answer is *no* — not using the Scripting Object Model and Design-Time Controls. You can only work with and update one record at a time.

For some applications, this may be a significant problem. I'm certain that Microsoft will be working hard to overcome this limitation in the next release of Visual InterDev.

Now when you run your application again, you can make changes to the data, go to the next row, and then come back, and you'll notice that the changes have been saved. The user doesn't even need to press a button! Every time you click the RecordsetNavbar to move to a different row, the current row is updated in the database first.

You can decide whether to use the Update button or the automatic update feature (or both) in your application. It all depends on how you want to design your user interface.

That's all there is to updating data in a database! No tracking changes or manually creating complex SQL Update statements. All that is done for you.

Adding records

To add rows, there are three steps:

1. **Insert a new row into the Recordset.**
2. **Fill the inserted row with data.**
3. **Update the database with by adding the new row and its data to the table.**

To change your application so that it can add new rows:

1. **Add a button to your page. Set the button's caption to Add and its name to btnAdd.**

   (For information on adding DTCs to your page and setting their properties, see Chapter 10.)

2. **Add the following code for the button's Click event.**

   ```
   Recordset1.addRecord
   ```

Replace `Recordset1` with your Recordset DTCs name, if the name is different.

Now when the user runs the application and clicks Add, all the fields are cleared. This allows them to enter data for the new record. Then the user can update the database by clicking the Update button or clicking to move to a different record (depending on which update method you chose).

Deleting records

Deleting records is even easier. All the user has to do is go to the row she wants to delete and tell the Recordset to delete it. You make that possible by adding — you guessed it — a Delete button.

To change your application so that it can delete rows:

1. **Add a button to your page. Set the button's caption to Delete and its name to btnDelete.**

   (For information on adding DTCs to your page and setting their properties, see Chapter 10.)

2. **Add the following code for the button's Click event:**

   ```
   Recordset1.deleteRecord
   ```

Don't forget to replace `Recordset1` with your Recordset DTCs name, if the name is different.

Now the user navigates to the offending record, clicks the Delete button, and the record disappears!

Using the Grid to display data

The Textbox and other DTCs are great when you want to create data-entry pages where the user works with one record at a time. However, you may find times when you want to see the data for several records at once. That's where the Grid DTC comes in.

To display database records with the Grid DTC:

1. **Add a Recordset DTC to your page and set it so that it retrieves the data you want from the database.**

   (For information on adding DTCs to your page and setting their properties, see Chapter 10.)

Other Recordset methods

In this chapter, I show you some of the essential Recordset methods you need to create data-entry pages. But you can use lots more that can be really handy.

For example, if you want more control over the record navigation, you can use these commands instead of the RecordsetNavbar: moveFirst, movePrevious, moveNext, and moveLast.

And, if you want to access the value of the data in a Recordset, you can also do that from your script with this line:

```
Name: <%
    =rsCust.fields.getValue("name")
    %><p>
```

The fields object is a property of the Recordset object. And it has a method, getValue, that returns the value of a field in a Recordset if you pass the name of the field.

For more information on cool Recordset methods and properties, check out the Visual InterDev online Help at:

MSDN Library Visual Studio 6.0⇨ Visual InterDev Documentation⇨ Reference⇨Scripting Object Model⇨ Script Objects⇨Recordset Script Object

2. **Drag the Grid DTC from the Toolbox and drop it where you want it to appear on the page.**

3. **Right-click the Grid and choose Properties from the pop-up menu.**

   The Grid Properties dialog box appears.

4. **Set the Recordset to point to the Recordset DTC on your page.**

5. **Click the Navigation tab.**

6. **Click the Row Navigation check box.**

   This feature enables you to navigate to different rows as well as to page through the data.

7. **Click OK.**

Now when you run the application, the page displays many rows of data and allows you to move a selection bar to change which row is currently selected. You didn't need to add a RecordsetNavbar because the Grid has one built in.

This is a very handy way to look at the data. The other tabs of the Grid Properties dialog box give you a wide variety of options for displaying the grid. It's actually nothing more than an HTML table, and almost all the table options are configurable for this control.

Using the Grid with other DTCs

Only one downside to the Grid control exists. You can't edit the data in it. It's for viewing only. So what do you do if you want to be able to view multiple records at once and also edit them? You use the Grid in combination with the other DTCs.

To create a Grid entry/edit page:

1. **Add a Recordset DTC to your page and set it so that it retrieves the data you want from the database.**

   (For information on adding DTCs to your page and setting their properties, see Chapter 10.)

2. **Drag the Grid DTC to your page and set its Recordset property.**

3. **Add Textboxes and other DTCs to your page below the Grid — one DTC for each field retrieved. Set their properties to use the same Recordset as the Grid.**

4. **Create Add, Delete, and Update buttons with the appropriate script.**

   (For instructions on creating these buttons see "Using Data-Bound DTCs to Display and Update Data" earlier in this chapter.)

When you run this application and use the Grid buttons to change records, the information in the DTCs below the Grid are always in sync with the Grid. That's because both are using the same Recordset DTC. You can also edit data as well as add and delete records.

Creating Your Own Queries

In the Recordset Properties dialog box, you can easily retrieve an entire table's data. But you don't always want all the columns in the table. And sometimes, you want columns from two different tables to appear in the same Recordset.

The way to accomplish both of these goals — and gain a *lot* of flexibility in the data you retrieve — is to create a query or a SQL Select statement for your Recordset.

If you already know SQL, you can click the SQL Query radio button and just start typing in your Select statement (see Figure 13-9).

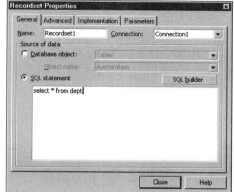

Figure 13-9:
Typing a
SQL Select
statement
for a
Recordset.

However, if you don't know SQL or if you could use some brushing up, the Query Builder was made for you!

By the way, the Query Builder works with both Access *and* SQL Server.

To access the Query Builder:

1. **Display the Properties dialog box for the Recordset.**

   (For information on adding DTCs to your page and setting their properties, see Chapter 10.)

2. **Click the SQL Statement radio button.**

3. **Click the Query Builder button.**

   The Query Builder appears (see Figure 13-10).

The Query Builder is a window that has four different panes. From top to bottom, they are:

✔ **The Diagram pane:** This pane shows a diagram of the tables (or views) that you want to retrieve data from. It looks a lot like a database diagram (which I discuss in Chapter 12).

✔ **The Grid pane:** In this pane, you can specify the criteria that limit the number of rows you get back. Here, you can tell Visual InterDev that you want to see only "Employees with a Salary greater than $30,000" or whose Position is "Manager."

✔ **The SQL pane:** This is where the actual SQL Select statement is created. Based on the information you enter in the previous two panes, this pane creates a Select statement. You can click here and modify the Select statement directly, if you want.

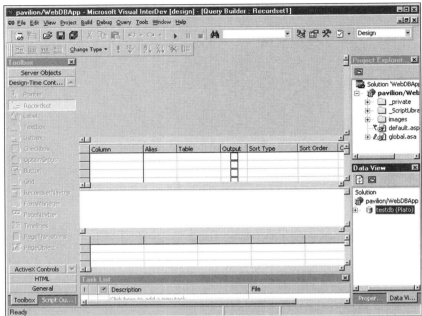

Figure 13-10:
The Query
Builder.

✔ **The Results pane:** This pane shows the results of the query. You can look at exactly what the query would retrieve right now. Seeing these results can help you make sure you've got all the information you need. If you like, you can edit the data in this pane and even add and delete records.

To create a query in the Query Builder:

1. **In the Data View window, open the Database icon and then click the Tables icon to view all the tables in the database you are connected to (see Figure 13-11).**

Figure 13-11:
The Data
View,
displaying
all the
tables in the
database.

2. Find the table or tables you want to retrieve data from. Drag those tables to the Diagram pane.

They appear as small windows listing all the columns in the table (see Figure 13-12). If foreign keys are defined, Visual InterDev automatically joins the tables using those foreign keys.

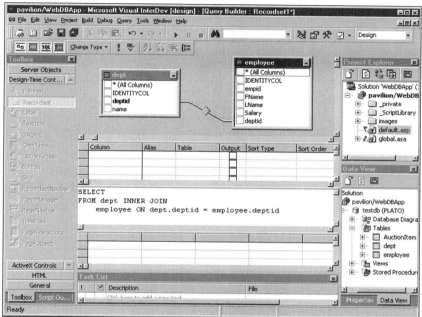

Figure 13-12:
The Diagram pane with tables in it.

3. Choose which columns you want to retrieve by clicking in the box beside the columns inside each table.

As you choose the columns, they appear in the Grid pane, along with their table and an indication that they should be output. In addition, you can see the Select statement in the SQL pane starting to take shape (see Figure 13-13).

4. Decide on your selection criteria.

Do you want to get all the records or just some part of them. What will determine which records you get and which you don't? Use this information to fill in the Criteria and Or columns of the Grid pane (you may have to scroll to the right to see these). For example, if you want only Employees with a Salary > $30,000, then scroll to find the Salary column, scroll over to the Criteria column, and type the following in the cell:

```
> 30000
```

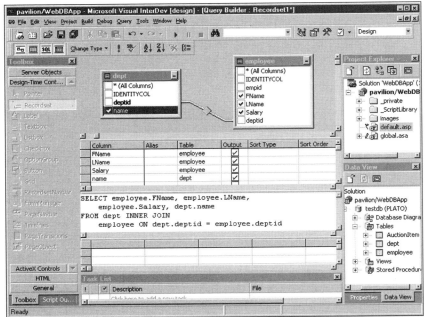

Figure 13-13: The Grid and SQL pane after columns have been added.

```
SELECT employee.FName, employee.LName,
       employee.Salary, dept.name
FROM dept INNER JOIN
     employee ON dept.deptid = employee.deptid
```

5. **Add all the criteria you want for all the columns.**

   Use the Or column to add additional criteria for the same field.

6. **Decide if and how you want to sort the records coming back. Go to the column you want to sort on, choose Ascending or Descending for the Sort Type, and then choose 1 for the Sort Order.**

   You can choose as many columns as you like to sort on, but the number in Sort Order determines which takes priority. For example, if you sort on State with a Sort Order of 1 and City with a Sort Order of 2, all the states are put in alphabetical order and then, within each state, all the cities are put in alphabetical order. (See Figure 13-14.)

7. **Click the Check SQL button on the Query toolbar.**

   Checking the SQL determines if your SQL is valid. Visual InterDev displays a message box informing you of the results (see Figure 13-15).

8. **Click the Run Query button on the Query toolbar.**

   Running the query actually executes your query and displays the results in the Results pane (see Figure 13-16).

9. **Check your results and make any changes necessary to fine-tune your query.**

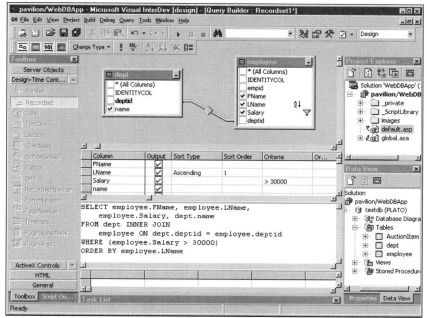

Figure 13-14:
Filling in the Criteria and Sort options.

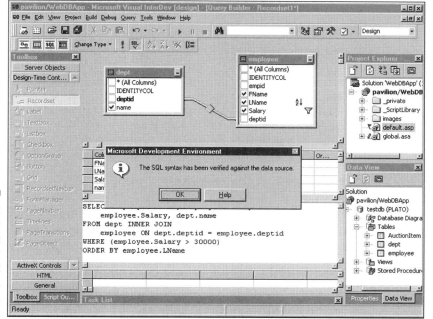

Figure 13-15:
A message box informing you that your SQL is valid.

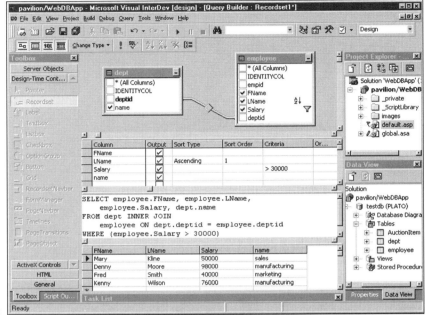

Figure 13-16:
The records
retrieved
are
displayed in
the Results
pane.

10. **Click the Save button in the Standard toolbar.**

11. **Close this window.**

    Your query now appears in the Recordset.

Even if you already know SQL, you may prefer to use the Query Builder. It is convenient, and it doesn't require you to remember table and column names off the top of your head. And, because the Select statement is always editable in the SQL pane, you can make it as complex as you like.

Using the FormManager

The FormManager is a very handy tool for easily creating data entry forms that have a distinct way of interacting with the user. It provides an alternative to coding events throughout the form to get it to act just as you want it to.

The best way to begin to see the power of the FormManager is through an example. So let me describe a situation for you to show you how to create a form that meets the requirements using only the FormManager — no supporting script.

How the View/Edit mode form works

By default, the text boxes that display your data are editable as the user browses through the records. Suppose that you don't want the text boxes to be editable all the time. Perhaps the user is in a hectic environment and you don't want to chance someone accidentally hitting the keyboard at the wrong time and entering garbage into a text box.

Instead, you'd like to disable the text boxes. This way, the user is free to browse through the data and view it all he wants. But if he wants to edit the data, he must specifically click an Edit button. Clicking the Edit button puts the user in Edit mode, enables all the text fields, and allows the user to type text to change the current record. Then when he clicks to go to another record, the current record is saved, and the user goes back into view-only mode.

This example illustrates how modes can be used to create forms that work in a distinctive way. In short, the FormManager enables you to easily:

- ✔ Create modes
- ✔ Determine what happens when you enter the mode
- ✔ Determine when you leave the mode
- ✔ Identify all the reasons you might move from one mode to another

Creating the View/Edit mode form

Here are the steps for creating a form like the one I describe in the previous section using the FormManager. You can use whatever database or table you want, but the fewer the columns, the quicker it goes.

First, create the form:

1. **Create a data connection and drop a Recordset on your form that retrieves data from a table.**

   (See "The Linchpin: The Recordset DTC" earlier in this chapter for a description of how this is done.)

2. **Drop Textbox DTCs for each of the columns, and set their properties to point to the Recordset.**

3. **Add a RecordsetNavbar and set it to work with the Recordset.**

4. **Finally, add a button. Name it** `btnEdit` **and set the Caption to** `Edit`.

   Don't bother writing any script for it at all. If you run the application now, it should display the data and allow you to navigate to different records.

5. Now add a FormManager.

It appears in Design and Source view as a simple bar. At run time, it won't appear at all (like the Recordset DTC). The final form should look something like Figure 13-17.

Now that all the pieces are in place, you are ready to set up the FormManager to do the special work of making the View and Edit modes a reality.

To create the View mode:

1. Right-click the FormManager and choose Properties from the pop-up menu.

The FormManager Properties window appears (see Figure 13-18).

2. In New Mode, type View **and click the > button.**

Default Mode is automatically set to View. Default Mode determines what mode this form will be in when the page is first displayed.

Now look at the grid at the bottom labeled `Actions Performed For Mode`. This is a list of things that you can do (either calling methods or setting properties) when the user first enters this mode.

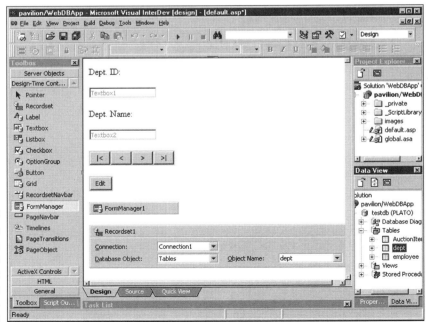

Figure 13-17:
The
complete
form in
Design
view.

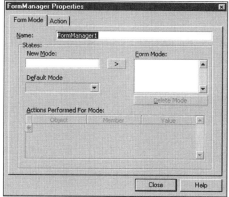

Figure 13-18:
The
FormManager
Properties
window.

To add actions to the View mode:

1. **Click in the first cell and use the drop-down button to find the first text box on your form. Choose it.**

2. **In the next cell, choose the `disabled` property.**

3. **In the last cell in the row, select what's there and type** true.

   This disables that text box whenever you enter View mode (see Figure 13-19).

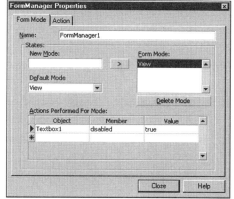

Figure 13-19:
The View
mode's first
action is
filled in.

4. **Continue on the second row with the next text box, setting its disabled property to** true.

5. **Keep going until all your text boxes are disabled.**

6. **Finally, set the** `btnEdit` **button's disabled property to** `false` **(see Figure 13-20).**

You want the Edit button to be enabled so that the user can click it to go into Edit mode.

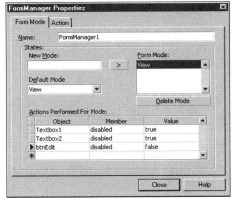

Figure 13-20:
All the
actions are
filled in for
View mode.

That's it. You've defined View mode. Now on to Edit mode.

To create Edit mode:

1. **In New Mode type** Edit **and click the > button.**

2. **Go to the first line of the Actions Performed For Mode grid and select the first text box. In the next cell, choose the** `disabled` **property. In the final cell, type** `false`.

You want to enable the textbox so that the user can change the data in Edit mode.

3. **Add all your text boxes to the grid, setting their** `disabled` **property to** `false`.

4. **Finally, set the** `btnEdit` **button's disabled property to** `true` **(see Figure 13-21).**

It doesn't make sense to let the user click the Edit button when she's already in Edit mode.

Now Edit mode is complete! The FormManager knows what modes you want and what to do when it enters those modes.

In the Form Mode list box, you can click the two modes to see the Actions Performed For Mode grid change. It always shows the actions for the currently selected mode.

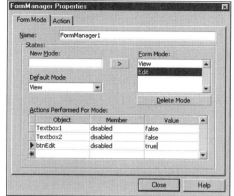

Figure 13-21:
All the actions are filled in for Edit mode.

You have just a couple of things left to specify:

- ✔ What will cause the form to change from one mode to the next?
- ✔ Do you want to do anything when before switching modes?

You can resolve both of those questions by clicking the Action tab of the FormManager's property dialog box (see Figure 13-22).

The grid at the top answers the first question. It assumes that an event always triggers a mode change. So you first enter the current mode, and then the object and event that cause the change and finally the new mode.

How should this one work? You know that it will come up initially in View mode, because that is already the default. How should the user get from View into Edit mode? The button!

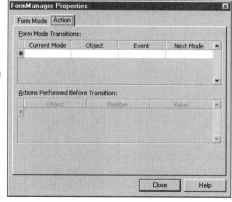

Figure 13-22:
The Action tab of the Form-Manager's Property dialog box.

To create the mode transition from View to Edit:

1. **Enter** View **in the first cell.**

2. **Choose** btnEdit **for the second cell.**

3. **Select** onclick **for the third cell.**

4. **Finally, enter** Edit **for** Next Mode **(see Figure 13-23).**

Now the FormManager knows to switch from View to Edit when the user has to click the Edit button.

But what does the user have to do to get back to View mode? He can click any of the buttons on the RecordsetNavbar. It turns out that each of the buttons on that control produces a different event, so you have to enter a row in the top grid for each one.

To create the mode transition from Edit to View:

1. **Set the** Current Mode **to** Edit.

2. **Set** Next Mode **to** View.

3. **Set the** Object **to** RecordsetNavbar1.

4. **Set the** Event **to** onfirstclick.

5. **Enter the next row exactly like the first except that the** Event **is** onlastclick.

6. **Enter the third and fourth row the same way except that the events should be** onlastclick **and** onnextclick **(see Figure 13-24).**

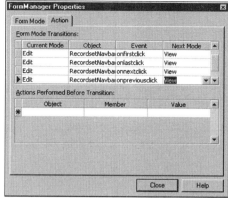

Figure 13-24:
All the
mode
transitions
are
complete.

That does it for the mode transitions. The user goes into Edit mode by clicking the Edit button and goes into the View mode by clicking one of the buttons on the RecordsetNavbar.

Only one more thing is left to specify. When the user is about to switch modes, you may want to specify that certain actions are executed before the mode changes. That's what the Actions Performed Before Transition grid is for at the bottom of the Action tab. This grid works exactly like the Actions Performed For Mode grid at the bottom of the Form Mode tab. You specify either

- ✔ The object and method to call
- ✔ The object, property, and value to set the property

In this form, you need to update the database when the user is in Edit mode and is getting ready to switch back to View mode.

To add the Actions Performed Before Transition for this form:

1. **Click the first Edit to View transition in the Form Mode Transitions grid at the top of the dialog box.**

   That should be the second line in the grid, because the first line defines the View to Edit transition (see Figure 13-25).

2. **Select the Recordset object in the first cell of the Actions Performed Before Transition grid.**

3. **In the second cell, choose the** updateRecord **method.**

   This method tells the FormManager to call the updateRecord method of the Recordset before transitioning from Edit mode back to View mode.

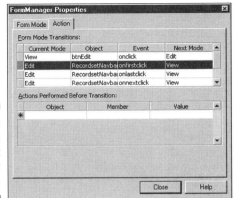

Figure 13-25:
Select the
first Edit
to View
transition.

4. **Now click the second Edit to View transition in the top grid.**

   Look in the third line this time.

5. **Choose the Recordset object and the `updateRecord` method here, too.**

6. **Click the third and fourth transitions and add the Recordset and `updateRecord` method for each of those.**

Whew! It's done. You have to become accustomed to a lot of mouse clicks and controls in the dialog box, but I think that after you're used to it, you'll find the FormManager a very intuitive way to set up your form.

And what's the alternative? If you were to create this effect using script, it would mean that you'd have to write small scripts in quite a number of different events all over the page. It's much easier to go to one place, define your modes, and let the FormManager work out the details. It's also a lot easier to maintain in the future!

Try running your application. It should work just as advertised. If you have any trouble, go back over the previous directions and make sure you followed them to a T!

Chapter 14

Billy-Bob's Internet Auction Application

*W*elcome to Billy-Bob's Internet Auction house. Get yourself a number, sit back, and get ready for some serious bidding!

Internet auctions have raised quite a stir in the last year or two — and for good reason. They allow anyone to put their stuff up for sale, and they allow people to choose from a huge variety of items. Online auctions enable you to easily compare prices on common items and also ferret out those unique collectibles. And most online auctions charge only a small fee for posting and nothing at all for bidding and buying. This is one area where online commerce, Internet-style, is already flourishing.

With that in mind, I created a real-world sample application in Visual InterDev to show you how it's done. Billy-Bob's Internet Auction is a fully functioning Internet auction that you can customize with your own categories and enhancements and then add it to your own Web site. There's nothing like a free auction to attract visitors and to keep them coming back regularly!

The Concept: An Internet Auction

As with any development project, a good application begins with a good design. Before you start creating pages, think about your application and decide what the best user interface for it would look like. And then begin thinking about how you could create it.

To get ideas, it's always a great idea to take a quick trip out to the Web and see how others are doing it. Here are a couple of great auction sites you can use as a guide as you customize this application to your use:

```
www.ebay.com
www.onsale.com
```

Of course, the application I include with this book is modest in comparison to those auction sites that have been online and making money for many months now.

However, I do provide all the basics so that you could use the Internet Auction as a foundation for your own auction or other Web commerce site. Here are the basic requirements I sketched out before I began:

- ✔ The site must allow visitors to enter new auctions, including item name, description, category, starting bid, and the seller's e-mail address. The seller must also choose whether she wants her auction to end in three days or seven days.

- ✔ The auction must provide listings of items by category. The user can choose an item from the list to see all the details about an item, and then choose to bid on the item.

- ✔ The application should accept new bids along with the bidder's e-mail address. Bids must be at least $1 higher than the current bid price. All bids are in whole dollar amounts.

- ✔ A seller who has one or more auctions must have a page that shows all his auctions — both those that are current and those that have ended. For those that have ended, the seller must be able to see the buyer's e-mail address and final bid so that arrangements for payment and shipment can be made.

My final application meets all these goals. You can choose to add many other features, of course. Look for suggested enhancements in the section titled "Ways to Make It Better" at the end of this chapter.

Designing the Application

When you're creating a Web application that makes use of a database, you always have two different sides to your design:

- ✔ **Front-end design:** This involves deciding what pages will make up your application, what each of them will do, and how you will navigate to them.

✔ **Back-end design:** You determine exactly what data needs to be stored and what tables you'll need to store it.

I discuss each of these sides separately for this project.

Front-end design: Designing the Web site

The first thing to do is decide what you want your Web site to do. In this case, I can imagine three primary scenarios:

✔ A person wants to browse through the current auctions by category

✔ A person wants to start their own auction of an item

✔ A person who has one or more auctions wants to see the status of those auctions

So from the Home page, I need at least three links to enable people to access these three processes.

But you probably will want to break it down further. You need to figure out exactly which pages you need for this project. When you get to this stage, it's a good idea to turn to the site diagram creator that's built into Visual InterDev. (See Chapter 5 for more information.) Even if you don't plan to use layouts or the PageNavbar to provide automatic links to your pages, a site diagram can be a great place to begin your planning process for a project.

For my example Internet Auction, I envisioned seven pages organized in a diagram like Figure 14-1.

You can see the three primary branches off the main page representing the three primary processes I mentioned previously. You can also see more detail within each of the processes. Here's a quick overview of how I foresaw each page working:

✔ **Home:** This opening page introduces the site and provides easy access to all the categories and provides the ability to add an auction and to review current and ended auctions.

✔ **AddAuction:** The user enters all the information about a new auction and submits it using this page.

✔ **CatList:** This page shows a list of all the current auctions in a particular category. The page accepts a parameter on the URL line and uses that parameter to determine which category of auctions to display. The user can then click any of the items in the list to see the detail for that item.

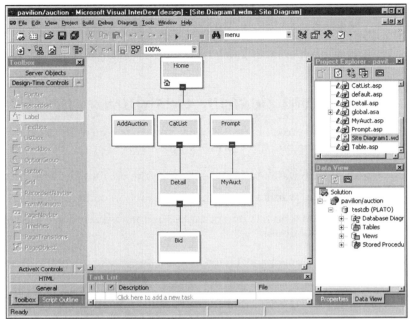

Figure 14-1:
The site
diagram for
the Internet
Auction.

✔ **Detail:** All the detail information for one specific item appears on this page. The page is passed the item number as a parameter on the URL line and retrieves only the item requested. It also contains a link to allow the user to bid on the item.

✔ **Bid:** This page shows the important details of the item along with the current bid price. The user can enter his e-mail address and a new bid. The page checks to be sure the new bid is higher than the old bid.

✔ **Prompt:** This page asks the user for her e-mail address. It then passes this address to the MyAuction page.

✔ **MyAuct:** This page takes the e-mail address entered on the Prompt page and searches for all auctions placed by that person. It lists the current auctions in one list and the closed ones in another list.

After I roughed out this detail, I moved on to database concerns.

Back-end design: Designing the database

By doing the front-end design, I figured out what pages I'm going to need and how they'll all connect together. Next, I needed to do the back-end design to figure out exactly what data I wanted to store and how to store it.

I decided to store the information in a Microsoft SQL Server database. If you don't have SQL Server, you won't be able to run this example as it is.

You can probably modify my Internet Auction fairly easily to work with Microsoft Access or any other database. The only sticking point may be how those other programs handle dates and times.

As for the data I needed to store, I ended up settling on this list:

- **Item Number:** Each item must have a unique number so that I can keep track of each item.

- **Name:** Each item also needs a name. The name can also include several words of description. This name will appear in the list of items and will make the user want to click it to get more detail.

- **Description:** I need to include a detailed description of the item with everything a potential buyer would want to know.

- **Category:** All items must be organized into specific categories for this site: Computers, Collectibles, Antiques, Jewelry, Furniture, or Other.

- **Seller Email:** I must know the e-mail address of the person who put the item up for bid.

- **Placed Date and Time:** I need to keep track of the date and time the item was put up for bid. Microsoft SQL Server has a `datetime` data type that stores both a date and a time in the same field.

- **Start Bid:** I need to know the amount that the seller chose to start the bidding.

- **Buyer Email:** When someone makes a bid on the item, his e-mail address is stored here.

- **Current Bid:** When someone makes a bid on the item, their bid goes here.

- **Expire Date and Time:** I need to determine when the auction will end. (I decided to offer only three and seven day auctions. I could have chosen to simply store how long the auction is and calculate the Placed Date and Time when the auction should end. But by keeping a separate date and time, I made it easier to add additional lengths of time in the future or even to allow the seller to choose whatever length she wants. Keeping a separate date also avoids the need to do calculations every time I need the end date.)

I decided to store all these fields in one table: the Auction Item table. As long as the functionality is simple, one table serves just fine. See "Ways to Make It Better" at the end of this chapter for ideas on extending the table's capabilities.

Notice that I decided *not* to keep a bidding history. With the structure I have now, I have no way of knowing who all the bidders were or how much they bid after an auction is closed. I keep track of only the last bidder and his bid. I do, however, separately keep track of the starting bid. You can decide to keep a bidding history, if you want.

Creating the Database Table

After I figured out what columns I needed and what tables the columns will be in, I created the structures in the database.

First, I created a Database Connection and a DSN to connection to an appropriate database in SQL Server. (See Chapter 12 for more information on doing this.)

Next I created a database diagram and created the table. (See Chapter 12 for more information.) Figure 14-2 shows you what the final table should look like in the diagram.

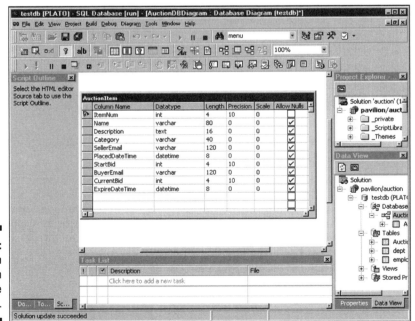

Figure 14-2:
The Auction Item table in a Database Diagram.

You should be able to see all the data types for the various fields you need to specify in Figure 14-2. The only thing you can't see in the figure is the ItemNum column. It should have the Identity column checked. With this column checked, Identity Seed and Identity Increment are automatically set to 1. This setting causes the database to automatically generate unique values for ItemNum whenever a new row is added.

Setting Up Billy-Bob's Home Page: Default.asp

The first thing Billy-Bob's Internet Auction needs is a page to greet the user, tell them what they've just stumbled into, and provide a few links to help them get around. Conveniently enough, Default.asp does just that (see Figure 14-3).

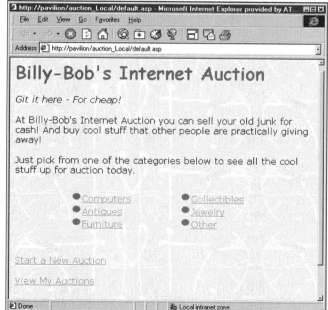

Figure 14-3:
The Home page for Billy-Bob's Auction.

You won't find anything tricky on this page — it's just headers, text, and a table to make two bulleted lists sit side-by-side (see Figure 14-4).

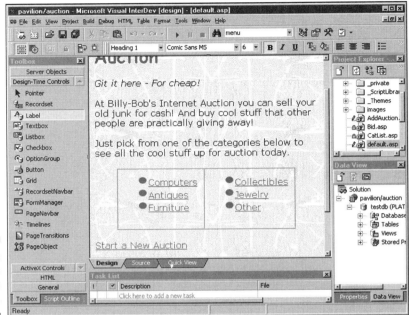

Figure 14-4:
Default.asp
in the
editor.

When I first created this page (and all the rest of the pages, for that matter), I didn't worry about the background, text fonts, colors, or any of that. I tagged text as different heading levels or bulleted or normal, but I didn't worry about any of the fancy stuff. At the end, I added a theme to the entire project that took care of all that for me!

Adding a New Auction: AddAuction.asp

An auction site wouldn't be much good if you couldn't add new auctions, so in this section, I discuss the AddAuction.asp page (see Figure 14-5).

This page includes a Recordset named rsAuctionItems that retrieves all the columns in the AuctionItem table.

The Design-Time Controls

Five data-bound Design-Time Controls are tied to the rsAuctionItems Recordset. These controls give the user a place to enter information that will be added as part of the newly inserted row.

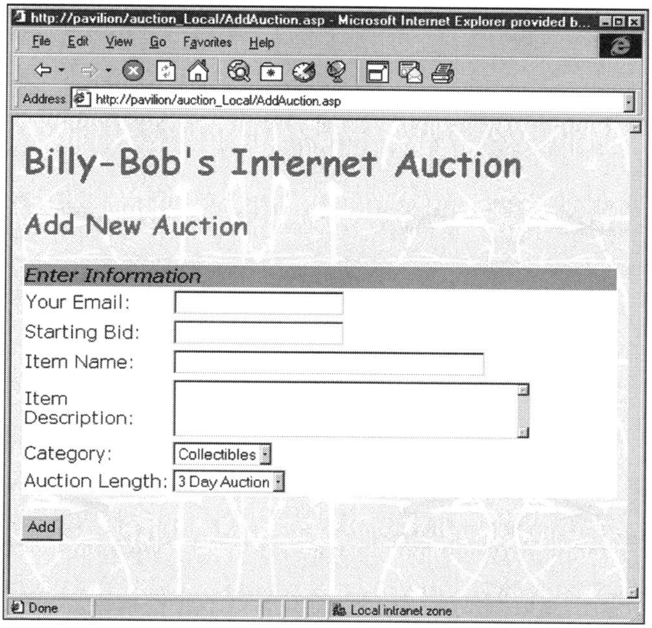

Figure 14-5:
The add auction page.

In addition to the five data-bound Design-Time Controls, I used one non-data-bound Design-Time Control: the last drop-down list box in which the user enters the auction length. You find out later in this chapter (in the section titled "The OnBeforeUpdate subroutine") how I used this control to fill in information in the AuctionItem table in a more indirect way.

The FormManager

I also include a FormManager on the AddAuction.asp page (see Chapter 9). The FormManager enables you to set up certain modes and determine what should happen when you enter and leave those different modes of operation. For example, you may have an Edit mode that allows you to edit existing rows and an Add mode that allows you to add new rows.

In this example, I don't need this page to be capable of handling multiple modes or anything nearly that complex. But I do need to do one tricky thing — I need the Recordset to automatically add a row and allow the user to enter the information to that row when she first comes to this page. This is, after all, an *add auction* page! Fortunately, the FormManager offers an easy way to make this happen. Figure 14-6 shows the properties for the FormManager on this page.

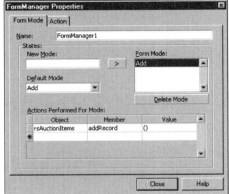

Figure 14-6:
The
FormManager
Properties
dialog box.

Only one mode is left: Add. The key is that I set the Add mode as the *default* mode, which means the page is put into this mode when the page first appears. And because of that, the *Actions Performed For Mode* listed at the bottom happen when the page first begins. A row is added with the AddRecord command. This is a sneaky and effective way of causing something to happen with the Recordset when the page is first loaded.

Filling in the information

After a row is added, the user can then type in the information that he wants for SellerEmail, StartingBid, Name, and Description.

For Category, the user must choose one of the options from the drop-down list box or simply go with the default value (Computers). Using a non-editable drop-down list box is a great way to ensure that the user doesn't enter invalid data.

Finally, the user must choose how long the auction will be online. The choices in the drop-down list box are three days and five days.

When the user is happy with what he typed in, he can click the Add button to finish the process of adding this row to the database.

Clicking the Add button

Clicking the Add button doesn't immediately update the database. As much as possible, you should always check data entered by a user to make sure it makes sense.

The server-side ASP code for the Add button's Click event is in Listing 14-1.

Listing 14-1   The ASP code for the Add button's Click event

```
Sub btnAdd_onclick()
if Trim(txtName.value) = "" Or _
   Trim(txtEmail.value) = "" Or _
   Trim(txtStartingBid.value) = "" Or _
   Trim(txtDescription.value) = "" then
      lblPrompt.setCaption(_
        "** Please Enter All Information **")
elseif not IsNumeric(txtStartingBid.value) then
   lblPrompt.setCaption(_
      "** Please Enter A Number For Starting Bid **")
elseif CInt(txtStartingBid.value) < 1 then
   lblPrompt.setCaption(_
      "** Starting Bid Must Be $1 Or Greater **")
else
   rsAuctionItems.updateRecord
   thisPage.navigateURL "default.asp"
end if
End Sub
```

This code shows you that the application first checks to see that the user has filled in the name, e-mail, starting bid, and description edit boxes. If they're not filled in, the prompt asks the user to please enter all information.

What's lblPrompt? Good question. It's the label that appears in the header of the table that initially says Enter Information. This text is replaced with one of the error messages in the If...Then structure shown in Listing 14-1 if something goes wrong (see Figure 14-7).

Including a label on your page to convey status or error information is a good idea. Because you can't do a message box as you can do in other development environments, a label can offer a nice replacement.

Back to the listing. If all the user entered was the necessary information, the application next checks to see if what was entered for the Starting Bid was, in fact, a number. If the user entered text there, the application lets him know that's a problem. The IsNumeric function does the trick.

Finally, if the Starting Bid is numeric, then I still have to test to make sure that it is greater than $1. Because I'm using the CInt function, fractional amounts (such as $0.99) are rounded up to $1 and accepted.

Finally, if everything is as it should be, the Recordset is updated and the user is sent back to the Home page.

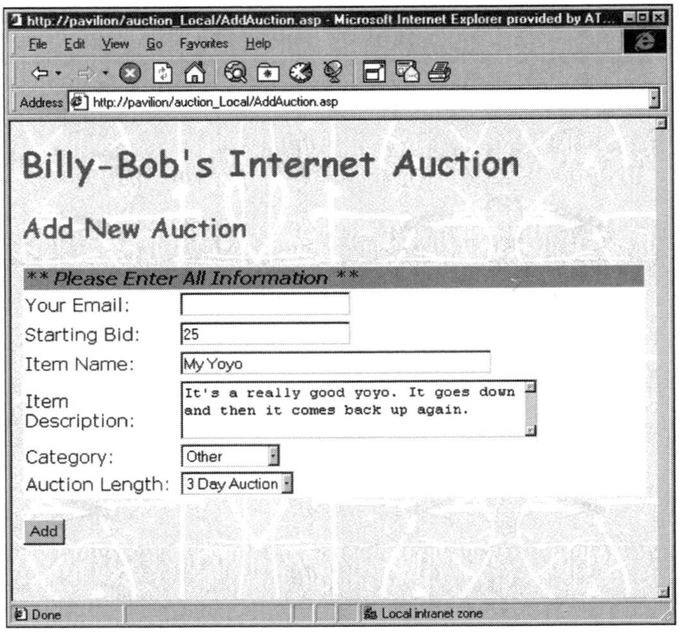

Figure 14-7:
The
lblPrompt
displays
an error
message.

The OnBeforeUpdate subroutine

One more important event gets triggered before the entered information is shipped off to the database: the OnBeforeUpdate event of the Recordset itself. I put code here that fills in the rest of the information in the row that isn't directly filled in by the user (see Listing 14-2).

Listing 14-2 The subroutine executed when the OnBeforeUpdate event of the Recordset is triggered

```
Sub rsAuctionItems_onbeforeupdate()
   rsAuctionItems.fields.setValue "BuyerEmail", _
      txtEmail.value
   rsAuctionItems.fields.setValue "CurrentBid", _
      txtStartingBid.value
   rsAuctionItems.fields.setValue "PlacedDateTime", Now
   rsAuctionItems.fields.setValue "ExpireDateTime", _
      DateAdd("d",CInt(lbxLength.getValue()),Now)
End Sub
```

You can use the `setValue` method of the `fields` object, which is a part of the Recordset object, to *manually* set the value of columns in a Recordset. This feature gives you the opportunity to change user input or calculate information based on user input before placing the final information in the Recordset and sending it off to the database.

Because no bid has been given yet, the Seller Email and Starting Bid values are dropped into the Buyer Email and Current Bid. The seller, by setting the starting bid, *is* the one who kicks off the bidding, after all.

The `PlacedDateTime` is filled in with the current date and time returned from the VBScript `Now` function. And the VBScript `DateAdd` function is used to calculate a date and time that is either three or five days after now and puts the result in `ExpireDateTime`. The list box `lbxLength` returns 3 or 5 as its values, so that value can be converted to an integer and used in the `DateAdd` function to add that number of days ("d") to `Now`.

You could easily modify the drop-down list box and these lines of code to allow the user much more flexibility in determining how long the auction goes for, if you want.

Finally, after this routine ends, all the necessary data is filled in satisfactorily, and the data is shipped off to the database and added to the AuctionItem table. It should, then, immediately appear in the listing of items in its category.

Displaying a List of Auctions by Category: CatList.asp

The Category List page (CatList.asp) is probably the page that will receive the most hits in the whole application. On this page, people browse through the dozens or hundreds of items in your auction by category (see Figure 14-8).

Notice that this *same* page is used to display items in the Computer category as well as the items in the Antique category. In fact, all the categories are displayed using only this page. Why did I give one page so many hats? Because it's a smart page!

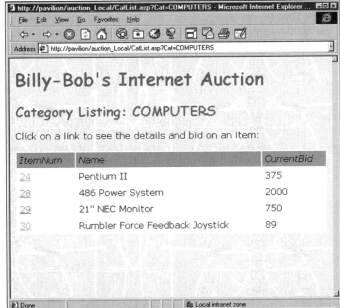

Figure 14-8:
The
Category
List page in
action.

Passing and receiving the category

Here's how it works. If you look back at the links on default.asp (see the section titled "Billy-Bob's Home Page: Default.asp" earlier in this chapter), you notice that the links that take the user to listings of each of the categories look something like this in the Source tab:

```
<A href="CatList.asp?Cat=COMPUTERS">Computers</A>
<A href="CatList.asp?Cat=ANTIQUES">Antiques</A>
<A href="CatList.asp?Cat=FURNITURE">Furniture</A>
```

The href does point to the CatList.asp page, but it adds something more. A URL parameter is passed after the ?. Cat is set equal to whatever category should be displayed.

Then that category can be referenced in CatList.asp like this:

```
<H2>Category Listing: <%=Request.QueryString("Cat")%></H2>
```

Request.QueryString provides easy access to the information passed from the other page.

Using a parameter with a Recordset

But in order to actually display only the rows that are in that category, you have to do more than simply pass the category to the page. You have to change how the query in the Recordset works. The easiest way to do this is to use a parameter in your Recordset.

The Recordset on this page uses this SQL statement:

```
SELECT * FROM AuctionItem
WHERE (Category = ?) AND
    (ExpireDateTime > GETDATE())
```

The WHERE clause is the place where the correct rows are selected and the rest are left behind. Ignore the second part — the part after the AND — for now. I discuss it in the next section.

Take a look at the first part after WHERE: Category = ?. You can include one or more ?s in your query when you want to replace them with parameters that are passed to the Recordset when the page is displayed. In this case, there is one parameter, and it will be used to determine which category is displayed.

There's only one question left to answer: How do you pass the parameter to the Recordset at run time?

```
Sub rsAuctionItemList_onbeforeopen()
rsAuctionItemList.setParameter 0,Request.QueryString("Cat")
End Sub
```

The OnBeforeOpen Recordset event happens immediately before the query is executed. This is the perfect place to tell the Recordset what to use to fill in any question marks in its Select statement. And the method to do that is the Recordset's setParameter. The first argument is which parameter you are passing. Because it starts counting at 0, you are passing the first parameter. The second argument is the value you want to pass. In this case, it's the category that was passed to this page.

Showing only the open auctions

There's only one more hitch with the query. You don't want to show *all* the auction items in the specific category. You want to show only the ones that are open. If the auction has already gone past its three or five days, then the auction is closed, and no more bidding is allowed. So those items shouldn't appear.

That's what the second part of the Select statement's WHERE clause is about:

```
SELECT * FROM AuctionItem
WHERE (Category = ?) AND
    (ExpireDateTime > GETDATE())
```

GETDATE() is *not* a VBScript function. It is a function that is built into SQL Server, and it returns the current system date and time (much like the VBScript Now function). After you have the current date and time, you can compare it to the ExpireDateTime column to filter out the closed auctions.

Displaying the Recordset rows

After you've coaxed the Recordset into retrieving the right data, all you have to do is display it. My first thought was to use the Grid Design-Time Control. This is a great way to display Recordset information in a multiple-row format and still retain all control of how it looks.

There's just one problem. You want the user to be able to click an item in the list to bring up a page with details about that item. To do that, a link must be associated with each row. You can't do that using the Grid.

So you're back to the drawing board. The only way to do it is to make your own grid that does have the ability to include links for each row. I created a subroutine to do this and included it in a separate file called Table.asp.

If you look near the top of CatList.asp, you see a line that looks like this:

```
<!--#include file="Table.asp"-->
```

This line brings all of Table.asp into this page at the location where this line appears. This is a handy way of including common subroutines and functions that you may want to use in more than one page.

I discuss the Table.asp file and the lines of code in CatList.asp that call it in the next section.

Displaying a List of Rows in a Table: Table.asp

Table.asp is never displayed directly to the user. It is, however, included in two other pages in this application — CatList.asp and MyAuct.asp. Because I used the same subroutine in both places, I made the subroutine into a separate file and simply used #include (which I discuss in the previous section) to make this code a part of those pages. This puts the code in a single file so that later, if I need to make changes to it, I can make them in Table.asp, and all the pages that use it will begin including the new version. Doing this avoids the problem of having to update the same code in many different places.

Table.asp contains one subroutine: DispalyTable. The purpose of DisplayTable is to take a Recordset and display specified columns from Recordset in a reasonably nice looking table (see Figure 14-9). It also makes the first column of each row a hyperlink that will take the user to a page that displays the detail for the row clicked.

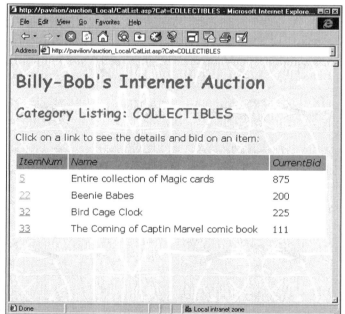

Figure 14-9:
The table
created by
DisplayTable.

The DisplayTable subroutine receives four arguments:

- ✓ **RecSet:** The Recordset object that contains the rows that are to be displayed in this table

- ✓ **Cols:** An *array* of strings that contain the name of the columns in the RecSet Recordset that are to be displayed in the table

  These names must correspond exactly to the column names in the Recordset.

    ✔ **NumCols:** The number of columns in the Cols array

    ✔ **DetailPage:** The name of the page that should be used to display the detail information when a row is clicked

There is one important assumption that is made when using this subroutine: the first column specified in the Cols array is assumed to be the primary key for the Recordset. This first column is always displayed as a link and will navigate to the DetailPage, passing the value of that column on the URL as a query string. This assumption works fine for this application as long as the first column passed in the Cols array is always the AuctionItem table's ItemNum.

How DisplayTable works

The `DisplayTable` subroutine held in Table.asp appears in Listing 14-3.

Listing 14-3   **The Table.asp DisplayTable subroutine**

```
<%
Sub DisplayTable(RecSet,Cols,NumCols,DetailPage)
Dim i

Response.Write "<TABLE bgColor=#ffffcc border=0 "
Response.Write "cellPadding=5 cellSpacing=2 width=100% >"
Response.Write "<TR>"
For i = 1 To NumCols
   Response.Write "<TD style='BACKGROUND-COLOR: #6699cc'>"
   Response.Write "<i>" & Cols(i) & "</i>"
   Response.Write "</TD>"
Next
Response.Write "</TR>"

RecSet.MoveFirst
Do While Not RecSet.EOF

   Response.Write "<TR>"
   For i = 1 To NumCols
      Response.Write "<TD>"
      if i = 1 then
         Response.Write "<a href=" & _
            DetailPage & "?ID=" & _
            RecSet.fields.getValue(Cols(i)) & ">" & _
            RecSet.fields.getValue(Cols(i)) & "</a>"
```

```
        else
            Response.Write RecSet.fields.getValue(Cols(i))
        end if
        Response.Write "</TD>"
    Next
    Response.Write "</TR>"

    RecSet.MoveNext
Loop

Response.Write "</TABLE>"
end sub
%>
```

I began creating this page by creating a table in the Design tab that looked the way I wanted my final table to look. I then switched over to the Source tab and started breaking the HTML apart and adding the VBScript loops around it.

The first loop cycles through all the column names in the Cols array and prints them in the cells of the row. In addition, a different background color is given to these cells. These are the column headers.

Next, a big `While` loop is created to loop through all the rows in the Recordset. Inside the `While` loop, a `For` loop runs through each of the columns for the current row.

The `If` statement inside the `For` determines if this is the first column. If it is, the item is turned into a link which references the DetailPage that was passed in, passing the value of that column to the page. Remember that the assumption is made that the first column is the primary key column and will be all the DetailPage needs to get the information for that record.

If this is not the first column, the data is displayed normally. The `MoveNext` at the end of the loop causes the next row to be processed. This continues until you are out of rows and `RecSet.EOF` becomes true.

How DisplayTable is called

When a page needs the functionality that `DisplayTable` provides, it must first include the Table.asp page using a line like this

```
<!--#include file="Table.asp"-->
```

Then in the location where the table should appear, the subroutine should be called. The following code shows, as an example, the call that appears in CatList.asp.

```
<%
Dim Cols(3)
Cols(1) = "ItemNum"
Cols(2) = "Name"
Cols(3) = "CurrentBid"
DisplayTable rsAuctionItemList,Cols,3,"Detail.asp"
%>
```

First, the Cols array is created. You can name it anything you like, but there's no point in getting fancy.

Then the elements of the array are filled in. The first one must be the table's primary key; the rest can be anything you want to display.

Finally, the subroutine is called, and the Recordset and the array are passed as arguments. The 3 in the third spot notifies the routine that there are three columns specified in the array. The "Detail.asp" string identifies what page should be executed when the user clicks one of the rows to see its detail.

Displaying the Details for an Auction: Detail.asp

After the user has browsed through a listing and found something that peaks his interest, he clicks the link to open Detail.asp (see Figure 14-10).

This page is designed to display all the information about the item. The user can look through all the information and then decide if it is something worth bidding on.

If so, a link is included at the bottom of the page that takes the user to Bid.asp.

So two things have to happen on this page:

✔ The single database record has to be retrieved and displayed.

✔ The bid link has to be created.

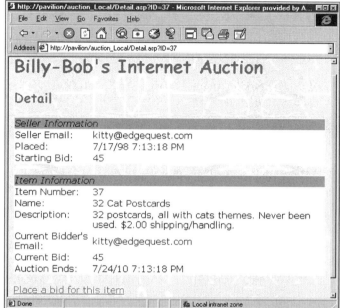

Figure 14-10:
The
Detail.asp
page.

Retrieving the record

This page only needs to retrieve one record. This page makes the assumption that when it is opened, an ID argument will always be passed on the URL to indicate which row to display. If an ID is not received, the page will fail.

Listing 14-4 shows the OnBeforeOpen event that sets the argument to whatever was passed in to the page. This works very much like the category passed to the CatList.asp page described earlier in this chapter in the section "Using a parameter with a Recordset."

Listing 14-4   The OnBeforeOpen event subroutine for Detail.asp

```
Sub rsAuctionItem_onbeforeopen()
rsAuctionItem.setParameter 0,Request.QueryString("ID")
End Sub
```

The Select statement in the Recordset, then, looks like this

```
SELECT * FROM AuctionItem
WHERE (ItemNum = ?)
```

The question mark is filled in with the ID passed to the page.

Linking to the bid page

You may think that linking to the Bid.asp page from this one would be a simple link. And it is, with only a couple of extras thrown in.

First, the Bid.asp page also needs to know which item it is that the user wants to bid on. So you have to pass on the ID that was passed to this page.

```
<A href='Bid.asp?ID=<%=Request.QueryString("ID")%>'>
Place a bid for this item</A>
```

Second, this Detail.asp page is used by two other pages in this application: CatList.asp and MyAuct.asp. All the items that come from CatList.asp can be bid on because CatList.asp filters out all the closed auctions. But MyAuct.asp includes a list of closed auctions. And the user may want to see the details for one of those closed auctions. But there's no way that you should allow bidding on that item. You can't bid on an item after the auction is over.

The solution is to put a little code around this link so that it is only displayed if the auction is currently open. All together, it looks like Listing 14-5.

Listing 14-5   The code to display the link only for open auctions
---

```
<%
' Only Show the option to place a bid if this
' auction is not expired
If CDate(rsAuctionItem.fields.getValue("ExpireDateTime")) _
    > Now Then %>
        <A href='Bid.asp?ID=<%=Request.QueryString("ID")%>'>
        Place a bid for this item</A>
<% End If %>
```

The link is displayed only if the ExpireDateTime is greater than Now.

Placing a Bid for an Item: Bid.asp

The Bid.asp page works much like the Detail.asp page. It receives an ID on the URL line and uses it as a parameter to retrieve the appropriate row. Then most of the details of the record are displayed (see Figure 14-11).

Two Design-Time Control edit boxes are also on the page: txtBidderEmail and txtBidderBid. This is where the user types her e-mail address and bid amount to place a new bid.

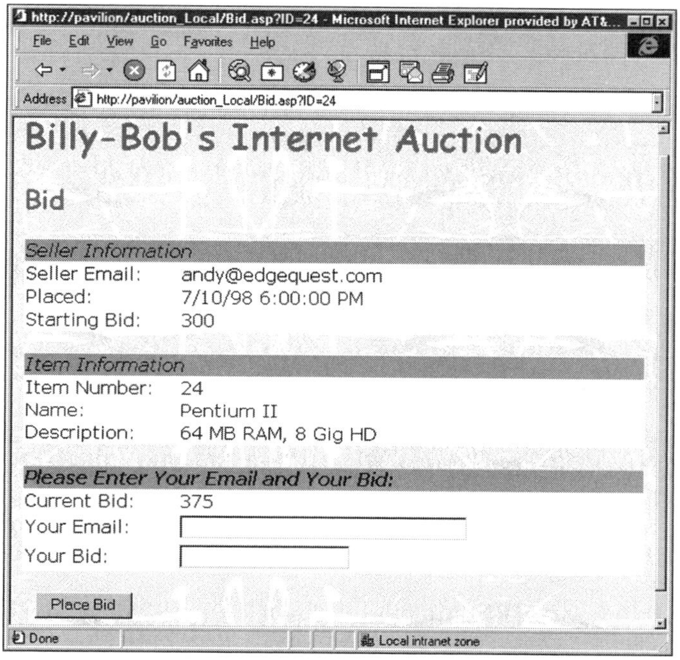

Figure 14-11:
The Bid.asp
page.

One important thing to notice is that these fields are not bound to the
Recordset. That's because I didn't want their current values displayed when
the page came up. I wanted them to be blank.

So instead of binding them directly to the Recordset, I handled the updating
of the Recordset with these values in the Click event of the Bid button (see
Listing 14-6).

Listing 14-6   The Click event of the Bid button

```
Sub btnBid_onclick()
If CInt(txtBidderBid.value) <= _
   rsAuctionItem.fields.getValue("CurrentBid") then
      lblPrompt.setCaption(_
      "** Your Bid Must Be Higher Than the Current Bid **")
Else
   rsAuctionItem.fields.setValue _
      "BuyerEmail",txtBidderEmail.value
   rsAuctionItem.fields.setValue _
      "CurrentBid",txtBidderBid.value
   rsAuctionItem.updateRecord
   thisPage.navigateURL "default.asp"
End If
End Sub
```

In this code, I first check to see that the bid is higher than the current bid. It'd be silly to accept a lower bid!

Then when I'm certain everything is okay, I use the Recordset's fields object to set the value of the BuyerEmail and CurrentBid columns to the information in the edit boxes. Finally, I update the record with the new information and go back to the Home page.

Prompting for the Seller's E-Mail Address: Prompt.asp

The one remaining process that hasn't been addressed is a page for sellers to view all their auctions. This is important because a seller needs to be able to view the *closed* auctions so that he can make arrangements with the buyer to make payments and then he can ship the product. This is the only place in the application that the user can go to see closed auctions.

But before the user can see all the auctions he's posted, you have to know who the user is. That's what the Prompt.asp page does (see Figure 14-12).

This simple page asks the user to enter his e-mail address and click the button. When he does, the following code is executed:

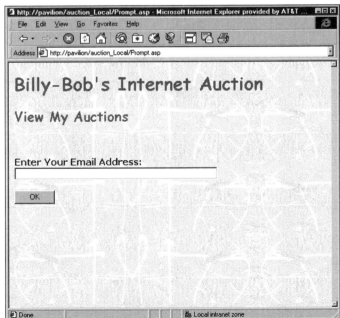

Figure 14-12:
The
Prompt.asp
page.

```
Sub btnOK_onclick()
    thisPage.navigateURL "MyAuct.asp?Email=" & txtEmail.value
End Sub
```

The MyAuct.asp page is opened, passing the e-mail address entered on the URL.

Displaying the Seller's Auction Status: MyAuct.asp

Finally, the MyAuct.asp page displays two lists — one of the current auctions placed by the user and one of the closed auctions placed by the user (see Figure 14-13).

At the top of the source, I include the Table.asp file described earlier in this chapter in the section titled "Displaying a List of Rows in a Table: Table.asp." It allows me to easily display a table with the rows from a Recordset that link to a detail page.

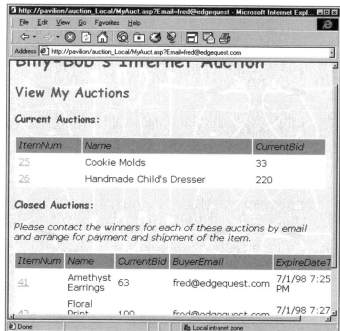

Figure 14-13: The MyAuct.asp page.

The current auctions

There are two Recordsets on this page. The first, rsMyCurrent has the following `Select` statement.

```
Select * From AuctionItem
Where (SellerEmail = ?) AND (ExpireDateTime > GetDate())
```

The e-mail address passed to this page is sent to this Recordset as a parameter and used to limit the rows retrieved to only those placed by this user. The second part of the `Where` clause assures that only open auctions are retrieved.

This Recordset's data is displayed using the `DispalyTable` subroutine I created and included in Table.asp. The code that calls it is in Listing 14-7.

Listing 14-7	The code that displays the current auctions

```
<%
Dim Cols(10)
Cols(1) = "ItemNum"
Cols(2) = "Name"
Cols(3) = "CurrentBid"
DisplayTable rsMyCurrent,Cols,3,"Detail.asp"
%>
```

This listing simply allows the seller to easily keep track of the progress of his current auctions.

The closed auctions

The second Recordset on this page, rsMyClosed, has the following `Select` statement

```
Select * From AuctionItem
Where (SellerEmail = ?) AND (ExpireDateTime <= GetDate())
Order By ExpireDateTime
```

Again, the retrieval is constrained to only those items placed by the user. This time however, all those where the ExpireDateTime is less than or equal to the current date and time are retrieved — in other words, all the closed items. This `Select` statement also sorts the items by their close date.

This Recordset is also displayed with the `DisplayTable` subroutine. The code that calls it is in Listing 14-8.

Listing 14-8	The code that displays the closed auctions

```
<%
Cols(1) = "ItemNum"
Cols(2) = "Name"
Cols(3) = "CurrentBid"
Cols(4) = "BuyerEmail"
Cols(5) = "ExpireDateTime"
DisplayTable rsMyClosed,Cols,5,"Detail.asp"
%>
```

This list enables the seller to get all the information he needs to obtain payment and ship the items to the highest bidder.

Ways to Make It Better

Billy-Bob's Internet Auction offers all the basic functionality you need to create an Internet auction. It does, however, have lots of areas where it could be improved.

For example, as it's written now, the application could be easily fooled. The only assurance that a user is who she claims to be is her e-mail address. So if you know someone's e-mail address, you could create auctions in his name and place bids in his name.

The best way to fix this would be to add some sort of registration facility where the user has to choose a password. Then whenever he wants to create a new auction or place a bid, he'd have to enter that password along with his e-mail address to confirm who he is. Or you could have him log in with his e-mail address and password once at the beginning and then recognize him for the rest of that session with a session variable or a cookie.

And if you add a log-in capability that uses session variables or cookies, you may want to break out the Buyer and Seller information into their own tables.

Here are some other ideas:

- ✔ If you wanted to be more flexible with the categories, you could break the categories in the list out into their own table.

- ✔ As I mentioned at the beginning of the chapter, the bidding history isn't tracked for a particular auction. You could easily add another table in the database and write some additional code to keep track of the bidding history. Then you could create a new page to display that history.

✔ In many cases, it would be nice if the seller could include a picture of the item when they created an auction.

✔ Some auction sites offer the seller the ability to set a reserve price. This is the lowest final bid that the seller will accept for an item. In other words, although the seller may start the bidding at $5, the person with the highest bid would only actually get the item if her bid meets or exceeds the reserve price of, say, $20. This allows sellers to protect themselves from an item going too cheap, but it also tends to annoy bidders.

✔ If you wanted to offer more detailed information about each item, you could ask the user for more specific information based on the category. For instance, if you had a Vehicles category you could ask for the type, color, make, and model of the vehicle as well as a description.

✔ You could add a search page that would allow the user to search within a category or across all categories for specific keywords like "bean-bag babies" or "card games."

There are, no doubt, many more ideas you'll come up with for expanding and enhancing this application for your own use. And feel free! That's why I included it.

Chapter 15

Data Commands and Stored Procedures

*W*ant to create some SQL and store it away for future use? Then you've come to the right chapter. Data commands and stored procedures are two very different things, but they both allow you to create SQL and then store it to be called in the future.

Data commands enable you to enter a SQL command and save it as an object in the Data Environment of your project. You can then easily call the data command as if it were a Data Environment method.

Stored procedures are compiled SQL subroutines that are stored in the database and can be called from your application to process or retrieve information.

By the way, in this chapter, I assume that you're familiar with basic SQL statements like Select, Insert, Update, and Delete. If you aren't, you can still get a lot out of this chapter, but you'll be able to do a lot more with the information if you know SQL. If you want to brush up on this topic, check out the book *SQL For Dummies,* 3rd Edition, by Allen G. Taylor (published by IDG Books Worldwide, Inc.).

Creating and Calling Data Commands

Your data connection object is held in the *DataEnvironment.* You can create one other kind of object in the DataEnvironment — the data command.

Data command? Ain't that just a fancy stored procedure?

If you're familiar with database stored procedures, you may think data commands sound awfully similar. Two very important differences between data commands and stored procedures exist, however:

✔ Data commands are stored on the client as part of your project, whereas stored procedures are compiled and stored in the database.

✔ A data command can be directly connected to a view or a table to retrieve that view or table's data. It can also hold a SQL statement. But a data command cannot hold multiple SQL statements — a stored procedure can.

You can think of data commands as simply a way to save a SQL command or query to be used later.

In fact, if you want to call a stored procedure in Visual InterDev, probably the easiest way to do it is to create a data command that, in turn, calls the stored procedure. The command then returns to your script whatever was returned from the stored procedure.

A data command is a SQL statement that accomplishes some task. It is stored as an object in your project, and you can call it just as you would a function or subroutine. You can even pass parameters and get a result back.

Creating a data command

To create a data command:

1. **In the Project Explorer, open the global.asa file to reveal the DataEnvironment object.**

2. **Open the DataEnvironment object to show your data connection object.**

3. **Right-click the data connection and choose Add Data Command from the pop-up menu.**

   The Command1 Properties dialog box appears (see Figure 15-1).

4. **Enter a command name and fill in the rest of the information to indicate what you want the data command to do.**

5. **Click OK.**

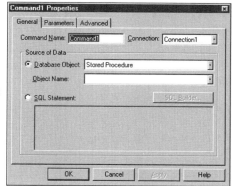

Figure 15-1:
The
Command1
Properties
dialog box.

The Command Properties dialog box is nearly identical to the Recordset Properties dialog box that I discuss in Chapter 14. For more information about how to fill in this dialog box, see that chapter.

The biggest difference between the Recordset Properties dialog box and the Command Properties dialog box is that with a command, you don't have to enter a SQL statement that returns a result set. In the SQL Statement text box, you can create an Insert, Update, Delete, or other valid SQL statement.

Whatever SQL statement you enter, it will be saved as a data command under the name you give it.

Running a command in Visual InterDev

You can execute a command from the Visual InterDev development environment to test it or to easily do some work for you.

To run a command from the development environment:

1. **In the Project Explorer, open the global.asa file to reveal the DataEnvironment object**

2. **Open the DataEnvironment object to show your data connection object.**

3. **Open the data connection to display all the data commands.**

4. **Double-click the data command.**

   The command is executed. If it returns a result set, the result set is displayed.

Calling data command — data command, come in please!

After you've created a data command and it works just as you want it to, you can easily call it from your script.

To call a data command from your script:

1. **Enable the Scripting Object Model for the page, if it isn't already enabled.**

2. **Add this line near the top of your script.**

   ```
   thisPage.CreateDE()
   ```

   It creates a DE (DataEnvironment) object in your script.

3. **Call the data command as if it were a method of the DE object. Pass any arguments inside parentheses.**

   ```
   DE.EmployeeRaise(10)
   ```

4. **You can continue to use DE throughout the script on this page to call as many data commands as you want whenever you like. To get a value back from a data command, call it just like a function.**

   ```
   NumEmp = DE.EmployeeRaise(10)
   ```

Using a data command in a Recordset DTC

Recordset DTCs, which I discuss in Chapter 13, enable you to use a query to retrieve information from the database.

If you have created a data command that returns a result set, you can use that data command as the source of data for a normal Recordset DTC.

To use a data command in a Recordset DTC:

1. **Create a data command that returns a result set.**

   See the section "Creating a data command" earlier in this chapter for more information.

2. **Drop a Recordset DTC on the page.**

3. **Right-click the Recordset DTC and choose Properties from the pop-up menu to access the Properties dialog box for the Recordset DTC (see Figure 15-2).**

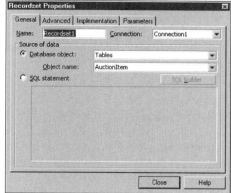

Figure 15-2:
The
Recordset
DTC
Properties
dialog box.

4. **Click the Data Object radio button and choose DE Commands from the Data Object drop-down list box.**

5. **In the Object Name drop-down list box, choose your data command's name.**

Now you can use the Recordset DTC along with the other DTCs to display data from the command's result set.

Accessing a data command result set

What if you create a data command that returns a result set? Can you access that result set from within script? Absolutely.

After you call the data command, there is a Recordset that is automatically created. The Recordset's name is

```
rsCommandName
```

where *CommandName* is the name of your data command. You can use this Recordset from script just as you would a Recordset DTC that had been dropped on this page. All the standard Recordset functions are available to navigate it, retrieve data, and so forth.

For example, suppose you created a data command called `Emp` that is tied to an Employee table. It simply returns all the fields of all the records of the Employee table. The code below would execute the command, loop through the Recordset, and display each employee's last name and salary.

```
<%
rsEmp.moveFirst
Do While Not rsEmp.EOF
    Response.Write rsEmp.fields.getValue("LName") & ", "
    Response.Write rsEmp.fields.getValue("Salary") & "<p>"
    rsEmp.moveNext
Loop
%>
```

The `moveFirst` method causes the Recordset to move to the first record. The loop continues until the `EOF` property is true, indicating that you've reached the end of the Recordset. Inside the loop, the `fields` object's method `getValue` returns the value of the name of the column passed. I use it here twice to display two different fields: last name and salary. The `moveNext` method causes the Recordset to move the next record to process it.

For more information on the Recordset object and its methods and properties, see the Visual InterDev online Help:

> MSDN Library Visual Studio 6.0⇨Visual InterDev Documentation⇨ Reference⇨Scripting Object Model⇨Script Objects⇨Recordset Script Object

Of course, in most circumstances, it's a lot easier to just use the Recordset DTC and the other DTCs to display and update data. As a general rule that's what you should do. However, if you ever need to access data more directly, the technique described in this section is the way to do it.

Creating and Calling Stored Procedures

A *stored procedure* is a feature supported by most client/server databases. It enables you to create something like a function or subroutine that is stored on the server and executed there when you call it.

You always write a stored procedure entirely in SQL. It uses whatever dialect of SQL your database uses. You can have as many SQL statements in a stored procedure as you like. You can pass parameters to a stored procedure, and it can return a value. It can also return a result set.

Different databases have very different dialects of SQL and different ways of handling stored procedures. Because of these differences, I focus on the Visual InterDev features that help you to create and use stored procedures in your projects.

See your specific database's documentation for more information about stored procedures.

Creating and editing stored procedures

To create a new stored procedure:

1. **In the Data View, open your project and your database connection.**

   Under the database connection, you see an icon labeled Stored Procedures.

2. **Right-click the Stored Procedures icon and choose New Stored Procedure from the pop-up menu.**

3. **The script editor opens, and a skeleton of a stored procedure appears in it (see Figure 15-3).**

4. **Enter the code for your stored procedure and click the Save button on the Standard toolbar.**

5. **Close the editor.**

   The name of your stored procedure appears in the Data View under Stored Procedures (see Figure 15-4).

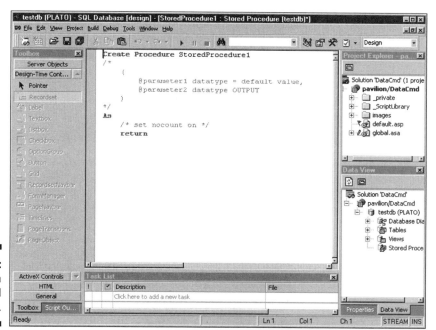

Figure 15-3: Editing a new stored procedure.

Figure 15-4:
The Data
View shows
your new
stored
procedure.

6. **If your stored procedure returns a result set, you can click the plus sign beside the stored procedure's name to open it and display any fields returned.**

To edit an existing stored procedure, just double-click the stored procedure's icon in Data View. The stored procedure is retrieved and displayed in the editor.

Running a stored procedure from within Visual InterDev

To execute a stored procedure from within Visual InterDev, right-click the stored procedure in the Data View, and then choose Execute. The stored procedure executes. If it returns a result set, the result set appears. An Output window appears at the bottom of the screen indicating the result of the execution of the stored procedure (see Figure 15-5).

Calling a stored procedure from script

In order to call a stored procedure from script, you have to create a data command that calls the stored procedure and then call that data command from your script.

To call a stored procedure from script:

1. **Create the stored procedure.**

   See "Creating and editing stored procedures" earlier in this chapter for more information.

2. **Create a data command, naming it something similar to the stored procedure name.**

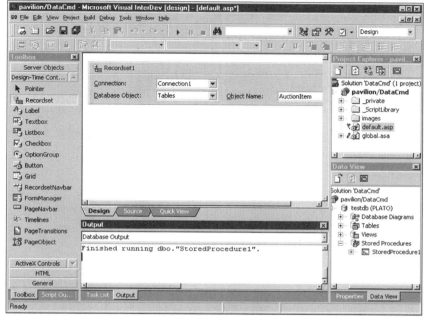

Figure 15-5:
An Output
window
appears
show the
result of the
stored
procedure
execution.

See "Creating a data command" earlier in this chapter for more information.

3. **Set the properties of the data command so that the Database Object is set to Stored Procedures and Object Name is set to the name of the stored procedure.**

4. **Save the data command.**

5. **Within your script, create the DE object and then call the data command as a method of DE.**

See "Calling a data command" earlier in this chapter for more information.

Using a stored procedure as a source for your Recordset

If your stored procedure returns a result set, it may be more convenient to display the data using the standard Recordset DTC and the other DTCs, rather than calling with a data command.

To use a stored procedure as a source for your Recordset:

1. **Drop a Recordset DTC on your page.**

2. **Set the Recordset's properties so that the Database Object is set to Stored Procedures and Object Name is set to the name of the stored procedure.**

3. **Add other DTCs as needed to display the data.**

Part IV
Wrapping It Up!

The 5th Wave — By Rich Tennant

@RICHTENNANT

"YO-I THINK WE'VE GOT A NEW KIND OF VIRUS HERE!"

In this part . . .

When the scripting ends, the debugging begins! In this part, you discover the Visual InterDev complete integrated debugger to help you chase down even the nastiest of insects.

And when you're done, you find out how to deploy your application so that your users can start putting the program to use in the real world.

Chapter 16

Getting the Bugs Out

*N*obody can write a complex computer application and get it perfect the first time. Most of us don't even make it on the second or third try. That's why *debugging* skills are so important. If software development were just a matter of writing the code, it would be a lot simpler. But the average developer probably spends as much or more time chasing down problems, tweaking, reworking, and rewriting code than it took to write the original code in the first place.

In this chapter, I provide a brief introduction to the Visual InterDev integrated debugger. It can make your debugging tasks go a little easier by giving you a peek behind the curtain to see your application as it is executing, line by line.

If you've ever worked with a debugger in another development environment, I'm sure you'll find the Visual InterDev debugger very familiar.

Debugging: When and Where

Just as when you are writing your scripts you must be aware whether you are coding for the client or the server, so you must be aware whether you are debugging on the client or the server.

The ability to debug client scripts is actually built into Internet Explorer. So you should find debugging client scripts on your desktop with the browser pretty straightforward.

When you debug server scripts, however, you have more to think about. First, which server will you use? You have Personal Web Server on your workstation if you are developing on Windows 95/98, and you have Personal Web Services if you are on NT Workstation. You also have Internet Information Server (IIS) on your Web server, which is probably running Windows NT Server.

Your best option, as you might guess, is to use your local Web server for your day-to-day debugging tasks.

Long Distance Extermination: Remote Debugging

Visual InterDev and IIS 4 also support *remote debugging,* which allows you to actually debug an application that is running on the production server from your workstation. You don't want to use this capability for your everyday debugging tasks. But it can be a very handy if you come across a quick problem that you must work out on the server, or if you see a bug that shows up only when the application is running on the production server.

If you want to do remote debugging, keep a few things in mind:

- ✔ When you use remote debugging, the debugger takes control of the server. Although the server may still work for other users, its performance is likely to be degraded significantly.

- ✔ Only one person can remotely debug the server at a time.

- ✔ You must do some extra setup on both the client and the server to get it working.

For more information on the setup necessary to get remote debugging working check out the online Help at:

MSDN Library Visual Studio 6.0⇨Visual InterDev Documentation⇨ Using Visual InterDev⇨Building Integrated Solutions⇨Integration Tasks⇨Debugging Remotely

After you have the client and server set up properly, server debugging works almost exactly as if you were debugging locally.

One alternative to remote debugging that avoids some of these problems is to simply install Visual InterDev on the server and debug the application right on the server locally.

Enabling ASP Debugging

Because local debugging is what you'll use in your everyday development work, I spend this chapter focusing on using that. After you have debugging set up properly on your workstation, debugging client script and debugging server script work pretty much the same way.

The first step in debugging is to tell Visual InterDev to automatically enable ASP scripting on your local server (PWS).

To automatically enable debugging:

1. **In the Project Explorer, right-click the project and choose Properties from the pop-up menu.**

   The IDispWebProject Properties dialog box appears.

2. **Click the Launch tab (see Figure 16-1).**

3. **Click the check box at the bottom of the dialog box labeled Automatically Enable ASP Server-side Script Debugging on Launch.**

4. **Click OK.**

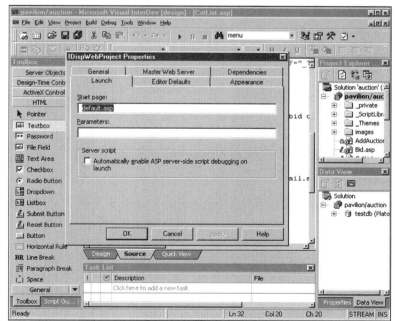

Figure 16-1:
The Launch tab of the IDispWebProject Properties dialog box.

Breakpoints: What Pressure Points Become When You Press Too Hard

When you run an application with the debugger, it runs just as it normally would until it hits a *breakpoint*. A breakpoint identifies a line of code where you want the application to stop so that you can begin using the debugger to examine what's going on. Usually, you set breakpoints a few lines before the area where you think the problem is taking place.

To set a breakpoint on a line of code:

1. **In the script editor's Source view, scroll until the line of code you want to break on appears on the screen.**

2. **Click the mouse in the gray bar along the left side of the editor, right beside the line where you want the breakpoint.**

   Right at the location where you click, a red octagon appears that looks, appropriately enough, like a stop sign (see Figure 16-2).

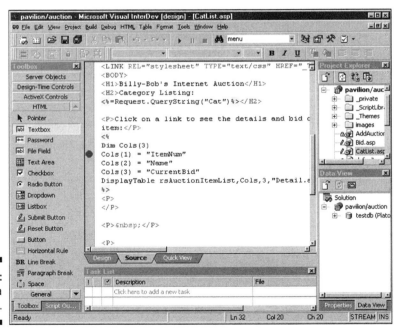

Figure 16-2:
Setting a
breakpoint.

Now when you run your application and this code executes, the application immediately stops just before it executes the line with the breakpoint. From the breakpoint, you can use the step controls (see the next section for information about step controls) to follow the path of execution.

To remove a breakpoint, simply click the stop sign. The breakpoint disappears.

Debugging a Page

To start debugging a page:

1. **Identify the page you want to debug. Right-click it and choose Set As Start Page from the pop-up menu.**

2. **Open the page in the editor and set any breakpoints that you want.**

   See "Breakpoints: What Pressure Points Become When You Press Too Hard," earlier in this chapter, for more information.

3. **Click the Start button on the Standard toolbar to run the application.**

   If this is the first time you have run the debugger for this project, you are prompted to enter user information to identify the debugging process on the server.

4. **Enter your domain, name, and password.**

   The page you chose appears in Internet Explorer.

5. **Execute the page triggering the events that have breakpoints.**

   When a breakpoint is reached, execution stops, and you can step through the code and interactively use the features of the debugger.

6. **When you have found the problem and made changes, you can click the End and Start buttons to restart the application, or you can simply choose Restart from the Debug menu.**

Be Careful Where You Step!

When your application stops at a breakpoint, you can watch the source code and execute it one line at a time, following the course of execution. This is called *stepping through* your code. Often this capability alone can help you find logic bugs in large If...Then...ElseIf structures or in complicated loops or nested loops.

To step through your code, follow these steps:

1. **Run your code as usual.**

   When a breakpoint is triggered, the current line appears with a yellow arrow beside it. That line is about to be executed.

2. **Click the Step Into button on the Debug toolbar, or press the F11 key on your keyboard.**

   The line is executed and the arrow moves on to the next line.

3. **Repeat Step 2 as many times as you need to.**

4. **If you want the application to quickly run through a number of lines and stop again, put your cursor where you want execution to stop and then click the Run To Cursor button or press Ctrl+F10 on the keyboard.**

In addition to Step Into, there is also a Step Over button. They work in much the same way — they enable you to move from one line to the next. You see the difference when you get to a subroutine or function call. If you choose Step Into when the arrow is on a function call, you immediately jump to the function's script and watch *it* executed line by line. If, instead, you choose Step Over, the function call is executed all at once as if it were a built-in command, and the arrow continues to the next line below the function call.

Watching and Changing Variable Values

You can discover bugs in another important place: in the values of the variables you use in your script. While you're stepping through your code, it's nice when you can actually see the value of important variables as they change and even change them yourself as the program runs to try out different scenarios.

That's what the Watch window does for you. It provides you with a list where you can place the variables you want to watch, and it shows you their value. You can even click the value to change it.

To view the Watch window, choose one of the following methods:

- ✔ Choose View➪Debug Windows➪Watch.
- ✔ Press Ctrl+Alt+W.

The Watch window appears at the bottom of your screen (see Figure 16-3).

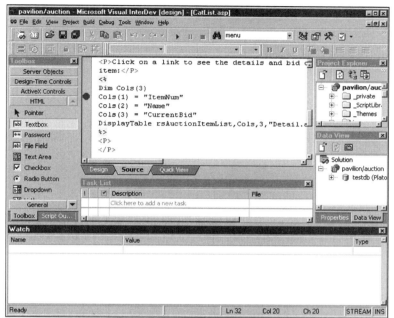

Figure 16-3.
The Watch
window.

To add a variable to the Watch window, select the variable name in the editor and then drag that selection down under the Name column of the Watch window. The variable appears in the list.

Or, if you prefer, you can just click the first blank line under Name and type the variable name yourself.

To change the value of a variable in the Watch window:

1. **While the program is running, click in the Value column on the Watch window beside the variable you want to change.**

2. **Type the new value and press Enter.**

   The value changes.

For More Information . . .

This chapter doesn't cover all the features of the debugger. It does show you enough of the features to get you started, and it shows you how to use the most common features that are likely to help you locate and nail your bugs.

For more information, check out the online Help at:

> MSDN Library Visual Studio 6.0⇨Visual InterDev Documentation⇨
> Using Visual InterDev⇨Editing and Scripting⇨Scripting Tasks⇨
> Debugging Your Pages

Chapter 17

Deploying Your Web Application

. . . .

In This Chapter

▶ Checking to see that the server is ready for the move

▶ Moving the application

▶ Testing to make sure all went as planned

. . . .

*A*fter you've designed, developed, debugged, and tested your application, it's time to deploy it, or in English — to let it out into the real world!

The production Web server is the final home for your Web application. It may be a public Web server with its own domain name that is accessible by anyone from the World Wide Web, or it may be on a machine that is internal to your company and serves up intranet applications to the users in your company. Either way, the application needs to be able to find its way to the right place on your server.

Making Sure Your Server Is Up to the Task

The first step in deploying your application is to make sure that your Web server is capable of hosting your application. Here are some of the most important items to check:

✔ In order for Visual InterDev to work with the server, you must have FrontPage server extensions installed on the server machine.

✔ If you are using Active Server Pages (ASP) or server components, then the server must either be running IIS 3.0 with the ASP extension installed, IIS 4.0 (or later), or another NT-based Web Server with Chili!ASP installed. (Chili!ASP is a third-party product that implements ASP on Web servers other than IIS. In fact, it is included on the CD in the back of this book. What a deal!)

✔ If you are using a client/server database, be sure that you install and deploy the final, production database correctly so that it is accessible from the Web server. Also be sure that the Web server itself has all the necessary database and ODBC drivers it needs.

✔ If your project depends on Microsoft Transaction Server (MTS), be sure it is installed on the server.

✔ Make sure that all server components used by the application are installed on the Web server.

Making the Move

After you're certain that everything on the server is ready to go, it's time to actually make the move. But how you make that move depends on whether the server you chose when you created the project is the same as the production server.

If your project server is the production server

If the Web server you identified when you first created your project is the production Web server, then deploying your application is simple.

In the Project Explorer, right-click the project and choose Release Working Copy from the pop-up menu. The current versions of all the files are copied up to the server, and the lock icon appears beside each of them.

If another server is the production server

The server you specified when you created the project may *not* be your production Web server. If you are working in a team development environment, for example, it may make sense to create a *development server*. This setup assures that half-done applications aren't wasting space on the production server and yet still provides a way that files can be shared among all the developers on the team.

In this case, Visual InterDev offers an easy way to deploy your application on a new server.

To deploy your application to a new Web server, follow these steps:

1. **In the Project Explorer, right-click the project and choose Release Working Copy from the pop-up menu.**

   The current versions of all the files are copied up to the server and they are locked.

2. **Choose Project⇨Web Project⇨Copy Web Application from the menu bar.**

   The Copy Project dialog box appears (see Figure 17-1).

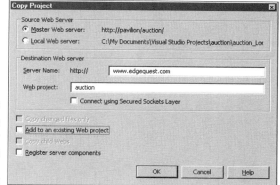

Figure 17-1:
The Copy
Project
dialog box.

3. **Click the Master Web Server radio button.**

4. **Enter the name of the server and the name you want for this project to have on that server.**

5. **Check whichever check boxes are appropriate for your situation at the bottom of the dialog box.**

6. **Click OK.**

   The project is copied to the new server.

Test, Test, Test!

After that application is on the new server, you must thoroughly test it. Be sure to check each of the following items as thoroughly as possible:

✔ All links, both local and external, go where they should.

✔ All graphics load, and all ActiveX components appear.

✔ The server script is executing appropriately and is not being passed down to the browser.

✔ Server components are being executed and returning the right results.

✔ All database retrievals and updates are working correctly.

Part V
The Part of Tens

The 5th Wave   By Rich Tennant

"I've been in hardware all of my life, and all of a sudden it's software that'll make me rich."

In this part . . .

Looking for help on a specific Visual InterDev question? Want to find source code for a common problem so that you don't have to recreate the wheel? In this part, you find a list of great resources for information, source code, Web links, and lots more.

You also find a list of really cool server components. Sometimes the best way to write a script is not to write it at all. Get a server component that does it for you, and you can spend your time on more important affairs — like golf!

Chapter 18

Ten Great Visual InterDev Resources

In This Chapter

▶ Really cool Web sites where you can find articles, tips, and source code

▶ Newsgroups, electronic newsletters, and listserves

▶ Cool server components and ASP examples

*W*ant to find the best resources to help you in you quest to develop Web applications with Visual InterDev? Well, look no further! I collected the best into this tidy little list that makes it easy for you to find exactly what you want.

The Official Microsoft Web Sites

Between the articles, tips, galleries, and downloads, it's hard to beat Microsoft's official Visual InterDev Web site. You can find it at:

```
www.microsoft.com/vinterdev/
```

But that's not the only place you'll want to visit! You can also find a whole site dedicated to scripting, including sections on VBScript and JavaScript:

```
www.microsoft.com/scripting/
```

And, of course, Microsoft Site Builder is dedicated to the Web developer using Microsoft technologies:

```
www.microsoft.com/sitebuilder/
```

Microsoft Developer's Network (MSDN)

The Microsoft Developer's Network (MSDN) is an annual subscription program that offers developers a way to keep up to date on all Microsoft's information and technologies. You can find different levels at different costs, but here's a list of some of the benefits offered:

- ✔ **The MSDN Library:** A comprehensive set of articles, sample code, documentation, conference papers, and technical specifications. This Library is a must-have for serious developers using Microsoft technologies.

- ✔ **The Operating Systems:** The current version of all the operating systems Microsoft produces, including Windows CE, Windows 95/98, Windows NT, and more. Also included is the current version of all the SDKs, like DirectX.

- ✔ **Back Office:** A powerful suite of enterprise tools including SQL Server, Exchange Server, Internet Information Server, Transaction Server, Site Server, and more.

- ✔ **Visual Studio:** The current release of all the Microsoft development tools, including Visual InterDev and Visual Basic.

ActiveServerPages.Com

This site has it all — tutorials, troubleshooting, tips, book reviews, links, and lots more. The topics range from scripting to IIS to Visual InterDev to database access. Lots of great source code for the taking, too!

Of course, you can find it at:

```
www.activeserverpages.com
```

User Groups

User groups are the best place to find others doing work like you are. You can share your thoughts, experiences, and ideas with others. You won't find a better way to get answers to common problems. To find a user group in your area, check out Microsoft's user group Web page at:

```
www.microsoft.com/msdn/usergroup/user/
```

15Seconds.Com

This site is a great source of news on the Visual InterDev, ASP, and IIS worlds. It also includes FAQs on a huge variety of topics as well as links to newsgroups, articles, and other great sites. They also keep a database of ASP consultants and available jobs. It's at:

```
www.15seconds.com
```

Newsgroups

Newsgroups are like distributed user groups where people with a common interest can discuss, share ideas, and help each other out. The Microsoft newsgroup server can be found at:

```
news://msnews.microsoft.com
```

Here are some of the newsgroups you can find there that you may be interested in:

```
microsoft.public.vinterdev
microsoft.public.vstudio.general
microsoft.public.vstudio.development
microsoft.public.inetserver.iis.activeserverpages
microsoft.public.scripting.vbscript
microsoft.public.scripting.jscript
microsoft.public.sqlserver.odbc
microsoft.public.sqlserver.programming
```

The ASP Hole

This is a very professional site for developers of Active Server Pages. It offers articles, downloads, and a whole lot more. It's at:

```
www.asphole.com
```

Electronic Newsletters and Listserves

One of the best way to get tips, ideas, tutorials, and up-to-the-minute news is through electronic newsletters and listserves. An electronic newsletter is just what it sounds like: a newsletter that contains articles, news, source code, and so on, that is sent to you via e-mail rather than through the postal service. A listserve is like a newsgroup except that all the messages are sent to you via e-mail.

To join the Visual InterDev Mailing List, send e-mail to `interdev@dwam.com` with the word `subscribe` in the subject line of your e-mail.

To join the Visual InterDev 6 Listserve, send e-mail to `listserv@connection.net` with a message body that contains

```
Subscribe VI6 Your Name
```

Replace *Your Name* with your name.

Books

A variety of books on technologies associated with Web development in Visual InterDev exist that can help you. Here are just a few (which are published by IDG Books Worldwide, Inc.):

- ✔ *Active Server Pages For Dummies* by Bill Hatfield
- ✔ *HTML 4 For Dummies* by Ed Tittlel and Stephen N. James
- ✔ *Visual Basic 5 For Windows For Dummies* by Wallace Wang

ServerObjects.Com

This is a great place to find lots of server components that do a huge variety of tasks. Some of them are free and some of them have timebomb demos, but they're all worth checking out. It's at:

```
www.serverobjects.com
```

Chapter 19

Ten Really Cool Server Components

In This Chapter

▶ Easy reports from your database data

▶ A calendar that remembers your dates

▶ A component that enables users to easily upload files to your Web server

Chili!Soft's Chili!Reports

The database capabilities that Visual InterDev provides are great. But there's one really big hole — Visual InterDev doesn't give you any good way to produce reports. That's where Chili!Soft's Chili!Reports comes in. Use this to organize your information exactly as your users want to see it.

For more information, check out:

```
www.chilisoft.com/support/default.asp
```

Easy-ODBC

If you are going to connect to a database from the Web server, you need to have an ODBC DSN entry created. Normally, you have to do this manually on the Web server machine itself. But with Easy-ODBC, you can do it remotely and automatically. Easy-ODBC even allows you to see a complete list of existing DSN entries and backup, compress, and repair Access 97 databases on the server — all from your workstation.

For more information on Easy-ODBC, check out:

```
www.15seconds.com/component/pg03377.htm
```

Easy-Edit

Easy-Edit is a server component that provides full access to files on the Web server and even allows you to bring up files in a Web page for editing. This component is a great way to provide a quick maintenance page for Webmasters.

```
www.15seconds.com/component/EasyEdit.htm
```

EZsite Calendar

Ever wish there was an easy way you could add a calendar to your site that would keep track of upcoming gatherings, deadlines, or other events that your visitors were interested in? Well, now there is with EZsite Calendar. Using totally server-side, in-process objects, the customizable calendar generates dynamic pages from database event information.

```
www.dougdean.com/
```

Conversa Chat Server

Want to add a personal touch to your Web site? How about a free chat room so that your visitors can communicate and share ideas. Conversa Chat Server 2.0 provides a powerful HTML-only solution that works with virtually any browser your users may have. Plus, you can moderate and log conversation threads. For more information, see:

```
http://www.adventia.com/
```

ASP MagicINI

INI files are a common, convenient way to store information in Windows. But before now, no easy way to access INI information from an ASP page existed. ASP MagicINI provides the functions you need to quickly store and retrieve information from server-side INI files.

```
www.dana-net.com/products.htm
```

ASP MagicRegistry

Since Windows 95 introduced the Registry database, it has been a popular place for applications to store information that needs to be remembered from one run to the next. Now your Web applications can have that same access to the registry with ASP MagicRegistry. In addition to reading and changing values, this tool enables you to create new keys and tree branches.

```
www.dana-net.com/products.htm
```

AspUpload

AspUpload enables users to easily upload pictures, applications, our source code to your Web site. Easy for you — just a few lines of script — and easy for your users!

```
www.persits.com/aspupload.html
```

AspNTUser

The AspNTUser component exposes your script to the full power of the NT domains, users, and groups. You can navigate the hierarchy of objects to look up users' names, rename domain users, determine if a domain account is disabled, and much more!

```
http://www.persits.com/aspntuser.html
```

Cookie Engine

This simple, free component generates unique numbers that you can assign to user cookies for identification.

```
www.15seconds.com/component/pg02877.htm
```

Part VI
The Appendixes

WHY DOGS DON'T USE LAPTOPS

THERE HE GOES AGAIN. I'LL BET IF I LEANED AGAINST A TREE, I COULD DO IT.

In this part . . .

Want some guidelines before you start installing the many, many megabytes of stuff on the installation disks? In this part, you find a few installation pointers before you set up your workstation and server environments with Visual InterDev.

You also get the help you need to brush up on your VBScript. Because VBScript is the default ASP scripting language and is the one that most developers prefer for server-side scripting, I thought it'd be a good idea to provide a quick course in this flexible, easy-to-learn language. If you've never done any sort of Basic programming before, trust me — it's easy. And if you *have* done programming in Visual Basic, VBA, TRS-80 Model I Basic, or some other variation, VBScript will be a walk in the park.

Finally, in this part, you also get a look at all the incredibly cool stuff I've packed onto the CD that you can find in the back of this book. What a deal!

Appendix A

A VBScript Tutorial

*T*his appendix provides a tutorial on the VBScript language, which is most often used as the server-side scripting language in Active Server Pages. If you have programmed in Visual Basic or Visual Basic for Applications in applications such as Word or Excel, then you already know most of these concepts. VBScript is just a subset of these languages. If you have not worked with any Basic-like languages before, then you'll want to read more carefully.

I'm on the Case

You can type commands and variable names in VBScript in uppercase and lowercase characters however you like. These three lines work exactly the same way in VBScript:

```
FOR FTSIZE = 1 TO 5
for ftsize = 1 to 5
FoR fTsIzE = 1 tO 5
```

MsgBox and InputBox are gone!

If you have used Visual Basic before, you've probably used the MsgBox and InputBox functions. They enable you to provide information to the user and get information back using standard dialog boxes.

But when you're creating Active Server Pages (ASP), you are writing code that runs on the server and does not have any direct interaction with the user. Because of that, these functions don't work in ASP.

But the best plan is to be as consistent as possible. I like to capitalize the first letter of all VBScript commands so that they stand out and keep the code easy to read. It looks like this:

```
For ftsize = 1 To 5
```

Your Comments Are Irrelevant!

Comments, or *remarks,* enable you to include notes to yourself or others inside your code.

HTML, uses `<!-` and `->` to enclose comments, and you can still use HTML comments in your pages. But if you want to comment VBScript code as you are creating it, you can also use the VBScript-style comment.

```
' This loop will print the same text
' five times
For num = 1 To 5
    Response.Write("Hello and Welcome!<br>")
Next
```

Instead of enclosing the comment with two different symbols as HTML does, VBScript always begins with an apostrophe and ends at the end of the line. So a new apostrophe is necessary at the beginning of each new line.

Comments can also go on the same line as code.

```
For num = 1 To 5 ' Do it 5 times
    Response.Write("Hello and Welcome!<br>")
Next
```

The VBScript comments, like all ASP code, are removed from the page before it is sent. So, unlike the HTML comments, these comments cannot be seen when the person browsing your page chooses View➪Source from the Internet Explorer menus.

Can I Get a Continuance?

If you have a line of code that is getting too long, you can break it in two using the line continuation character, which is an underscore. This character lets VBScript know you're going to continue on the next line and not to understand it as two separate lines.

```
If Age > 18 And _
   Age < 65 Then
```

To type the underscore character (_), just hold Shift while typing the dash. Use this character wherever you'd normally put a space in your code.

It's a good idea to indent the second line so that it's clear that it is part of the first one.

Using Variables and Constants

In VBScript, you declare new variables using the Dim statement (don't ask why it's Dim and not something sensible like Var — it's a long story).

Numbers and forced declaration

The following code creates three variables called Rent, Months, and Annual.

```
Dim Rent, Months, Annual
Cost = 500
Tax = 12
Annual = Cost * Tax
```

You can list as many variables after Dim as you want. Or you can write multiple Dim lines — it's up to you. You assign a value to a variable by using the equal sign, and you can do math on variables using + and - for addition and subtraction and * and / for multiplication and division. Use the ^ symbol for exponents.

One important thing to notice: VBScript doesn't have variable types. Declaring variables identifies them as variables and nothing else. You can hold any type of information you want in them. You can even change the type of information they hold over the course of their life (although this isn't usually a good idea).

By the way, you can actually get away with using variables and not declaring them at all. But this is, of course, a bad idea. Your code can become confusing fast if you start using variables no one has ever heard of before!

In fact, the best thing to do is to force yourself to always declare variables. Just include this line at the top of your page, even before the <HTML> tag.

```
<% Option Explicit %>
```

This line causes VBScript to give you an error any time you use a variable without first declaring it on that page.

Strings and concatenation

In addition to holding numbers, variables can hold strings.

```
Dim Prefix, Word, Suffix, Complete
Prefix = "Un"
Word = "constitution"
Suffix = "al"
Final = Prefix & Word & Suffix
```

String literals are always surrounded with quotes. The & is the string *concatenation* character. In other words, you use it to stick strings together. The previous code would display the word

```
Unconstitutional
```

Constants

Constants in VBScript work as they do in other languages — they are like variables, but after you give them a value, that value can't be changed.

You declare a constant just like a variable, replacing Dim with Const. You must also give the constant a value when you declare it.

```
Const Weight = 153.5
Const NameOfGod = "Bill Gates"
```

Calling Statements and Functions

VBScript has two types of commands — *statements* and *functions*. A statement stands on its own and simply does something. Dim is a statement.

```
Dim Artist, CD
```

A function is different because it always *returns a value* for you to use in your code. An example of a function is Date.

```
Dim ThisDate
ThisDate = Date
Response.Write "It is now " & ThisDate & ".<p>"
```

In this code, you create the variable ThisDate and then assign the value that is *returned* from the Date function. Then the value of ThisDate is used to inform the user of the date.

Use Response.Write to send HTML to the browser so that you can communicate with the user. For more information on Response.Write, see Chapter 9.

A function can also have *arguments*. An argument is a value that is passed to the function when it's called.

```
Dim Weight, NewWeight
Weight = 153.5
NewWeight = Int(Weight)

Response.Write "The weight is about " & NewWeight
```

The Weight variable is assigned a value and then passed to the Int function. Int chops off any fractional part of the number and returns an integer. In this case, it returns 153. This value is returned into the NewWeight variable and displayed.

When passing arguments to a function, you always put those arguments in parentheses after the function name. If you have more than one argument, separate them with commas. However, when you are executing a statement (such as Dim), you do *not* use parentheses.

Making Decisions with If . . . Then

The If...Then statement in VBScript works much like it does in any other language. Here's the basic form:

```
If condition Then
    statement
    statement
    ...
Else
    statement
    statement
    ...
End If
```

The *condition* can be any comparison you want to make. You can use any of the conditional operators listed in Table A-1.

Table A-1	Conditional Operators for `If...Then` Statements
Symbol	*Description*
=	Equals
>	Greater than
<	Less than
>=	Greater than or equal to
<=	Less than or equal to
<>	Does not equal

Here are some examples:

```
If Amount > 5000 Then
    ...
End If

If Name = "Fred" Then
    ...
End If

If Price <= 5.99 Then
    ...
End If
```

If the condition evaluates to True, then the statements after `Then` are executed. If it is False, the statements after `Else` are executed. You can leave out the `Else` and its statements if you want. In that case, if the condition evaluates to False, execution simply continues on the next line after `End If`.

If you have a simple If...Then statement that has only one command as its statement, you can get by without using an End If, if you put the whole thing on one line.

```
If NumMinutes > 15 Then Wait = "Long"
```

Compound If . . . Then statements

You can put more than one condition together in an If statement by using an And or an Or to create a *compound* If...Then statement.

```
If Pressure <= 85 And Type = "Terrain" Then
    ...
End If
```

Multiple conditions with ElseIf

The If...Then statement in VBScript is flexible enough to handle situations in which you have multiple conditions to check. VBScript does this with another keyword: ElseIf.

```
If WindSpeed <= 30 Then
    Description = "Calm"
ElseIf WindSpeed <= 50 Then
    Description = "Gust"
Else
    Description = "Tornado"
End If
```

If the first condition is true, the statement is executed and then VBScript continues to whatever is after End If. If the first condition is false, then the second condition (after ElseIf) is checked. If it is true, its statement is executed. If not, the statement in the Else part is executed. You can have as many ElseIf clauses as you want, but at most, only one will ever be executed — the first one that evaluates to True. The Else is optional, but if it is included, it gets executed only if *all* the conditions fail.

Simplifying Decisions with Select Case

Like the ElseIf statement, the Select Case statement enables you to check multiple conditions, one after the other.

```
Select Case DayCode
Case "Mo"
    ThisDay = "Monday"
Case "Tu"
    ThisDay = "Tuesday"
Case "We"
    ThisDay = "Wednesday"
Case "Tr"
    ThisDay = "Thursday"
Case "Fr"
    ThisDay = "Friday"
Case Else
    ThisDay = "Weekend"
End Select
```

The variable at the top (in this case, `DayCode`) is the same variable that is evaluated throughout the statement. So `Case "Mo"` looks at `DayCode` to see if it is equal to `"Mo"`. If it is, the line (or lines) below are executed. In this case, I set `ThisDay` to a more readable version of the weekday. If none of the conditions match, then the optional `Case Else` is executed.

You can also use comparison operators in a `Select Case`. Here's an example:

```
Select Case WindSpeed
Case Is <= 30 Then
    Description = "Calm"
Case Is <= 50 Then
    Description = "Gust"
Case Else
    Description = "Tornado"
End Select
```

Notice that when you use the < or > sign you must also include the `Is` after `Case`. This is just a quirk of the VBScript `Select Case` statement. You don't need the `Is` when you check to see if something is equal (you don't even use the equal sign). But you do need it if you are using any of the other comparison operators.

`Select Case` and `If...Then...ElseIf` do very similar things. How do you know which one you should use? Use the one that makes the code clearer. Remember that you can only use `Select Case` when you are comparing against one variable (the one that appears at the top after `Select Case`). If you need to compare against more than one variable, you have to use `If...Then...ElseIf`.

In C and C++, the statement that works like `Select Case` actually runs faster than an `If...Then...ElseIf`-type statement. VBScript doesn't show a significant difference in execution speed between the two. So, use whichever makes your code easier to understand.

Flying Loops

Loops enable you to execute the same section of code again and again. VBScript loops are easy to use and offer all the flexibility you should ever need.

VBScript has two basic types of loops. The `For...Next` loop counts off a certain number of times and then quits. The `Do...Loop` uses a condition to determine whether it should continue looping each time.

The For . . . Next loop

The `For...Next` loop makes executing a loop a set number of times easy while automatically keeping track of a counter.

```
Dim Num, Total

For Num = 1 To 5
    Response.Write "10 times " & Num & _
        " is equal to " & 10 * Num & ".<p>"
Next
```

This code produces the following output.

```
10 times 1 is equal to 10.

10 times 2 is equal to 20.

10 times 3 is equal to 30.

10 times 4 is equal to 40.

10 times 5 is equal to 50.
```

The `For` line marks the beginning of the loop. It also identifies the *index variable* (`Num`), the number of the first loop (1), and the number of the last loop (5). The `Next` line marks the end of the loop. Everything between the `For` line and the `Next` line is a part of the *body* of the loop and gets executed again and again.

The first time through the loop, Num is set to 1. The second time it is set to 2, and so on, up through 5.

Most of the time, your loops start with 1, but they don't have to. You can create a loop like this:

```
For Times = 10 To 100
```

This loop sets the variable Times to 10 the first time through, to 11 the second time through, and so on, up to 100. The first number can be 0, and it can even be negative, if you want. In any case, it always starts with the first number and counts by one up to the last number.

Using step

When you use the keyword Step with your For...Next loops, you can tell VBScript what number the For loop should count by.

```
For Num = 2 To 10 Step 2
```

In this loop, the first time through, Num is assigned 2, then 4, 6, 8, and finally 10.

```
For Weeks = 0 To 36 Step 7
```

Weeks is assigned 0 the first time, then 7, 14, 21, 28, and 35.

Do . . . Loops

The VBScript Do...Loop is a very different kind of looping structure from the For...Next loop. The Do...Loop enables you to loop *while* a condition is true or to loop *until* a condition becomes true.

```
Dim Num
Num = 0
Do While Num < 3
    Num = Num + 1
    Response.Write "I'm looping!"
Loop
Response.Write "I'm done looping."
```

Do always begins the loop, and Loop always marks the end. Everything in between is the loop's *body*. In this case, a While and condition appear after Do. So this is a *top-tested* While loop. In other words, VBScript tests the condition *before* the loop begins. If it is true, the body is executed. If not, VBScript skips the entire loop and it's never executed. You could move the While to the bottom, after Loop.

```
Dim Num
Num = 0
Do
    Num = Num + 1
    Response.Write "I'm looping!"
Loop While Num < 3
Response.Write "I'm done looping."
```

This is a *bottom-tested* While loop, which means that VBScript executes the body of the loop *first* and then it checks the condition. If the condition fails, the loop is exited and "I'm done looping" is displayed.

So you can see the difference between the top-tested and bottom-tested loop only when the condition fails the *first time*. If the condition fails the first time in a top-tested loop, the body is never executed. If the condition fails the first time in a bottom-tested loop, the loop gets executed once before jumping out.

You can also put an Until in either the top or bottom position. Until reverses the logic. For a While, the loop continues as long as the condition is *true*. For an Until, the loop continues execution as long as the condition is *false* (and exits when the condition becomes true).

Here's an example:

```
Dim Num
Num = 0
Do
    Num = Num + 1
    Response.Write "I'm looping!"
Loop Until Num = 3
Response.Write "I'm done looping."
```

Finding the Exit

There are times when you want to jump right out of the middle of a loop. You want to get out of the loop entirely — no matter what else is going on. VBScript makes this possible with the Exit command.

```
For Count = 1 To 100
   ...
   If Temp > Threshold Then Exit For
   ...
Next
```

Exit For is almost always found within an If...Then statement that checks some special case where the loop should end. You can use Exit Do in exactly the same way to exit a Do...Loop.

I Work Hard. I Need Arrays.

An *array* declares a whole group of variables at once. An array declaration looks like this:

```
Dim Dog(10)
```

This line creates ten different variables. Each variable has the same name — Dog. You refer to the variables individually by using their number. You can assign a value to Dog number 3 by using this syntax:

```
Dog(3) = "Fido"
```

Being able to refer to variables by number has the advantage of allowing you to search through them one-by-one using a loop.

```
Dim DogNum, Found
Found = False
For DogNum = 1 To 10
    If Dog(DogNum) = "Coco" Then
        Found = True
        Exit For
    End If
Next
If Found = True Then
    Response.Write "I found Coco!<p>"
Else
    Response.Write "I didn't find Coco.<p>"
End If
```

Assume that this code is executed after all ten dog names are filled in. The code searches through the entire list to find one particular dog — Coco. All you need is a For...Next loop. The index of the loop is used in the array to check each and every one, one at a time.

Dynamic arrays

A *dynamic array* is an array that doesn't have a set number of elements defined when it is created. When you declare a dynamic array, it looks like this:

```
Dim Codes()
```

The empty parentheses after the variable indicate that it is *dynamic*. This option enables you to wait and determine later how many elements you need. After you know how many you need, you use ReDim.

```
ReDim Codes(15)
```

If you find out later that you actually need more elements than that, you can even ReDim again.

```
ReDim Preserve Codes(20)
```

The Preserve keyword asks VBScript to preserve any data that had been put into the array previously. If you don't use Preserve, all the data is wiped when you use ReDim.

UBound

When working with dynamic arrays, you don't always know what the highest array element is, especially if you keep ReDim-ing it. The UBound function allows you to get this information.

```
Dim Cats(), Highest
...
ReDim Cats(17)
...
Highest = UBound(Cats)
```

After the ReDim, Highest holds 17.

Multidimensional arrays

Arrays are a list of variables that all use the same name. But arrays can be more than a list. They can be a *grid*.

```
Dim TicTacToe(3,3)
```

This array has two dimensions. Instead of a list of values, this is more like a grid — each with its own two coordinates. `TicTacToe(2,2)` would be right in the middle of the grid, `TicTacToe(1,1)` would be in the upper left, and `TicTacToe(3,3)` would be in the lower right.

And, yes, you can have a three-dimensional array, too, if you want.

```
Dim Rubics(3,3,3)
```

This is like a cube. You can even go with four, five, and six dimensions — but don't ask me what shape those look like! In practice, it's uncommon to use an array with more than two dimensions.

Creating Your Own Functions and Subroutines

With VBScript ,you can create your own functions and subroutines and call them again and again from throughout your page or throughout your Web application.

Creating subroutines

A subroutine in VBScript is a named portion of code that accepts arguments and does something. A subroutine does not return a value. You create a subroutine using the `Sub` command.

```
Sub ShowName(FirstName, LastName)
...
End Sub
```

The `Sub` line identifies the name of the subroutine, and the parentheses contain the arguments that the subroutine expects to have passed in. The `End Sub` line identifies where the subroutine ends. All the lines of code between `Sub` and `End Sub` are the body of the subroutine.

Creating functions

A function is exactly like a subroutine, except that it also returns a value.

```
Function SumValues(FirstVal, SecondVal, ThirdVal)
...
SumValues = FirstVal + SecondVal + ThirdVal
End Function
```

This code works just like the declaration of the subroutine. The only difference is that the name of the function can be used like an already-declared variable (like `SumValues` in this example). And that variable contains the value that is returned when the function ends.

Calling subroutines and functions

Calling subroutines and functions works in about the same way as calling built-in VBScript commands and functions.

```
ShowName "Fred","Smith"
Total = SumValues(12,18,33)
```

When you call a VBScript function, you use parentheses around the arguments; when calling a VBScript statement, you don't. The same is true when calling functions and subroutines you create.

Using Common Commands and Functions

The rest of this appendix introduces you to some common functions in VBScript. You can get more details on each of these functions in the online Help system. You can also find lots more functions in Help. This list is just intended to give you an idea of where to start.

To get more help on VBScript, choose Help⇨Contents from the Visual InterDev menu bar. Then open the topic titled Platform SDK. Under Platform SDK, open Internet/Intranet/Extranet Services. Open Scripting, and then open VBScript Language Reference. Whew! Why is it buried so deep? I have no idea.

Doing Math

In this section, I describe the more exciting math functions and leave the rest for your own research, if you are so inclined.

Rnd and Randomize

You can use Randomize and Rnd to add a creative or unexpected element to your Web pages. These functions are particularly useful when creating games or puzzles.

Rnd

Here's the general form for Rnd:

```
var = Rnd
```

Rnd returns a random number between 0 and 1 into the variable named var. These values generally look like 0.4214255 or 0.2443286.

The problem with Rnd is that every time you reload your page, the same series of "random" numbers appears. For instance, imagine you have a dice-rolling page that rolls the dice three times and shows you the results. You load the page and it generates a 5, a 3, and a 1. Then you refresh the page. You get a 5, a 3, and a 1 again. The numbers are random, but you get the same sequence every time.

Randomize

To solve the same-sequence problem, you need Randomize. Here's its general form:

```
Randomize
```

Because computers can't create a number out of thin air, they use a complex formula to generate random numbers. The only problem is that they have to feed that formula a value to get it started. The value fed to the formula is called a *seed*. The reason Rnd normally gives you the same random numbers every time is because it always starts with the same seed.

Randomize causes VBScript to use the system's clock as the seed for the random number. Because the clock is very likely to be different every time you run the program, you always get a different sequence of numbers.

Use Randomize once, before you ever call Rnd. Doing so seeds the generator, and you get a different sequence every time.

Generating useful random numbers

The problem is that these numbers between 0 and 1 aren't very useful. How do you get useful numbers (like numbers between 1 and 6, or 1 and 10, or 1 and 100)? You multiply the return value from Rnd by the maximum number you want and then use Int to chop off any decimal part of the number. Then you add 1.

```
var = Int(Rnd * highnum) + 1
```

You can use that formula to generate random numbers between 1 and any number.

Now suppose you want to generate random numbers between 100 and 200. Is there a way to do that? Sure.

```
var = (200 - 100 + 1) * Rnd + 100
```

Or, more generally:

```
var = (topnum - bottomnum + 1) * Rnd + bottomnum
```

where *bottomnum* and *topnum* are the lowest and highest numbers you want to be in the range.

Int and Round

Int and Round are the functions VBScript uses to convert numbers that include a fractional part (like 5.2 or 3.14159 or 7.632) to whole numbers. You can do that a couple of different ways, so a couple of different functions exist (actually, there are more than a couple, but these are the important ones).

Int

Int takes the most straightforward solution to this problem:

```
var = Int(expression)
```

The *expression* can be any formula that ends up producing a number with a fractional part.

Int does no rounding of any kind. It simply removes (or truncates) the fractional part and returns the whole number part.

Round

The general form for Round looks like this:

```
var = Round(expression)
```

Again, expression can be any formula that ends up producing a number with a fractional part.

Round rounds the fractional number just as you would expect. If the number is 1.7, it's rounded to 2. If it is 3.3, it's rounded to 3. If it is 4.5, the rule says that it goes to the higher number: 5.

Other math functions

A host of other math functions are available. All the standard ones are here and then some. Here's a list of all the VBScript math functions I haven't discussed in this chapter. You can look up the details in the VBScript online Help.

- ✔ Trig Stuff: Atn, Cos, Sin, Tan
- ✔ Other Stuff: Exp, Log, Sqr, Abs, Sgn, Mod, Hex, Oct

Manipulating Strings

Because strings are so important, many commands and functions exist to deal with them. Some of the most important ones follow.

FormatCurrency, FormatDateTime, FormatNumber, FormatPercent

You can format the look of a string holding currency values, dates and times, numbers, and percentage values in almost any way imaginable. These functions are very flexible. All four of them also give you the option of simply formatting the information based on the computer's regional settings.

You can look up all the different arguments that are available for each of these functions. Believe me, a lot of them exist.

InStr

InStr searches a long string to see if it can find a shorter string within it. If it finds the shorter string, it returns the position within the larger string where the shorter string can be found. The general form for InStr looks like this:

```
var = InStr(searchedstr, strtofind)
```

The var is a variable that holds the position where strtofind was found within searchedstr.

Here's an example:

```
Dim LongString, FindString, Position
LongString = "So long and thanks for all the fish."
FindString = "thanks"
Position = InStr(LongString, FindString)
```

Position would hold the value 13, because "thanks" appears 13 characters from the beginning of LongString.

Len

The general form for Len looks like this:

```
var = Len(stringvar)
```

You send a string to Len as an argument, and it returns a number indicating how long stringvar is.

```
Dim TheString, TheLength
TheString = "The Eagle has landed."
TheLength = Len(TheString)
```

MyLength would hold 21, because that's how many characters are in the string.

LCase, UCase

The general forms for LCase and UCase look like this:

```
var = LCase(stringvar)
var = UCase(stringvar)
```

LCase and UCase both take one string argument. They both return that same string converted to lowercase or uppercase, respectively.

LTrim, RTrim, Trim

The `Trim` functions, `LTrim`, `RTrim`, and `Trim` each receive a string as an argument and return a string. The string returned is the same as the string sent except that:

- ✔ `LTrim` chops off any leading spaces (those that appear on the left side of the string).
- ✔ `RTrim` chops off any trailing spaces (that appear on the right side of the string).
- ✔ `Trim` chops off both leading and trailing spaces.

Space, String

The `Space` function provides an easy way for you to create a string with lots of spaces in it. Just send a number indicating the number of spaces you want, and `Space` returns a string of that length, filled with spaces. For example, `Space(17)` would return "   " (17 spaces).

`String` is an enhanced and more generalized version of `Space`. It enables you to create a string of any length with any character. You simply send the number and the character you want to use. `String(2,"#")` returns "##", and `String(5,"%")` returns "%%%%%".

Left, Mid, Right

`Left`, `Mid`, and `Right` are three of the most useful string functions in VBScript. They enable you to tear apart a string into smaller strings.

`Left` and `Right` have these general forms.

```
var = Left(stringvar, num)
var = Right(stringvar, num)
```

`Left` takes two arguments — a string and a number. It returns a string that is comprised of the left-most characters of the string sent. For example, `Left("cat fashion",3)` returns "cat". `Left("Squidly",5)` returns "Squid".

`Right` works exactly the same way, but it takes the characters from the right side of the string.

Mid takes characters from anywhere within a string. It has this general form:

```
var = Mid(stringvar, start, num)
```

The second argument, start, determines where in stringvar to begin, and num determines how many characters to use. Mid returns the string that results. Mid("My lovely lady",4, 6) returns "lovely". It starts with the fourth character ("l") and takes six characters total (including the fourth).

Getting a Date (And Time)

The following VBScript functions provide key date and time access and manipulation functions.

Date, Time, and Now

Date, Time, and Now are all functions that take no arguments and return a single value, swiped from your computer's system clock.

- ✔ Date returns today's date.
- ✔ Time returns the current time.
- ✔ Now returns the current date and time together.

Weekday and WeekdayName

Weekday accepts a date as an argument. It returns a number between 1 and 7, indicating the number of the day that date falls on.

WeekdayName conveniently accepts a number argument between 1 and 7 and returns the name of the associated weekday, as a string.

Other Date/Time Functions

VBScript provides a lot of date and time functions. Here are a few more of the more interesting ones:

- ✔ DateDiff: Returns the number of days, weeks, months, or years that exist between the two dates passed.

- ✔ DateAdd: Adds a certain number of days, weeks, months, or years to a date and returns the new date.

- ✔ Day, Month, Year: Each of these takes a date and returns a number that indicates the part of the date associated with their name.

- ✔ MonthName: Takes a month number (1 to 12) and returns the name of the month (January through December).

Appendix B
Visual InterDev Installation

● ●

In This Appendix

▶ Finding out what you need to know before you get started

▶ Figuring out what to install on the Web server

▶ Installing Visual InterDev

▶ Installing all the other stuff you need on your workstation

● ●

*U*nfortunately, getting started with Visual InterDev is a little more complicated than just installing and running Visual InterDev. That's because Visual InterDev is designed to work with a Web server, which is where the pages and applications you create will finally be stored. You must know ahead of time which server you will use, what operating system it runs, and what server applications and components have been installed on it.

The Web Server

If you are working for a company, the server you use may be your company's Web server. Or it may be the internal intranet server. Or perhaps your company works with another company that provides space for your site on *their* server. You must have several server components installed on the server you use before Visual InterDev will work.

In any case, to use all the features of Visual InterDev, you need several components installed on your Web server. These include:

✔ **Microsoft FrontPage 98 Extensions:** These extensions provide all the components needed for FrontPage 98 and Visual InterDev to create Web projects on the server and track those projects' information. These extensions absolutely *must* be installed on your Web server before Visual InterDev can work with it.

✔ **Visual InterDev Server Components:** The server components add all the Visual InterDev-specific components that enable you to easily interact with the Web server from Visual InterDev.

✔ **Microsoft SQL Server:** If you plan to do database access using SQL Server, then SQL Server must be installed either on your Web server or on another server machine that is connected to the Web server.

✔ **Database Components:** These components enable easy access to database information from the Active Server Pages created in Visual InterDev.

All these components (except SQL Server) come on your Visual InterDev installation CDs. Just run the Setup program on the server and choose the Server Applications and Tools option. (SQL Server is a separate application. For more information on installing that product, see the SQL Server documentation.)

After your server has all these components installed, you can turn your attention to your workstation.

Your Workstation

Although your server is probably running Microsoft Windows NT Server, your workstation can run any Windows operating system you like. But more than likely, you are running either Windows 95/98 or Windows NT Workstation.

On your workstation, you must first install Visual InterDev itself. You do that by inserting your Visual InterDev installation CDs, running Setup, and choosing the Workstation Tools and Components option.

Then you need to install Personal Web Server if you are running Windows 95/98 or Personal Web Services if you are running Windows NT Workstation. To do that, locate the Windows NT Options Pack on your Visual InterDev installation CDs.

Believe it or not, even if you are running Windows 95/98, you still need the Windows *NT* Option Pack. When you run the NT Option Pack, it automatically checks to see what operating system you are running. If you are running Windows 95/98, it installs Personal Web Server. If you are running Windows NT Workstation, it installs Personal Web Services.

Personal Web Server/Personal Web Services is a local, scaled-down Web server application. It enables you to test your Web applications on your local machine without having to copy your pages up to the Web server and then download them into the browser every time you want to make a change and see how it looks.

And because you are using your own machine as a mini-Web server, you also need to install many of the same components on your machine that you installed on the Web server, including Microsoft FrontPage 98 Extensions and Visual InterDev Server Components. You do not need to install Microsoft SQL Server on your local machine, however, because your local Web server accesses SQL Server on whatever server it resides on, just as the main Web server would.

Appendix C

About the CD

* *

On the *Visual InterDev 6 For Dummies* CD-ROM:

▶ Microsoft Internet Explorer and Netscape Communicator

▶ A huge variety of server components that can make your scripting life easier

▶ A complete online auction application, including all source code

* *

System Requirements

Make sure your computer meets the minimum system requirements listed here. If your computer doesn't match up to most of these requirements, you may have problems using the contents of the CD:

- ✔ A PC with a 486 or faster processor.

- ✔ Microsoft Windows 95/98 or Microsoft Windows NT Workstation/Server.

- ✔ At least 8MB of total RAM installed on your computer. For best performance, I recommend at least 16MB of RAM installed.

- ✔ At least 80MB of hard drive space available to install all the software from this CD. (You'll need less space if you don't install every program.)

- ✔ A CD-ROM drive — double-speed (2x) or faster.

- ✔ A monitor capable of displaying at least 256 colors.

- ✔ A modem with a speed of at least 14,400 bps.

If you need more information on the basics, check out *PCs For Dummies,* 4th Edition, by Dan Gookin; *Windows 95 For Dummies,* 2nd Edition by Andy Rathbone; or *Windows 98 For Dummies,* also by Andy Rathbone (all published by IDG Books Worldwide, Inc.).

Using the CD

To use the CD that came with this book:

1. **Insert the CD into your computer's CD-ROM drive.**

   Give your computer a moment to take a look at the CD.

2. **Open your browser.**

   If you do not have a browser, follow the easy steps as described in the "Installing a Browser" section later in this appendix to install one. For your convenience, I have included Microsoft Internet Explorer as well as Netscape Communicator.

3. **Click File⇨Open (in Internet Explorer) or File⇨Open Page (in Communicator).**

4. **In the dialog box that appears, type** D:\default.htm **and click OK.**

   Replace the letter D: with the correct letter for your CD-ROM drive, if it is not D.

   This action displays the file that walks you through the content of the CD.

To navigate within the interface, simply click any topic of interest to take you to an explanation of the files on the CD and how to use or install them. After you are done with the interface, simply close your browser as usual.

To run some of the programs, you may need to keep the CD inside your CD-ROM drive. This is a Good Thing. Otherwise, the installed program would have required you to install a very large chunk of the program to your hard drive space, which would have kept you from installing other software.

Installing a Browser

To install Internet Explorer on your PC:

1. **Double-click on the folder on this CD titled Internet.**

2. **Within that folder, double-click on the folder titled MS Internet Explorer.**

3. **Inside that folder, double-click on Ie4setup.exe.**

4. **Follow the instructions that appear on your screen.**

After you have Internet Explorer installed, you can double-click on Default.htm on the CD to see a Web page describing the contents on the CD.

What You'll Find

Here's a summary of the software on this CD.

Billy-Bob's Internet Auction

The complete Billy-Bob's Internet Auction application described in Chapter 14 is included on the CD. It includes all the source code for the ASP pages as well as scripts to create the database table and even fill it with test data!

See "Setting Up Billy-Bob's Internet Auction" later in this appendix for information on installing this application on your machine.

Chili!ASP

ASP is a technology developed by Microsoft for use with Internet Information Server (IIS). However, Chili!ASP is a product created by Chili!Soft and gives *other* Web servers the ability to run ASP pages. This means that you can use Visual InterDev to develop applications for those servers by using Chili!ASP. The demo included on this CD gives you a taste of the possibilities.

Note: This product was especially designed for and will install with Windows NT 4.0 and later.

Chili!Reports

Although the Visual InterDev database interaction capabilities are very complete, you can't easily create complex reports from your Web applications using Visual InterDev. Chili!Reports (also from Chili!Soft) fills that gap.

Conversa Chat Server 2.1

Online chats are just a component away! This server component implements chat rooms on your Web site. And it provides broad reach to virtually any HTML browser.

AspNTUser

This program provides a hierarchy of objects that you can access in script that let you view and manipulate the NT users database.

Easy-ODBC

This server component enables you to create DSNs on the server machine without actually going to the server machine. This feature can be a time saver for busy Webmasters.

Easy-Edit

You can add this editor to a Web page to allow Webmasters full access to the server's directories and files remotely. Using this editor is great for making quick changes while skipping the usual download and upload steps.

Internet Explorer 4.0

This is the latest version of Microsoft's premier Web browser. It offers full Dynamic HTML support and client-side scripting in both VBScript and JavaScript. It's an excellent test platform for your Web applications.

Netscape Communicator 4.04

This is Netscape's very popular Web browser. If your Web applications don't look good in this browser, they won't look good to a large portion of your audience! Always test any pages you're creating for the World Wide Web with Netscape Communicator before you put them out there.

Setting Up Billy-Bob's Internet Auction

The Internet Auction is more than a few Web pages. It includes ASP scripting and database access. Because of that, it requires a few steps to set it up on a new computer. Fortunately, I outline these steps in detail in the next couple of sections.

Setting up the auction database

In order to create the table you need to use the Auction application, AuctionItem, you can either create it yourself using the information in Chapter 14 or you can use the script I included on this CD-ROM in a text file named AuctTabl.txt. The script is a normal SQL script that you can run from Microsoft SQL Server ISQL or ISQL_w (the Windows version).

You can put the table in any database you like, but make sure that the database you choose doesn't have a table named AuctionItem. If it does, this script will delete the existing table and all its data.

To create the AuctionItem table with ISQL_w:

1. **Run ISQL_w by choosing its icon in the Start menu⇨Programs⇨ Microsoft SQL Server 6.5 Utilities.**

2. **Log into the server using your login information.**

   A Query window appears.

3. **Choose the database where you want to store the new table from the drop-down list box at the top of the window.**

4. **Click the Query tab and copy the text from AuctTabl.txt into the big text area on that tab.**

5. **Click the green Play button on the top right of the window.**

   The window automatically switches to the Results tab and displays this line:

   ```
   This command did not return data, and it did not return
       any rows
   ```

6. **Go back into Visual InterDev and right-click Tables in the Data View. Choose Refresh from the pop-up menu.**

   The new table should appear under Tables.

To add the sample data to your newly created table, I included a data file called AuctData.txt. In order to add this data to your AuctionItem table, you have to use the Microsoft SQL Server BCP utility. This utility is designed to enable you to easily import and export data from the tables in your database. The only bad news is that BCP is a DOS utility. So you have to launch a DOS box to run it. After you do, use a line like this to execute it:

```
bcp dbname..AuctionItem in auctdata.txt -S server
-U username -P password
```

Replace *dbname* with the name of the database where you placed the AuctionItem table. Replace *server* with the name of your server machine hosting the SQL Server database. Replace *username* and *password* with your login information.

After you enter this command, it asks you an almost endless series of questions. Just press Enter to take the default for *all* of them.

Finally, you see:

```
Starting copy...
26 rows copied.
Network packet size (bytes): 4096
Clock Time (ms.): total =220 Avg =8 (118.18 rows per sec.)
```

Of course, some of your specific numbers will be different, but it should look something like this. Now you can go in to Visual InterDev and double-click the AuctionItem table under Tables in your Data View, and you should see all the data there.

Creating the Auction Application

You could add the Auction application to your own Web server in a number of ways, but this one is probably the easiest.

To add the Auction application to your server:

1. **Create a new project in Visual InterDev on your server and call it** *auction*.

2. **Drag the Web pages and site diagram from the CD-ROM on to the name of your project in your Project Explorer window.**

   Doing so adds these pages to your project.

3. **Ctrl-click each of the newly added pages. After they're all selected, right-click and choose Add to Master Web from the pop-up menu.**

   (If the option doesn't appear on the menu, you probably have something selected in addition to your new files. Make sure you don't select global.asa, too.)

   The little flags beside the page icons turn into little locks.

4. **Right-click default.asp and choose Set as Start Page from the pop-up menu.**

5. **Right-click the project and choose Apply Theme and Layout.**

6. **Click the Theme tab, and then click the Apply Theme radio button.**

7. **Scroll down and select Street Writing.**

8. **Click OK.**

   The theme is added to the project. You may receive an errors about being unable to apply the theme to a file. If you do, just click the Skip button. It won't affect your application.

9. **Add a Data Connection to your project.**

It should point to the server and database where you put the AuctionItem table and its data. Name the Data Connection **dbconnect**.

If You Have Problems (Of the CD Kind)

I tried my best to compile programs that work on most computers with the minimum system requirements. Alas, your computer may differ, and some programs may not work properly for some reason.

The two likeliest problems are that you don't have enough memory (RAM) for the programs you want to use, or you have other programs running that are affecting the installation or running of a program. If you get error messages like `Not enough memory` or `Setup cannot continue`, try one or more of these methods and then try using the software again:

- ✔ Turn off any anti-virus software that you have on your computer. Installers sometimes mimic virus activity and may make your computer incorrectly believe that it is being infected by a virus.

- ✔ Close all running programs. The more programs you're running, the less memory is available to other programs. Installers also typically update files and programs. So if you keep other programs running, installation may not work properly.

- ✔ Have your local computer store add more RAM to your computer. This is, admittedly, a drastic and somewhat expensive step. However, if you have a Windows 95 PC, adding more memory can really help the speed of your computer and allow more programs to run at the same time. This may include closing the CD interface and running a product's installation program from Windows Explorer.

If you still have trouble with installing the items from the CD, please call the IDG Books Worldwide Customer Service phone number: 800-762-2974 (outside the U.S.: 317-596-5430).

Index

(continued)

IDG Books Worldwide, Inc., End-User License Agreement

READ THIS. You should carefully read these terms and conditions before opening the software packet(s) included with this book ("Book"). This is a license agreement ("Agreement") between you and IDG Books Worldwide, Inc. ("IDGB"). By opening the accompanying software packet(s), you acknowledge that you have read and accept the following terms and conditions. If you do not agree and do not want to be bound by such terms and conditions, promptly return the Book and the unopened software packet(s) to the place you obtained them for a full refund.

1. **License Grant.** IDGB grants to you (either an individual or entity) a nonexclusive license to use one copy of the enclosed software program(s) (collectively, the "Software") solely for your own personal or business purposes on a single computer (whether a standard computer or a workstation component of a multiuser network). The Software is in use on a computer when it is loaded into temporary memory (RAM) or installed into permanent memory (hard disk, CD-ROM, or other storage device). IDGB reserves all rights not expressly granted herein.

2. **Ownership.** IDGB is the owner of all right, title, and interest, including copyright, in and to the compilation of the Software recorded on the disk(s) or CD-ROM ("Software Media"). Copyright to the individual programs recorded on the Software Media is owned by the author or other authorized copyright owner of each program. Ownership of the Software and all proprietary rights relating thereto remain with IDGB and its licensers.

3. **Restrictions on Use and Transfer.**

    (a) You may only (i) make one copy of the Software for backup or archival purposes, or (ii) transfer the Software to a single hard disk, provided that you keep the original for backup or archival purposes. You may not (i) rent or lease the Software, (ii) copy or reproduce the Software through a LAN or other network system or through any computer subscriber system or bulletin-board system, or (iii) modify, adapt, or create derivative works based on the Software.

    (b) You may not reverse engineer, decompile, or disassemble the Software. You may transfer the Software and user documentation on a permanent basis, provided that the transferee agrees to accept the terms and conditions of this Agreement and you retain no copies. If the Software is an update or has been updated, any transfer must include the most recent update and all prior versions.

4. **Restrictions on Use of Individual Programs.** You must follow the individual requirements and restrictions detailed for each individual program in Appendix C of this Book. These limitations are also contained in the individual license agreements recorded on the Software Media. These limitations may include a requirement that after using the program for a specified period of time, the user must pay a registration fee or discontinue use. By opening the Software packet(s), you will be agreeing to abide by the licenses and restrictions for these individual programs that are detailed in Appendix C and on the Software Media. None of the material on this Software Media or listed in this Book may ever be redistributed, in original or modified form, for commercial purposes.

5. **Limited Warranty.**

   (a) IDGB warrants that the Software and Software Media are free from defects in materials and workmanship under normal use for a period of sixty (60) days from the date of purchase of this Book. If IDGB receives notification within the warranty period of defects in materials or workmanship, IDGB will replace the defective Software Media.

   (b) **IDGB AND THE AUTHOR OF THE BOOK DISCLAIM ALL OTHER WARRANTIES, EXPRESS OR IMPLIED, INCLUDING WITHOUT LIMITATION IMPLIED WARRANTIES OF MERCHANTABILITY AND FITNESS FOR A PARTICULAR PURPOSE, WITH RESPECT TO THE SOFTWARE, THE PROGRAMS, THE SOURCE CODE CONTAINED THEREIN, AND/OR THE TECHNIQUES DESCRIBED IN THIS BOOK. IDGB DOES NOT WARRANT THAT THE FUNCTIONS CONTAINED IN THE SOFTWARE WILL MEET YOUR REQUIREMENTS OR THAT THE OPERATION OF THE SOFTWARE WILL BE ERROR FREE.**

   (c) This limited warranty gives you specific legal rights, and you may have other rights that vary from jurisdiction to jurisdiction.

6. **Remedies.**

   (a) IDGB's entire liability and your exclusive remedy for defects in materials and workmanship shall be limited to replacement of the Software Media, which may be returned to IDGB with a copy of your receipt at the following address: Software Media Fulfillment Department, Attn.: *Visual InterDev 6 For Dummies,* IDG Books Worldwide, Inc., 7260 Shadeland Station, Ste. 100, Indianapolis, IN 46256, or call 800-762-2974. Please allow three to four weeks for delivery. This Limited Warranty is void if failure of the Software Media has resulted from accident, abuse, or misapplication. Any replacement Software Media will be warranted for the remainder of the original warranty period or thirty (30) days, whichever is longer.

   (b) In no event shall IDGB or the author be liable for any damages whatsoever (including without limitation damages for loss of business profits, business interruption, loss of business information, or any other pecuniary loss) arising from the use of or inability to use the Book or the Software, even if IDGB has been advised of the possibility of such damages.

   (c) Because some jurisdictions do not allow the exclusion or limitation of liability for consequential or incidental damages, the above limitation or exclusion may not apply to you.

7. **U.S. Government Restricted Rights.** Use, duplication, or disclosure of the Software by the U.S. Government is subject to restrictions stated in paragraph (c)(1)(ii) of the Rights in Technical Data and Computer Software clause of DFARS 252.227-7013, and in subparagraphs (a) through (d) of the Commercial Computer–Restricted Rights clause at FAR 52.227-19, and in similar clauses in the NASA FAR supplement, when applicable.

8. **General.** This Agreement constitutes the entire understanding of the parties and revokes and supersedes all prior agreements, oral or written, between them and may not be modified or amended except in a writing signed by both parties hereto that specifically refers to this Agreement. This Agreement shall take precedence over any other documents that may be in conflict herewith. If any one or more provisions contained in this Agreement are held by any court or tribunal to be invalid, illegal, or otherwise unenforceable, each and every other provision shall remain in full force and effect.

Installation Instructions

1. **Insert the CD into your computer's CD-ROM drive.**

   Give your computer a moment to take a look at the CD.

2. **Open your browser.**

   If you do not have a browser, follow the easy steps as described in the "Installing a Browser" section of Appendix C to install one. For your convenience, I have included Microsoft Internet Explorer as well as Netscape Communicator.

3. **Click File⇨Open (in Internet Explorer) or File⇨Open Page (in Communicator).**

4. **In the dialog box that appears, type** D:\default.htm **and click OK.**

   Replace the letter D: with the correct letter for your CD-ROM drive, if it is not D.

   This action displays the file that walks you through the content of the CD.

To navigate within the interface, simply click any topic of interest to take you to an explanation of the files on the CD and how to use or install them. After you are done with the interface, simply close your browser as usual.

80025 75540

Discover Dummies Online!

The Dummies Web Site is your fun and friendly online resource for the latest information about ...*For Dummies*® books and your favorite topics. The Web site is the place to communicate with us, exchange ideas with other ...*For Dummies* readers, chat with authors, and have fun!

Ten Fun and Useful Things You Can Do at www.dummies.com

1. Win free ...*For Dummies* books and more!
2. Register your book and be entered in a prize drawing.
3. Meet your favorite authors through the IDG Books Author Chat Series.
4. Exchange helpful information with other ...*For Dummies* readers.
5. Discover other great ...*For Dummies* books you must have!
6. Purchase Dummieswear™ exclusively from our Web site.
7. Buy ...*For Dummies* books online.
8. Talk to us. Make comments, ask questions, get answers!
9. Download free software.
10. Find additional useful resources from authors.

Link directly to these ten fun and useful things at
http://www.dummies.com/10useful

For other technology titles from IDG Books Worldwide, go to
www.idgbooks.com

Not on the Web yet? It's easy to get started with *Dummies 101*®: *The Internet For Windows*®*98* or *The Internet For Dummies*®, *5th Edition*, at local retailers everywhere.

Find other ...*For Dummies* books on these topics:
Business • Career • Databases • Food & Beverage • Games • Gardening • Graphics • Hardware
Health & Fitness • Internet and the World Wide Web • Networking • Office Suites
Operating Systems • Personal Finance • Pets • Programming • Recreation • Sports
Spreadsheets • Teacher Resources • Test Prep • Word Processing

IDG BOOKS WORLDWIDE
BOOK REGISTRATION

We want to hear from you!

Register This Book and Win!

Visit **http://my2cents.dummies.com** to register this book and tell us how you liked it!

- ✔ Get entered in our monthly prize giveaway.

- ✔ Give us feedback about this book — tell us what you like best, what you like least, or maybe what you'd like to ask the author and us to change!

- ✔ Let us know any other *...For Dummies*® topics that interest you.

Your feedback helps us determine what books to publish, tells us what coverage to add as we revise our books, and lets us know whether we're meeting your needs as a *...For Dummies* reader. You're our most valuable resource, and what you have to say is important to us!

Not on the Web yet? It's easy to get started with *Dummies 101*®: *The Internet For Windows*® *98* or *The Internet For Dummies*,® 5th Edition, at local retailers everywhere.

Or let us know what you think by sending us a letter at the following address:

...For Dummies Book Registration
Dummies Press
7260 Shadeland Station, Suite 100
Indianapolis, IN 46256-3945
Fax 317-596-5498

™

BESTSELLING
BOOK SERIES
FROM IDG